Underdogs

Anguish and Anxiety:
**Eighteen men and women
write their own case-histories**

Edited and introduced by
PHILIP TOYNBEE

HORIZON PRESS
NEW YORK
1962

© 1961 by Philip Toynbee
First American Edition – 1962

Library of Congress Catalog Card No: 61–17808

PRINTED IN GREAT BRITAIN

Contents

CONTENTS

INTRODUCTION

MY FIRST step in compiling this symposium was to send a letter to some of the weekly and Sunday papers in which I appealed for 'underdog confessions'. It was soon clear that if a competition had been held to discover the surest method of increasing one's daily post my letter to the papers must have won a prize. For nearly all of us have a hard-luck story to tell, or to tell again, and a case can be made out, with the aid of modern psychology, for supposing that the world is inhabited entirely by underdogs. Even Adler's 'superiority complex' turned out to be simply another manifestation of its apparent opposite. And as for the confessional aspect of my request that, too, has become more acceptable in recent years when traditional reticences have been so vigorously assaulted by our new habit of baring our wounded bosoms to the world.

The problem of selection was both severe and painful. It was hard to solve because, at this point, I had no clear criterion in mind. It was never a question of finding the most literate among my correspondents and compiling a work which was to be judged by literary standards. On the other hand literary ability has much to do with articulacy, and articulacy with a proper degree of honest self-examination. The commonest form of literary failure is not a rough freshness of diction, a clumsiness which may itself be an instrument of vivid expression. The commonest form is a staleness of vocabulary which contributes to a dishonest conventionality of thought. The worst written contributions were the least revealing, and among the final survivors Mrs Kaye is perhaps alone in achieving an appalling vividness without any pretensions whatever to literary equipment. I would have had more such pieces if I could have found them, but the ability is, of course, a rare one.

7

What seemed to be needed, in the first selection, was certainly some degree of eloquence—enough at least to convey the nature of the experienced distress. But it was not necessary that all the contributors should have the exceptional literary ability of Mr Other. This discovery was a welcome superaddition to what was primarily intended to be not a literary but a sociological and psychological symposium. The distinction is difficult to draw, but there were certainly many rejected contributors who wrote with more trenchancy and eloquence than many who appear here.

The first weeding-out involved all those sad monomaniacs with a single, overwhelming but more or less incomprehensible grievance to describe. Mr X had lost his job with an engineering firm in the year 1927. With his long and confusing letter he included a thick pile of documents, including the blank little letters he had received over the years in answer to his constant appeals that the Great should pay attention to his case. These cases are not funny, or if they are funny they are certainly sad as well. Perhaps if my intention had been purely documentary I would have felt obliged to include at least one specimen even of this least appetising form of complaint. But such stories, whatever the impenetrable rights and wrongs of them, are dull, and it was certainly one of my intentions that the readers should not be bored.

On the other hand I had made it plain in my letter to the press that I would regard 'imagined' grievances with quite as welcoming an eye as those which could be shown to be objective. It would not have mattered in the least whether Mr X had *really* been unfairly treated, provided that he believed himself to be a victim. When I was in Israel I tried to arrive, by constant enquiry, at some adequate definition of a Jew, and it was agreed in the end that anyone was a Jew who believed himself to be one. How much more is everyone an underdog who sees himself in this light. And what other criterion could we possibly adopt? I had hoped to receive a communication from some obviously 'successful' man, some well-born tycoon with a marvellous wife and family who, in spite of all appearances, had recognized his inalienable status as an underdog. No such piece of good-fortune came my way, but it would have been an odd criterion which would have denied its right to inclusion on the ground that such a man had no legitimate title to the label.

At a later stage of selection I found myself biased in my choice simply by the need to create some sort of pattern, or at least an adequate variety. This led to a preference for the odd and unexpected complaint—that of Mrs Vaughan, for example, or that of Mr Goe. There was no wish to present a statistical survey of the underdog's condition in modern Britain, but there was a felt pressure to avoid too much of the same thing and to show the condition in as many aspects as I could. I am aware that this has led to a curious lack of social balance in the final result, but this was due to what happened to be available as much as to any deliberate choice on my part. There is nothing in this book by any victim of racial persecution or discrimination; there is nothing by any representative of our largest group of unfortunates, the old; there is nothing, perhaps less surprisingly, by an alcoholic. The balance could have been corrected by commissioning contributions from known members of these groups, but that would have led to a different kind of book. What appears here is selected only from what was made willingly available. And besides this I confess to a prejudice against the inclusion of the familiar. If a coloured or Jewish sufferer, or a white sufferer among Africans, had offered an article which shed a new light on this condition I would gladly have included it. But nobody did so. The sad old story was told many times again, but I preferred what may seem like the comparative triviality of Mr Goe's complaint to the restatement of a familiar impeachment.

The resulting book, then, is in no sense a comprehensive survey of our underdogs: it is not even a representative selection from the main complaints which have been made. But it does contrive, I think, to deal with the familiar in a new way and to reveal a great deal of suffering which we seldom contemplate. We pity, when we think of them, the children of drunken fathers, but Mr Lacey describes this condition to us in a way which compels us to think of it in detail. Mrs Lorne, whether she be right or wrong in her estimate of her own charms, may make us think with pity as well as with irritation of those whose personalities repel us.

There is some sense in the ordering of the book. The first four contributions deal with a more or less general sense of failure; the next four are all concerned, however differently, with sex, and the next three with physical disabilities. After that there is a lapse into the miscellaneous, and the book is brought to a close by the only contribution by an underdog who is also a gay dog, a Miller of Dee who is perfectly contented with his apparently outcast condition. Perhaps I ought not to have included Mr Powell, since my chosen terms of reference suggest that the gay acceptance of his condition removes the victim from the category of underdogs. Yet it seemed to me fitting that Mr Powell should have the last say. He suggests, by his tone of vigorous yet amiable defiance, that line where the underdog and the rebel meet each other and dubiously salute. They are by no means the same creature, though the bitterness of 'A Reluctant Pensioner' suggests another ground on which they coalesce. Trotsky in exile was never an underdog, whether before or after his brief years of power. Mr Fawley, threatened with prison for a psychical or physical peculiarity, seems to accept his grim fate without many rebellious reactions.

In this connection it is worth quoting a strange comment on this enterprise which was provided by a columnist in *The Daily Telegraph*.

IDOLATRY

Mr. Philip Toynbee is appealing for contributions to a symposium of 'underdog confessions'. The contributors' 'condition of supposed mistreatment of inferiority', he says, 'may be racial, sexual, mental, criminal or any other'.

This book should become a 20th-century classic, the contemporary equivalent and reversal of Samuel Smiles's Victorian manual *Self Help*, a park-bench-side book for those who want to go down in the world and are looking for the most up-to-date forms of maladjustment and failure.

In the past, the worship of the criminal and the underdog has mostly been confined to intellectuals and rich Bohemians. Now there are ominous signs that it is beginning to permeate the mass of the nation and gain approval in the highest quarters.

More and more books and films are appearing which express and encourage this taste. It will soon be impossible to find a London theatre which is not presenting some farrago of drivel about thieves, pimps, hooligans, prostitutes, sex-maniacs and class-maniacs.

There is a frenzied search for new varieties of the under-privileged, from misunderstood working-class under-graduates to perverts of every kind. It is a raging disease which will end in complete identification with the object of idolatry. It will be our fate to become what we love.

Then the symbolic figure of England will be a half-witted, impotent, armless, half-caste pickpocket, continually grumb-ling about his mistreatment by one-armed foreign rivals.

Is it only personal pique which makes me think that this is as unpleasant a comment as it is confused? We are not con-cerned in this book with beatniks or with any of those who boldly strive for attention or self-expression in our society. There is much to be said for such figures, and much to be said against them, but they have little relationship to underdogs. Mrs Kaye was making no gesture against society when she made a disastrously mistaken marriage. It was no deliberate act on Mr Lacey's part to be born to a father who was always in his cups. Nor are we intent on purveying admiration for those who happen to be unfortunate. The underdog is someone who deserves our pity if only because he pities himself. In many of the cases in this book he deserves our pity because he is, even by Peter Simple's standards, a pitiable man. There are, of course, our neo-Nietzcheans who abominate the whole emotion, believing that pity is debilitating to those who experience it and humiliating to those who receive it. Let them read this book, then, without compassion: the contributors have supplied their stories and it is not for the editor to decree the reception which they deserve.

But it is worth pointing out that only about half of the contributions to this book are cases in which 'society' might plausibly be blamed for the condition of the victims. There are, of course, a few utopians in our midst who believe that in some future state of universal bliss all husbands will be kind to their wives and all women will be charming. But to most of us cruel husbands and charmless women seem to be an incurable aspect of the human condition as we know or can foresee it. At least we may be agreed that no legislative measure of our own time can ensure that the Mrs Kayes shall all be happy in their married lives or that the Mrs Lornes shall contrive to delight their companions. And although medical science may well find a means of curing the future Mr Goes it can hardly be blamed for having not yet achieved their cure. On the other hand it is immediately available to our legislators to remove Mr Fawley from the category of underdogs, simply by implementing the recommendations of the Wolfenden Committee. Mr Lacey, on the other hand, would not be helped by this legislation, and it is questionable whether pederasty should be described as a socially ameliorable condition. Nor will most of us believe that it was environment alone which decided that Mr Cules or Mr Other should regard themselves as failures. So long as there is success there will be a relative condition of failure, and the procrustean society in which neither will be permitted has been rightly attacked by several of our prophets.

Opinions will certainly differ about the degree to which these cases of distress are amenable to social cure. They will surely differ less about the degree to which all the conditions described here have been at least aggravated by our individual faults of intolerance and selfishness. If it is true that Mrs Lorne lacks charm, then some responsibility must lie with those who refused to find her charming. It is no part of my editorial function to preach a sermon here, but it does seem that man's inhumanity to man is the real villain of all these sad stories.

And how *that* is to be removed is beyond the widest editorial terms of reference.

In one sense, of course, not one of these contributors deserves to be included. All, as I claimed at the opening of this introduction, are in various degrees articulate and by their articulacy all are saved from the worst human condition of all—which is to suffer without words to express or relieve it: to suffer alone and without the possibility of communication. The saddest cases were among those whose offerings had to be rejected. 'Please, *please* let me write and let the world know the anguish which I suffer every night.' I did, of course, allow it, and the result was a piece of ornamental flamboyance in which the real anguish of this woman was almost wholly concealed by her devastating affectations. Some, of course, became harsh to the editor when their offerings were regretfully refused. 'I just thought to ask whether you really consider it consistent with your position as a serious literary journalist to refuse my article simply on the ground that it does not satisfy the demands of the Establishment.' Alas, it was wholly other demands which it failed to satisfy, and this failure is added to the condition of the sufferer.

It is another part of Peter Simple's simplicity to suppose that to plan a symposium by underdogs implies some peculiar respect for that condition. It is true that Jesus Christ showed just such a respect, but there are not many of us who can follow Him in this unless we hold to the neo-christian persuasion that suffering ennobles and that pain is good for us. Suffering may ennoble still further those who are already noble, but most of us know very well that it has the opposite effect on ourselves. 'The Reluctant Pensioner's' tone is by no means admirable, and there are, perhaps, rather few of these contributors for whom we are likely to feel an immediate affection. They are presented here according to no theory of their superiority to the successful, but simply on the right to their chosen title of underdogs.

Mrs Kaye will forgive me if I write that I would have welcomed a contribution from her husband as well as from herself. It may well be that he has nothing to say for himself, but it is at least possible that he too believes himself to be an underdog. And we do not know—how can we!—whether Mr Sainsbury was really guilty of the offence of which he was accused. Guilty or not his right to be included seems to me to be clear enough—as clear, that is, as the right of 'Joe', who is a self-confessed criminal.

What is, of course, true, is that a book of this kind could only have been produced, with any hope of welcome, in a society which no longer equates failure with moral error, or criminality with wickedness. It is fashionable to believe that there is no such thing as human progress and that we become, if anything, worse as time passes and the legacy of Adam's sin accumulates. But we have learned, not least from Freud, to be less odious to each other than were those eighteenth century magnificos whose recreation was to bait the lunatics in Bedlam. This is not the place to argue about moral responsibility; our ideas are nowhere in a state of more bewildering flux. But we are at least more chary of ascribing fault than most of our predecessors were. We see it as at least arguable that 'Joe' would not have remained a thief if society had had a different attitude to criminality. We shall not readily condemn Mrs Dean because her early seduction led her into paths of sexual confusion. What has certainly happened in the last hundred years is that more of us have adapted the famous heart-cry of John Bradford. There, but for some accident of upbringing or circumstance, go we ourselves. And the fact that almost all of us sometimes regard ourselves as underdogs is not necessarily a foolish indulgence or due to a fit of meaningless depression. We are given, at these moments, an opportunity to ally ourselves in spirit with those who are more constantly unfortunate. In fact the Pharisees are not so powerful as they used to be and the sufferers in our society are not so easily dismissed either as people of exceptional good fortune or as the proper victims of their own weaknesses or wickedness. And it is unlikely that many readers will automatically divide up these contributors into those who have and those who have not deserved their misfortune.

Yet it is worth remembering that precisely such a division

would have been the first task of a great many readers in the nineteenth century. The first four contributors would all have been condemned on the harsh old principle that failure is deserved. Mr Fawley and the Pederast would have deserved the fate of Oscar Wilde, and Mrs Dean is an obvious example of a Fallen Woman. The Reluctant Pensioner and Mr Goe would indeed have received sympathy for their physical afflictions, but many would have added that it provided them with an unusual opportunity for the development of character. Mr Sainsbury and 'Joe' would have received the benefit of the doubt only from a small minority of readers, and Mrs Colyer would have been harshly criticised for not thanking God for his mere munificence in providing her with so many children. Mrs Lorne's condition would not, I think, have been either discussed or thought about, and only Mr Lacey, 'Jackie' and Mrs Kaye would have fitted easily into the pattern of Victorian pity.

Many would say that we have carried our indulgence too far, both to ourselves and to others. But at least we are agreed in not knowing quite where it should stop, if indeed it ought to stop at all. So far as our *feelings* are concerned nearly *all* these underdogs will receive at least our sympathy. And since it is we, in our capacity as 'others', who have contributed so much to their misfortune it may even be that we shall match our feelings with a few good resolutions. At least we may find that this book has enlarged the reach of our imagination.

I

Crammer and Failure

by 'CALDER GENN'

The hye montaynis ar blastyd oft
When the lowe vaylye ys myld and soft;
Ffortune with helthe stondis at debate;
The ffall ys grevous ffrome Aloffte
And sure, circa Regna tonat.

Sir Thomas Wyatt

THE TRAVELLER on the high mountains reaches their summit in middle life, and, however grievous the fall, the view must be splendid while it lasts. Even if the sun has passed meridian, its decline will be slow, and what the glories of the sunset, the expanse of the night sky? In the valley bottom there is already shadow; the hills grow steeper as the valley narrows; and fogs are rising.

To translate the metaphor, at the age of forty-five you are a crammer—English and History for the General Certificate, all levels—while your contemporaries and equals are head-masters and dons, senior civil servants, junior cabinet ministers, and successful novelists. This is the age at which you awaken to find your ambitions escaping and your prospects cramped. Success—the high mountains—is no longer in view, and yet energy is still abundant and ability, so you feel, is still culminating. You become, for the first time, conscious of status as what you haven't got. The young are scrupulously respectful, contemporaries are mortifyingly tactful, and your elders eye you with the sad puzzlement of one who watches a rocket fizzle out on its stick, or else with gratified disdain. Acquaintances and colleagues dissolve in radiance from your sight, you are no longer invited to parties, and complicated diffidences obstruct your cultivation of new friends. And if only some of this is true, the sentiment of its truth has nonetheless settled within you. And is not that the essence of under-doggery— the self-conviction?

Such a predicament is approximately mine, and its very familiarity is my excuse for this essay. An attempt to elucidate a specific instance of a commonplace phenomenon may have a degree of clinical interest; what is more important, it may a little help my fellow victims. I began by putting to myself certain questions: one was: 'What am I really missing?' And another, 'How did it happen?'

A difficulty in the way of answering the first is, of course, the temptation to facile consolation. It is tempting, for instance, to suppose that grapes on high mountains almost certainly never ripen. It is also too easy to remember that however high a mountain, there are others still higher, and that valleys are themselves often far above sea-level. Yet though the climber of Snowdon may be yearning for the Matterhorn, the fact remains that valleys and mountains are always clearly distinguishable, whatever their respective elevations. There can be no doubt, either, that mountains of any height are always worth climbing, in fact or in metaphor, because, in fact and metaphor, the achievement enhances the personality. The resistance to effort in the climb, the spacious view at the top: that affords definition, this scope, to the personality. By living down among shadows, the valley dweller is apt to become, in his own feelings, shadowy.

But then, to this first question, there is an inevitable supplementary: 'What is the criterion of success, and why should I subscribe to it? Have I no compensations, and is there no other achievement that merits the name?' As to the compensations, Wyatt evidently believed in them. 'Ffortune with helthe stondis at debate'—at least I have no ulcers; my digestion is good, and I sleep well. 'The ffall ys grevous ffrome Aloffte'—no doubt. But Wyatt wrote these lines from his own tragic experience of the high mountains; the valley dweller has no right to use that sombreness to refract upon himself the beams of solace. There are other compensations. 'Oxbridge residents are terribly conformist,' remarked an acquaintance to me once. 'What,' I asked (being one of them), 'do they conform to?' To which she no doubt returned a tacit '*Sancta simplicitas*' beneath her genial laugh, but at the moment of the question I was genuinely puzzled, and of course to some extent fortunate in my puzzlement. The valley dweller is often freer to form his own soul, and I know at least one who prefers the condition for exactly that reason. But in order to shape one's soul, one must first contemplate it, and much depends on how much contemplation it bears. This is a matter which would lead us straight to my second question; but first I would like a few more words on success.

The success that a failure misses is not after all foremost the achievement of good status, though that is enviable; it is not, either, money or power. All these may be absent, and yet a man may be 'successful'; that is to say, inferior in his own feelings about himself to no one. The sense of inferiority arises from a different lack, one that breeds an emotion akin to guilt; a lack not of what ought to have been received, but what ought to have been given. The failure has withheld himself—not altogether and from the whole of life, unless he is in a madhouse, but nonetheless crucially; he has not made the necessary effort.

He has not withheld all effort. I myself am proud of my marriage, though its success is no doubt due more to my wife, and of my children, though what gives me pride in them—their superiority to myself—ought perhaps to be a cause of humility. Wherever the credit is mainly due, I have made some effort to make my family happy, and my ability to tell my children stories is one of the few talents of which I feel inclined to boast. In my work I am conscientious and even imaginative, so that I have surmounted in it, though not mountains, yet some considerable hillocks which give me chronic satisfaction. Nonetheless, over me I feel the shadow of the mountain I did not climb. It keeps me chilly on the warmest days; and all because at some time, without knowing it, I chose the 'vaylye myld and soft'.

For long, like so many middle-class failures, I blamed my schools. That they were on the whole poor, is true: private schools and a second-rate public school, petty cosmoses where little boys were encouraged to cultivate a self-importance quite out of scale with the rôles in the outer world that most of them would become qualified to fill. I clowned my way through them, envious of the hierarchies into which I seldom dreamt of being able to break, satisfied with a tolerance which sometimes resembled popularity, and always rather dreading than desiring to make friends. But my schools had one advantage usual to those outside the state system: the classes were small, so that the teaching, for what it was worth, was bound to reach the pupils. All the same, it did me little good; from eight to eighteen it never occurred to me to see my school career as anything but an ordeal to be survived; and all the while the lines of anxiety on the brows of my poor parents deepened. It did not occur to them, I think, that since they were seeing me for no more than a quarter of every year, their understanding of my nature might be growing dim. But for this there was another, profounder reason, and to reach it I must summarize my earlier life.

The first eight years of my life were spent in the care of a devoted nurse. I saw much more of her than of anyone else, because my parents were so occupied with my father's work—he was an eminent Congregational minister—and my three brothers were much older. She cared for me in a London flat three floors above the street. In the mornings, she in her neat grey uniform and I a meticulously toileted dandy, we went to Hyde Park. There she made sure from the first that I played only with 'the best babies'. In the afternoons we went to Regent's Park which, for some reason, the best babies did not patronize, so that there I rarely played with anyone. But I was good at playing with myself, and never thought of my world as constricted. My nursery had two windows. One looked on to the well of the block, an intricate affair in besooted white brick, where only the top storeys ever saw the sun, and which to me was a mysterious world for satisfied contemplation; the more fascinating because, except for sonorous pigeons and for sparrows whose sharp chirping echoed resonantly, it seemed to be utterly forsaken.

The other window looked on to the street which had a slum at its farther end. There I would stand, time and again, contentedly and unenviously watching the dirty children quarrelling, shouting, and playing their ingenious games. Directly across the street towered another block of flats, more aspiring in every sense. From a window one storey higher than my own, a little boy would sometimes lean out and talk to me, or we would blow bubbles that hovered and burst above the heads of the street children, who stared up at us, frowning in perplexity at beings so much of other worlds. His world was indeed a little higher than mine; not only could he look down on my nursery table and tell me what I had had for tea, but his parents did not, I believe, regard me as a suitable visiting acquaintance; a street's breadth remained our social distance. They might have thought differently had they known that, though entirely owing to the democracy of nannies, I sometimes took tea in St James's Palace.

I look back on those first eight years as a time of sober colours and rich tones. I remember moments of extraordinary contentment, as when the tawny midday fog shut out even the lighted street-lamps, perfectly isolating the brilliant womb-life of my nursery; or, again and again, lying awake in the early morning, watching the light grow above the drawn curtains, and listening to the music of hooves through the otherwise deserted streets—I think they must have been a detachment of cavalry on the way to exercise in the park. I believe that whereas one child may learn a chair to be an object for climbing upon, sitting on, jumping off, another may learn it as an object with its own mysterious inscape—its wood with visible depths, and the grain like currents and eddies of a living stream; its shape a personality, inimical or friendly. The first child will quickly tire of chairs and of the room which they inhabit; I think my own children are such, and on the whole I am thankful. The second child will have the advantage that he will seldom be bored or lonely. His world will remain outwardly confined, but it will be inexhaustible. I doubt whether I was basically introverted; I took, in my life-stream, the course which offered least resistance to the current.

Accordingly, when I reached the age of eight, my parents, in what must have seemed like wisdom, sent me away to my first boarding school.

There were obviously two great dangers in my contented nanny-sheltered existence. A fond nurse has many advantages, but she has two disadvantages: she is not the mother, although she performs the functions of one; and, in contrast to a mother, she is unlikely to have a motive for wanting to see the child grow up. The consequences are that if the child, as I did, embraces the relationship, he is faced with unfair torment when the nurse leaves him; and if her influence over him has been profound, he has no motive for embracing a future. Rarely in my life have I felt any sentiment about the future except fear. What to others has been the excitement of opportunity, to me has been menace, the greater for the reverberation of any great expectations—'And sure, *circa Regna tonat.*' I date my first vivid consciousness of this fear from the time when my nurse left me. If the mother can step in at such a time, and greet the child with equivalent love and responsible foresight, all, no doubt, comes well; but this my own mother was unable to do.

To understand one's parents, one must, I suppose, understand their marriage, particularly if, like that of mine, it was at once a difficult and successful one.

History in our time transforms human nature so quickly that I wonder whether there will ever be a man much like my father again. He was devout, and a puritan. When I grew up I liked to think of him as a puritan of the seventeenth as distinct from one of the nineteenth century; I suppose I only meant that he was without primness, that his beliefs were passionate without fussiness, and that he loved the Bible. He was a man with no weak qualities—he had gaps in his character but no ghosts—and no nuances; he could never restrain his vigorous movements, saw no reason to doubt his ethics or his creed, never understood anyone who did, and yet was perfectly humble. Since my mother's nature had grown different organs of perception, so that she belonged to a different spiritual genus, I do not think that he can ever have understood her. However,

22

he never ceased to adore her, and the combination accounts for the success of their marriage. My mother had taste and discernment; she once told me that we had been put into the world to learn to discriminate. But in consequence she was one of those who are much more certain of their feelings than of their beliefs, and for whom a religion was an image of felt values rather than a doctrine of metaphysical facts; she may even have thought that the facts as such were unimportant. But she loved my father, partly for his physical beauty of which she was fully conscious, partly for his goodness, and partly no doubt because she enjoyed in his attitude to her the mixture of chronic perplexity and incessant admiration.

Because she loved him, and was, in herself, completely Victorian in her sense of duty, she forced herself to act as his curate in his large London church. The church itself was ugly, and the people who came to it were commonly drab, dull, smug, and lower middle class, though it is true that there were exceptions especially in the social category. I remember, for instance, a distinguished surgeon whose son is now a cabinet minister, and a leading politician whose son became a missing diplomatist. Perhaps, to be fair to the general run, they had the distinction of a typical unguardedness; the smugness, when it predominated, was the by-product of a dignity which itself implied courage, and at worst was ridiculous rather than odious. I think of them as vulnerable, and therefore human. My mother at all events made herself indispensable, but whatever the compensations of the work she must often have found it repugnant. She hated the ugliness that was so ingenious that it could not be alleviated; she must have hated the drabness, and, since her nature was retiring, she must have dreaded the gregariousness. She had snobberies, and though the chief of these was intellectual, she was Victorian enough to be a social snob as well; she must have suffered a little from the shortage of that sort of distinction. Yet once when I asked her if she ever regretted her earlier prospects as an art student, she only said, 'No, it wouldn't have been life.'

I was born when my father's career was near its height; he was something of a national figure, and the work, on which his health flourished, was for my mother too heavy. They lived, until my birth, in a large house which was difficult to run, and then came the war. During it my mother's digestion broke down, and though she never became a complete invalid, I remember her as usually tired. It is true that 'the reed bends when the oak falls', and she was to outlive my father by many years. The fact, nonetheless, as I see it affecting my birth, was that by that time she had had enough. She had already borne three children, and I doubt whether I was part of the design. I remember her saying that suckling me had to be abandoned because it caused her intense pain, and she must have renounced me to my nurse with thankfulness.

Parents of today, of the same intelligence, would, I think, be anxious about a child born into these conditions. Psychology has drilled into us so many warnings; a modern mother, acting as my mother did and with her feelings, might consider that she was forsaking her child, as in a sense she would be. Her consequent worry might be immediately worse for the child than my parents' obliviousness was, but it might also lead to later remedies. At any rate, though my mother was a constitutional worrier—I remember that in a chair she would always sit forward and tense as though expecting imminent news—my infancy was too cosy to distress her mind. I doubt whether she doubted that she loved me, and indeed I still have no idea whether she did. It is a difficult point in justice; she may have been less oblivious of my needs than I am inclined to suppose, and much torn between her duties to me and to my father.

Moreover, as a family we suffered from a handicap which may have impeded her from recognizing her true feelings for me, and so judiciously compensating for their shortcomings. Not only were we far too northern to be demonstrative, but we were also too Victorian—except for my father who rather was too imperceptive—to be outspoken. Above candour we valued loyalty, and loyalty with us took one especial form which I refer to in my own mind as 'the conspiracy'. We all understood the difference between my parents; we should have been crass if we hadn't. We realized, that is to say, that my father's philosophy was untranslatable into my mother's terms,

24

and that my mother was determined that he should never perceive this. It was not that, apart from his perplexities, my father was unaware of the difference—I have a book inscribed on the flyleaf from my father to my mother: 'To Olivia, who led me along the broader way to the fuller life'—nor that she tried to avert open disagreement with him. Indeed she sometimes rather relished it, though she often preferred an extreme tact; for instance, I was seventeen before I discovered that my mother, unlike my father, was not a convinced teetotaller. Her real concern was more that my father should not be thrown into utter bewilderment. It followed that, as a family, we were united, but stealthy in our movements, and somewhat inclined to nervous outbreaks. We developed a tendency to violent utterance, because at the root of the family lay the unutterable. And because true relationship was in consequence frustrated, we practised rôles. It was simpler and far safer to revere my mother for her wisdom and my father for his goodness, both of which were authentic and intrinsic, than to raise the dilemma that these qualities might, as they were represented, be incompatible.

The conspiracy which protected my father also protected my mother. She must not recognize herself as a conspirator, even though it was for him and not against him, for what would then become of his prestige in her eyes and ours? He did not, it is true, demand prestige; on the contrary, such a reward was to him the merest by-product, easily dispensable. But recognition of incompatibility of outlook could easily lead to a war, destructive of more than the issue was worth. What my mother and we all loved in my father was not his theology, his sabbatarianism, and his total abstinence, but his goodness, his ardour, his strength and his generosity. Protectiveness is the concomitant of loyalty, and what Victorians protected in one another is invisible to analysis. We, as a rule, can see no logic in their assessments, and we trust analysis to the point of exposure; we are not altogether the worse for it, and yet the price we pay may be too dear, for the latent hatred in all human relationships is thereby released, at the expense of the love, which is implicit there too.

The practice of what I call 'the conspiracy' was not only an added strain on my mother psychologically, but I think made it easier for her to transmute her love for me, in whatever degree it may have existed, into duty. One difference between the two is that duty can be delegated. So first I was given a nurse, and then I was sent to boarding school; I was subjected to a process which should have turned me into a rewarding product. But a product in process is necessarily passive, and in my case an unexpected consequence was that by the time I was fifteen I was finding my mother increasingly difficult to talk to. I used to try, but while I was speaking I could watch her gaze looking past my words with the distress of a seeker; either there was something she had lost in me, or something which she had not found, and which she constantly expected without much hope. It was, I believe now, her son. She would have recognized him had she perceived ambitions. She was too discerning to estimate these as indispensable, but they would have enabled her to recognize a personality taking shape, and, for all her discernment, I doubt whether she ever clearly distinguished between the shape of a personality and that of a career. My three brothers had rewarded her early by a number of promising shoots in the soil of their youth, but as she looked into mine she saw nothing but a tangle of weeds which she had never planted. Had she, perhaps, forgotten to plant anything, and did she ever ask herself the question? I believe now that she had been content, without realizing it, to leave me in the hands of her deputed gardeners.

The result in me was a devotion enforced by a strong strain of guilt. Like all children, I felt the need for love, and, from my eighth year, in my hidden recesses I felt its absence—or what that recessive self took to be its absence, for duty is as cold as charity. Instinctively I concentrated my efforts on trying to attain it. It seemed to me wrong to have a feeling, a taste, of which she disapproved. Unaware that she hated dogs, at the age of ten I badgered her until she told me the breed she disliked least—it was airedales; I then made them my favourites, though I would have preferred her to have said spaniels. Should she slight a book which was fascinating me, I gave up reading it; and I was haunted by a painful, inexorable need for confession. I would search my life for a misdeed, or even an ill-thought, and produce an imaginary peccadillo as if it were a crime or a blasphemy, to be received of course with embarrassed bewilderment. I liked my own company, but considered that she had a prior right to it, and so I would impose myself on her when she would herself have preferred to be alone. Parting from her to go to boarding school was agony, and not quickly forgotten when once the severance was completed.

The pain of school was due above all to the absence for me of the usual compensation—enjoyment of the company of other boys. Most children, I suppose, spontaneously enlarge their bond with their parents into friendship with their kind, but I felt no such impulse because I had no such starting point; if I could not have my mother's society, I preferred to be alone, and my infancy had trained me to relish solitude. This lack of instinct for friendship has lasted all my life, and I regard it now as one of my deepest deprivations. I have not found it difficult to attract friendship, but again and again I have betrayed it by purest negligence, only to realize the importance of the loss much later.

Guilt, indifference to people, fear of the future—I have mentioned them all as features of my nature, and I trace them all back to that family *lacuna*, for what was missing between my mother and myself was as deficient between myself and the rest of my family. My brothers were out of my reach in my years of infancy, and when I was old enough for them, my own sense of unworthiness baffled them. My father tried hard in his own way to communicate with me, but I was too much in my mother's mould for us to understand each other. When my wife came to probe into the constraint, I tried to explain it in these words: 'I feel as though I have come late to a party, and am wondering whether I was ever invited.' At the time, I meant my family; but I think it is true also of my feeling for life.

Our parents give us life, but their most valuable gift to us is the sense of the right to be alive. My nurse lavished her love on me; to that extent my infancy was if anything overprivileged

Thereafter I became an interloper, intrinsically unworthy, in anyone's company ashamed. Hence my sole concern became how to construct an illusion of permanency in a nest of congenial circumstance. Some people would have found a system of habits enough for this purpose, but I, realizing that ambitions were expected of me, needed something more, and since ambitions were impossible to me I substituted their deadly *simulacra*—daydreams. 'I hitched my waggon to a star,' I once explained to an acquaintance, 'only to find that stars are useless for drawing waggons.' In reality astronomy teaches us that they rush them into outer space. Vestiges of these dreams still operate upon me; is the waggon still rushing? This essay is in part an attempt to apply a brake.

So far I have tried to explore the factors which first constituted my plight. For part of what remains, I wish to define more closely what I take that plight to be, but first I must say a little in justification of my reminiscences. There are, I suppose, several sorts of underdog, but one among them seems evidently bogus. Whereas the true underdog, of whatever breed, is authentically underprivileged, has a just grievance, can point to a more or less identifiable oppressor, the false kind merely has a chip on his shoulder. The man who blames his failure on to his parents or his schools, or else upon society, instead of taking the burden upon himself, is drearily familiar, and up to a point his evasions are very easily exposed. For clearly, all parents since the first have been imperfect, and no schools have ever been very satisfactory; and since no schools are always worse than bad ones, what can a man hope from society? Every man is a victim of injustice, so that injustice must be exceptional not to be boring. But yet I must insist that it is the familiar that is important, and it is only superficiality in the treatment of it that ever makes it seem trivial. I only wish not to leave my parents in the mire of my smears, for I think that, in many ways that scarcely appear in this essay, they were exceptionally good. As human beings I remember them with pride; as parents with indulgence and compassion—with indulgence, because whatever wrongs they did to me were the price of the dues they paid to each other and to others, and with compassion because, whatever their shortcomings, I cannot accuse them of not, with how much suffering effort, having tried.

In what sense have I a claim to be included in this symposium? Only that I have described a moral crippledom of, I feel sure, a very usual kind. Now congenital cripples do not, if they are otherwise healthy, require any pity; on the contrary, they resent it as a gratuitous contribution to their handicap. They do not, either, need to be told that it is for them to overcome their limitations and lead a normal life; the disease itself provides all the needed pressure in that direction. But what if the cripple does not recognize his disease, feels himself somehow shameful in his inferiority? It is to counter just such a mysterious and needless shame that I have written this analysis. I do not know what the benefits of it, if any, will be; but perhaps I may escape the complications of such a disease—the resentments which are the more bitter because they arise out of the unknown, and in later years turn a tormented man into a tormenting one.

One must also in these days face the possibility that one's self-analysis is unscientific; I may be referred to a psychoanalyst for orthodox treatment. Indeed I tried one once; but I bored myself—if the reader will believe it—by talking about myself, and I bored my analyst so far that twice he fell asleep. I cut short the treatment, which was, I'm afraid, of slight profit to either of us; no doubt in the end he would have concluded that I suffer from the effects of an *Oedipus Complex*. However, I am not much concerned with whether an analyst would endorse my diagnosis, for its importance to me is precisely that it is my own—that I have just so far set myself against the obstacle that hitherto constituted myself; in that sense perhaps I have overcome one mountain, after all.

2

Ghost-writer and Failure

by 'H. E. R. CULES'

A LITERARY ghost is, according to a successful author whose name, however, escapes me, 'a writer whose talent is insufficient to earn him a living unless he masquerades as somebody else.'

I am a ghost. Reflection on a successful writer's description of the motive rankles because it is true. The advantages of spectral writing are probably obvious but one gets pleasure out of describing them. First of all, it is comparatively well paid, thus enabling one to pose as a successful citizen with a car, refrigerator, dinner jacket, and similar symbols of economic triumph. One may privately gloat with masochistic delight over one's defects but there is nothing an inferior person hates so much as displaying his inferiority by his possessions or lack of them.

A second pleasure, and this I find the greatest of all, is to savour the clayish qualities of a popular idol's feet. I have ghosted books for entertainers, a famous novelist, an ageing playwright, one or two criminals, a Scotland Yard Holmes, a spy, a member of the nobility and a handful of politicians. If any of them had valets (one did) I would have shared in their conspiratorial glee of knowing how stupid, bumptious, phoney, hypocritical and uncultured they were—some in perhaps only one category but most in all.

A deeper delight, of the hair shirt variety, is the way the sycophantic plaudits of the notoriety's friends and relatives pass by the ghost who is mainly responsible for the literary activities being applauded.

Only very exceptionally has my help been publicly acknowledged, usually in inverse ratio to the proportion of work I did.

By contrast I recall with renewed delight the bone-headed colonel for whom I wrote an extremely dreary and pedantic history of his regiment, full of incidents of crass incompetence and futile bravery in unpronounceable districts of India, the Crimea, Zululand, Flanders and Burma. There was a 'do' in the regimental mess to launch the book. Possibly to keep my lips sealed or to obtain confidential support if awkward questions arose I was invited along in my usual rôle of 'research assistant'.

The hesitant, slightly self-conscious description by the ostensible author of his 'writing op', with his 'found it pretty easy once I got down to it, you know; must have a knack for it', with turgid references to his literary muse, 'a nice turn of a phrase', and hints about a parallel talent with Churchill's, were all splendid hearing.

He was by no means the only client I have had who has quite genuinely convinced himself (less frequently herself—women are most honest) that he did in fact write 70,000 words or so in grammatical and fairly readable English.

The smug sensation of knowing one has the power to debunk the whole set-up is, of course, first rate Walter Mitty daydream provender. But one never does.

A long-suffering wife and one or two hardened friends are the sole audience for my soul-searching and complaining. A psychiatrist would know what's coming next. For the interested layman who may be unskilled in travelling along all too familiar by-roads of the psyche I would say that it goes something like this:

'I'll chuck the damned thing, money or not. If the stuff's good enough to get into print under what's-his-name then it's good enough to appear under mine. This sort of literary schizophrenia can get out of hand. I'm beginning to find I identify myself with these passée tarts, would-be dictators, and has-been crooks. Anyway, I'm hitting a new low in ghosting for these bloody women in the Sunday papers. I'm getting into a sort of hermaphrodite condition.'

The friends usually make sympathetic and encouraging noises

on the lines of 'you're wise. Take the plunge, old boy! You can write; you know that. Half a dozen publishers know it too.'

My wife, wiser than they, keeps quiet until I run out of self-pity. Then she takes the line of 'don't worry about it, darling. You know you're better than they, and I know it. That's what really matters.'

I don't know it. In fact I'm pretty convinced otherwise by the materialistic standards of the twentieth century which boil down to the size of the bank balance, and the number of paragraphs in the gossip columns. The mystification as to why A is popular, rich, important and respected, while B, so far as I can see virtually identical in physique, mental powers, and background, is and will remain a nonentity, gradually turns into a neurosis.

The strange thing is that a renewal of admiration and veneration is irrepressible, though of tender growth. I find myself going starry-eyed to the first interview with a prospective client, as all these people, whether they are notorious white-slave traffickers destined for the Sunday Press, or archaeologists hoping to interest the mob of telly-watchers in something about the background to the civilization which they grace, have enormous charm which they can turn on or off at will.

Understandably they turn it on in order to get the donkey section of their literary task done for them, and to cut my share of the financial reward by ten per cent or so. I find that I succumb to their extrovert personalities every time and for quite three meetings subsequently feel convinced that the whole Secret of Success is involved in that word Charm with all its inferences of magical powers.

Any degree of intimacy destroys this rosy-hued regard. The charm is so obviously artificial that I cannot believe it works during the crises and opportunities of my falling idols' careers.

It is impossible, for instance, to think that a lady novelist's oozy insinuations that I am so clever work equally well with her publisher or can somehow permeate her literature so that 120,000 factory girls read her serial versions every week. One begins to doubt that a politician's charmingly implicit trust in one's discretion so that he is impelled to reveal scandalous goings-on among Cabinet Ministers has also been his method of getting entrusted with a government department and marrying the nubile daughter of a wealthy diplomat.

The nearest I have come to a solution to this problem of greatness is to suspect that in this world one achieves what one expects, and never what one deserves. Without exception the 'names' whose careers, or at least whose vanity, I have assisted regarded the benefits I provided as their due.

How one acquires this beneficial attitude I wish I knew. Possibly it's something to do with the glands, and is obviously inheritable. I greatly doubt whether it can be inculcated by training or education, though envious underdogs among the underprivileged classes will insist that it is, regretting their lack of public school education and wasting their money on correspondence courses purporting to be a substitute.

This I know to be futile for I am a public school product—a fact concealed by the school and, normally, by myself. But in theory I should have emerged as a youth who worships the Protestant Christian God, the Establishment and the Straight Bat. I would have been trained not to think, to be class-conscious, and to regard the British, or rather the English, as the Chosen of the Creator. I did not.

In practice I believe the public schools fail miserably in their objective if this is as popularly supposed. My retiring personality attracted few chums at school, and all such slight acquaintanceships evaporated when I left. It was impossible, however, not to remember fairly well at least the thirty-odd youths with whom I progressed, or was shifted, through my public school education.

Only one ever appears today in the Press as a man of substance. And this would be questioned by many, as he is a trouble-making Socialist MP who protested about Suez, visits Russia, marches from Aldermaston, and sympathizes with the hierarchy of the ETU. The remaining twenty-nine have presumably found the oblivion of mediocrity which I myself enjoy.

As a matter of comfort to my inferior ego my *Alma Mater,* as everyone who hasn't been to one calls it, seemed to specialize in inferiority. I recall the names of only two people whose scholastic careers made them objects of admiration as fellow scholars, though of a previous era. One was an Admiral who was inveigled into a speech-day ceremony. His attendance at the school had been terminated at the age of fifteen by expulsion for fighting errand-boys in Smithfield Market. The fight was not, of course, the occurrence objected to; he did it for money contributed by the meat porters, thereby confounding his amateur status.

The second, never mentioned by the staff but gloated over in the evening papers by the pupils, was a key witness in the Mr A. Indian Rajah blackmail case of the nineteen-twenties. He was apparently a blackmailer too. He shot himself in a taxi.

It would probably be nearer the truth to say that the public schools specialize in turning out mediocre human beings so smugly disciplined that they rather like their intellectual sterility. Really the percentage of worldly, spiritual or artistic successes is fantastically small. The majority aim no higher than to hang on to the social standards they were born in, and sending their own sons to the school. Incidentally, only a fraction of ex-boys seem to make enough money to do this. And if one could not send one's son to the school the next best thing was to return to it oneself—as a master.

The man who I admired was an ex-pupil. He was a more or less unfrocked clergyman who shared with me a hearty dislike of the twentieth century. I caught from him the sense of the Glory that was Greece and the Majesty that was Rome.

Like all day-dreamers, he glossed over the defects of his dream worlds. Consequently I never heard much about the conditions of the slaves in Athens or indeed of the political intrigues which menaced free men too. My education omitted anything about the degeneration of Rome or the defects of a dictator state. My mind was cultivated to accept the past as splendid and the present as disgusting. I have not, of course, changed my opinion since.

This master liked me because, I suspect, I was one of his kind. He had been quite a brilliant classicist at Cambridge and should have made a worldly triumph in at least one of several ways according to the ostensible public school plan. He could have stayed at Cambridge. He could have become a headmaster of a public school. He could have behaved with the discretion that in time confers a Bishopric on holy clerks or at least a well-endowed parish in the shires.

He had, at fifty when I knew him well, done none of these things. He was a teetotaller which probably kept him out of university life. He despised sport which invalidated anything more than a classical post under some headmaster who appreciated the benefits of a moving ball. He had such objective views on Christ and such a hatred of the Papacy that promotion in the Church (seeing that Dean Inge was then safely ensconced in the Deanery of St Paul's, seemingly for ever) was out of the question.

I worshipped this man as one who had made the best of second best. I continued to venerate his views for years after I left school. I always regarded him as my idea of a happy man who counted the world well lost for learning. I tried, and have continued to try, to model my own mentality on what I believed to be his.

Just after the war I saw his extremely ugly little face, with its wispy hair stretched over his bald pate, staring at me from page one of the *Daily Mirror*. He was then in his sixties, and he had just died. He had, it seemed, married a mere child—some simple country girl of busty beauty but vacuous face. And he had, for reasons unrevealed at the inquest, thrust himself head downwards into the well of the rural hovel where he had set up his amorous ménage.

We of the inferior classes can understand that. We neither pity nor condemn. The inevitable climax of banal disaster is acceptable.

'You'll do; yes, you'll do,' this master had observed as we said goodbye on my last day at school. It was all I wanted, or expected, to hear—the password of the underdog the world over.

I needed this modest encouragement, for I was alarmed as to what it was I would do. A few weeks before I left school, the Great Western Railway had one of those periodic outbursts of initiative when vast organizations run by badly educated but very successful tycoons decide to grab whatever value there might be in the much vaunted and little exploited public school man. The Railway let it be known that they were open to take boys from the public schools 'with a view to executive appointments'.

I travelled daily to and from Paddington and loved the railway. The opportunity seemed a fair version of the basic 'I want to be an engine driver' outlook. I put my name down—the only boy, incidentally, in the whole school fool enough to believe the statement about the executive appointments at its face value.

From whatever director the notion had originally come it had clearly been forgotten or deliberately ignored by those at Paddington Station whose job it was to keep the trains running.

I found myself in a large and depressing office at the end of Platform One with half a dozen boys younger than myself. They were what I then called working-class and were quite obviously already working. Two or three were, in fact, in the blue serge of the GWR uniform; porters, lamp boys or something, and chosen as literate.

We were given a foolscap sheet of questions which consisted chiefly of mathematical problems concerned with pay loads of excursion trains, the feasible tonnage of coal in a train hauled in sixty trucks, and mysterious abbreviations like FOB and CIF.

I did not even attempt the arithmetic questions as soon as I discovered that I did not know my tons-cwt-pounds table. I had a go at the geography question and probably destroyed my chances of an eminence in the Transport Commission today by describing Newport as in the Isle of Wight. I had not heard of a more important town of the same name in Mon, and had been mystified at the GWR's interest in an island they did not serve. Most of the other places I had never heard of, or was unaware of the county which they graced.

I failed, of course—and so fascinated was the Superintendent of the Line, a large and kindly man with a beard, at this sorry proof of the futility of the public school system that he had me in for an interview. Whatever thought he may have had about a hefty, muscular young patrician of the ruling classes being a potential asset if only for prestige and decorative value, I knew by his face after we had met that these had been quickly banished.

Though over seventeen I looked about fourteen. As usual in moments of crisis my nostrils had filled with mucus and I had to hang my mouth open to breathe. Later, in the gents' lavatory, I saw that in my mystification about tons of coal from Cardiff to Birkenhead, my inky fingers had streaked blue-black on my temples and down my right cheek.

'I'm afraid you've failed our simple examination,' the Superintendent said. 'It was for junior booking clerks or parcels traffic staff. A pity. Good afternoon.'

For some reason I was delighted at knowing I would not work for the GWR, and I thanked him effusively. This non-plussed him so much that he remained speechless, merely crossing the room and opening the door for me.

My ignorance about Newport (Mon) and Newport (IOW) was, in reality, one of those pieces of disguised luck which have embellished my existence. I would have been far too supine ever to have extricated myself from a railway job and might by now have attained perhaps the first class booking office (stations beyond Reading) at Paddington. One has to be mediocre, but it is better to enjoy failure in something more to one's liking.

I drifted into journalism, via that peculiar and venal section of the Fourth Estate known as trade paper publishing. It was as corrupt as anything could be without falling foul of the Law. The amount of advertising decided without right of appeal whether a product was good or bad in the editorial columns.

Slanting of news was on a petty scale in the trade press. When I progressed or descended to daily newspaper work I found the odour of corruption different but stronger. Here money might not buy editorial opinion, but power did. I was young enough to feel so deeply about this disillusionment of my ideals that I left for the comparatively clean atmosphere of the film industry.

I can claim without risk of being refuted that I was the lowest paid press manager in the London film industry of the mid-thirties. My firm, incidentally, made the worst films themselves and imported the worst made in Hollywood. The flood of treasure poured out by the public, the banks, and the insurance companies to the benefit of men like Korda and Pascal was so great that a few trickles inevitably ran our way too. It was a period not without its financial benefits.

However, after a couple of years, the shareholders at last caught on to the truth that the considerable turnover somehow got absorbed in the hordes of production units, studio companies, film renting organizations and so on which were conglomerated together for the purpose of getting a cheaply made quickie from Hollywood's outback to the screen of a miners' welfare hall in South Wales. An economy drive began.

The advertising manager, my superior, getting £18 per week, was sacked. I got his job, while retaining my own, with an increase which brought my salary up to £10. I was thus able to retain my position as the lowest paid film executive between Oxford Street and Shaftesbury Avenue. I was also the hardest worked. I was so busy doing the actual work that I was an abysmal failure at the main purpose of film publicity, which was to make friends and enemies of everyone in the same job or with the vaguest connections with Fleet Street.

Plenty of men who had been employed for years or were misfits like myself subconsciously looked forward to the war. I believe it is said to be a suicide-proneness endemic in the human race. More superficially it seemed at the time like a time when courage, patriotism, determination and similar virtues of the Samuel Smiles type would bring their own reward.

In fact, at the outset, nepotism, the old school tie, the right club, and all the rest of it meant far more than in civilian life. My unwillingness to boast of any of the last-named, plus an inherent poverty of the aforementioned virtues, meant that I floundered in the 'other ranks' until better and braver men wearing the same coloured uniform as I settled the whole business and ensured the continuance of the pattern jeopardized in 1939.

I left the RAF as unostentatiously as I had sidled in, and

faced the infinitely greater terrors of civilian life. My previous employers, with a Government order about re-engagement of employees prodding them to be generous, gave me a year's salary not to come near them again.

I registered with the Appointments Bureau of the Ministry of Labour in January 1946, and was flatteringly told that a high-powered executive position would soon be mine. I have not heard from this establishment since.

The complete absence of discipline, time-keeping or responsibility in uniform had ruined me for any civilian employee relationship, with its rules, demands for individuality, enterprise and what-not. I became self-employed as a convenient method of evading the need to compete in a contest where I knew only too well anyone younger, brighter, indeed virtually anyone, could outwit me.

It was, of course, a temporary action until things settled down, until the way ahead was clearer, and similar responsibility-evading clichés. It was temporary in 1946; it is still temporary in 1961.

One may always miss the bus; but, thank God, there's no natural or man-made law against leaning on the bus stop post pretending you haven't. . . .

3

Inadequate Education

by 'BRIAN COLEMAN'

IT IS not without good reason that the 'S.J.' after a Jesuit
priest's name is sometimes thought to mean Soldier of Jesus.
Since its foundation by Ignatius Loyola more than four
centuries ago, battalions of Jesuits, armed with their ferulae,
have marched to almost every country in the world and educated its people. Or tried to.

Their aim is spiritual perfection, not only for themselves but
for everyone and, wisely, they teach that spiritual and secular
knowledge are complementary. Despite persecution which has
often led to martyrdom, the Society of Jesus has continued its
set course, improving the world quality and quantity of
Christians with one hand and with the other adding to the well
of human knowledge. The Society's work in astronomy,
geophysics, meteorology and seismology is famous. But their
aim is to teach, to pass on what they know. They have taught
in Japan, China, Mexico, Cuba, the Philippines, Brazil; during
the course of the centuries they have found their way to un-
charted lands, to teach.

It is not the fault of the Society of Jesuits that in England
their lay teaching colleges must concentrate primarily on
forcing their boy pupils through the General Certificate of
Education—the infamous 'School Cert.'

For the great majority of English children, education has
only two stages; elementary school and secondary modern
school—or, if one takes and passes the scholarship, then it's
a County, technical, grammar school, or college. Perhaps, as
in my case, a Jesuit college. Each of the two stages is terminated
by a crucial examination, the first at eleven when a boy thinks

only of food, fooling about and fighting, the second at sixteen when he substitutes females for fighting.

So the Jesuits in their colleges and the teachers in their County, technical and grammar schools do their level best in the five years they have the children in their power to get as many as possible over the hurdle of the final examination, the School Cert. Within the stark confines of their curriculum they are astonishingly successful. What happens next? In the early Summer of each year and in the budding Spring of their lives, thousands upon thousands of young girls and boys, their School Certs thrown in the bedroom drawers containing the padded brassières and flashy evening ties, drift aimlessly into the gaping maws of insurance offices, banks, shipping companies, the Civil Service. Any white-collar job will do. You need a School Cert to get it, so you might as well make the best of your education.

Anyway, that is what happened to me.

My five years at College were from 1938 to 1943—war years, certainly; conditions change. But something never, never changes, and that is the cocky, know-it-all woolliness of a pubescent child's mind. I can remember only two boys who had some vague notion of what they were going to do when they left school, and they were two who intended to stay on for another couple of years and try for the university entrance examination, eventually to become teachers. Their parents must have put them up to it. We thought they were crazy. We were educated. We knew that sin was something to do with trigonometry, could struggle through Caesar but bogged down somewhat on Virgil; could scan *The Hound of Heaven,* and it had been good fun in the coach going to see that year's School Cert Shakespeare play. I know that I, for one, had nothing more to learn. The world, my oyster, was waiting; so wide open that it seemed too easy to reach out for the pearl.

My father was a hard-handed man, often on the dole between the two World Wars, and was naturally delighted when his only son achieved the status of clerk in a London bank. An ambition which was the realization of thousands of proud parental dreams. From Glasgow through Tyneside; from the

Ridings through Orwell country and the Potteries; from the Valleys through the Midlands to London, a white collar job meant security. Security. No dole for my son. Good parents could not possibly have higher aspirations. A university was no more thought of than taking the children, with their buckets and spades and home-made swimming costumes, to Capri for the summer holidays.

Secure with white collar, tight suit, season ticket and luncheon vouchers, I joined the herd of daily commuters. It took me five years (broken by National Service, a numbing nightmare which did little except increase my vocabulary), to wake up to the fact that I had missed something. Was still missing something. The Latin I had half-learned at college was intended to develop logic, so they told us. Logically then, I worked out that my mind had been filled like a dustbin with bits of English Literature; mathematics, pure and impure; oddments of French and Latin; the Greek alphabet (of all things); scraps of history and geography; and a hotch-potch of physics and chemistry sweepingly labelled 'science'.

Logically, I decided that the old adage about half knowledge being worse than none was correct. But the awful fact that I had this half-knowledge remained. Logically, it was easy to conclude that it had achieved its object—the School Cert followed by the certainty of the permanent, pensionable, secure job. All right: but the scraps of knowledge are still there, firmly whacked in, and utterly useless in the daily task of earning the crust; and they itch and nag.

An itch cannot be ignored—that was even beyond Bottom's remarkable prowess—and dissatisfaction grows and cankers. My first sign of unrest was a novel, which took a year to write and was full of (to me) obscure words culled from Roget and Chambers and scarcely ever conveying the intended meaning. When this and all the short stories and poems were duly rejected, I would not at that time consider studying the art of writing at an established school. Oh dear, no. I had had my education. I had my School Cert to prove it.

At this stage in my soul-searching I got married and suspended the search for a short while, telling myself that this was all that mattered. I was probably convinced, too, then.

From the time I left school at sixteen until I was called up for National Service, I was employed by Barclays Bank (Dominion, Colonial and Overseas)—I believe it has a less archaic title now —and my work consisted mainly of sorting out certified invoices, bills of exchange, bills of lading and other shipping documents. These documents arrived from the export agents in batches of anything from duplicate to sextuplicate, and it was my job to separate them neatly and methodically, and list them all on long forms headed 'Bills Outward' for despatch to the overseas branch handling the goods. A reasonably sane child of twelve could have done the job just as efficiently; certainly my knowledge of the Greek alphabet was no help. Even good handwriting was not necessary for the forms were checked by another clerk, then sent down to the typing pool to be typed, then checked by another clerk. 'Bills Outward' was my main job: to complete my day's work I spent about an hour each morning in the post room, opening and sorting letters. One has to be able to read to do that.

The astonishing aspect of my banking experience was that so few of the enormous number of clerks employed seemed to take the slightest interest in their work, in either enthusiasm or mortification; or to treat it as anything but a felicitous way of simply earning a living. It was not until later that I discovered that most of them regarded the daily round as only a means to an end, a way of providing enough money to enable them to pursue their main interests—buying for the home, holidays abroad, motoring, golf, angling, boating. The commuter's hobbies. And I had naïvely supposed on leaving school that one's daily work was in itself important.

Clerical work in massive organizations like banks and the Civil Service is efficiently broken down, almost to the point of mass-production; so that one man will do a routine job for a certain number of years, then, unless he is unusually feckless or crass, he is promoted to another routine job. And so on. Salary increases and bonuses are automatic; knowledge of clerical procedure, unique to the organization and built up over the years, is only acquired through experience. It comes automatically. The college education, even if it includes commerce, is as much use as a third arm.

As a member of my college Old Boys' Association I was well in touch with my contemporaries, and found that most of them on drifting away from school had been swallowed up by vast offices. Office fodder. Routine jobs, just like mine. Knowing how to decline *mensa* and to prove Pythagoras was not really important. No kind of office work requires secondary school knowledge in its actual performance, but one has to have a secondary school education to attain it. But with the bank clerks and Old Boys all so complacent, I had that painful, queasy sensation that I must be the one out of step.

Three years in the Royal Artillery passed away like a long walk through a bog, up to the eyebrows. I went in with the lowest possible rank and came out with it. Then a year in another bank, during which the novel was worked out of my system, then marriage. But still the feeling persisted that something had gone wrong somewhere. I had an oppressive sense of inferiority, and tried hard to convince myself that the restlessness I suffered was entirely my own fault. It was not that I considered the world owed me a living—the Jesuits, like the good educationalists they are, leave their pupils in no doubt that the benefits and blessings of this world have to be worked for as well as those of the next—but that I was a victim of circumstance, of mistreatment. I felt that I was capable of doing work that required a much greater mental effort than that expected by the bank, yet I was not academically qualified to tackle it. I had been cheated by the educational system. With a wife, cramped lodgings, a child expected, and a bank clerk's salary, to think of starting to study for entrance to a university was quite out of the question.

An outlet was vital or I would burst. My mind, almost inert during the day's calculation of dividend warrants, fairly bubbled over in the evenings. A second novel was written in three months; stories and poems were scribbled down as fast as my hand would move over the paper. I confess that this helped a great deal, but the itch persisted. I was unfulfilled.

As a possible step further towards expression, I joined an amateur dramatic society. Imagine my amazement when I discovered that nearly all of the society's members were young people just like myself, half-educated, not realizing that their minds had been opened up but nothing put in them, trying to glean some sort of intellectual satisfaction through amateur dramatics. It is people like those, like myself, who form the music appreciation societies, amateur dramatic companies, art groups and literary and debating societies; who fill the Old Vic gallery, the Promenade Concerts and public library lecture rooms, who hover about the art galleries and read the posh Sunday papers, dim-eyed suburban culture-vultures.

This was a revelation indeed. I had thought the itch was personal, but the disease, like Antigone's, is catching.

The most common medicine for the disease is cynicism, and I have had to fight against the temptation of this bitter pill with far greater perseverance than I have had to struggle with a sense of injustice. There is no man more unhappy than the sour, jaded cynic. In order to appreciate music, the theatre, literature and art, one does not need a college education; in fact it is probably better to be without it and start from scratch, so that the love is natural, not a calculation of the mind. For a person with a college education which he considers is not properly used, to take up one or another form of art merely as an outlet for frustration, seems to me to be a dangerous step towards cynicism.

If, in order to live I must serve Mammon, as most of us have to, then it seems that I should devote the best of my ability and knowledge to that task.

The vicious circle of high school as a means to an end followed by the safe job as a means to an end embraces thousands of us. Having myself been a victim of the educational system I read with wry misgivings the accounts of battles over the raising or lowering of the present school leaving age. By all means raise it, and keep on raising it; but develop the children's natural qualities, fine them down until they are sharp enough to push through to university for final shaping and refinement. A child's head is not a rag-bag to be stuffed to bursting point until he or she is set loose on the world in a flat spin at fourteen, fifteen or sixteen, with or without the ridiculous success-symbol of the abominable School Cert.

Ever since those great comic scribes Defoe, Swift and Bunyan said what they wanted to say by saying something else, uncountable young men have tried to do the same, and uncountable manuscripts lie stuffed away in drawers after three or four rejections. A very kind literary agent took the trouble to point out some of the major flaws in my second book and made meticulous suggestions for rewriting. It was generous and considerate of her, and I shall always be grateful for her encouragement. But that novel, like the first, was a song sung. Nevertheless, I began to think that my writing could be improved at an evening institute, and enrolled in a class for 'Writing for Publication'. The tutor, quite rightly, scoffed at my novels as being unsaleable, and told me that every one of the forlorn writers in his class had at least one dejected rejected outpouring of blood-sweat behind him. Now they were writing for money. Not in the least embittered by the loss of the will to continue with creative writing, the students were learning how to manufacture stories for the weeklies of the world, articles on anything from church brasses to cookery recipes, and commercial library romances, thrillers and westerns. Most of the students were successful, but I could not stay with them. It was not for this that I underwent a college education. Hack writing is a refuge more soul-destroying than amateur dramatics, for the desire to create has to be stifled or titillated to suit the audience. Amateur actors can ham away as much as they please. There are rules; but they are the actor's servants, not his masters.

An intellectually unrewarding job is a humiliation of the mind. I left the bank with a feeling of relief, which was doubtless shared by the staff department, and was lucky enough to find employment in a publishing house. By learning the system, and happening to be around during staff reorganization, I have progressed well, and now constantly meet extremely pleasant young men in flannels with jolly good accents who know exactly what they want out of life and have the confidence of their qualifications to go ahead and get it. So now I must combat a humiliation of the spirit. There, but for the lack of guidance at the proper time, encouragement or initiative, go I.

We live in suburbia, we whose education has been a lick and a promise. Oh, how those university chaps who mock at their education amuse us! How pleased we are with *Lucky Jim, Hurry On Down*—even Jimmy Porter had a redbrick: Holden Caulfield ran away from a simply wonderful school. But, oh, how we envy them their chance! We are the non-catchers in the rye. We have missed.

And what of my children, all too soon to be hurled into the rat-race? How can I with my own nagging sense of failure hope to teach them anything but decency, charity, morality; attributes of the senses rather than the mind? Perhaps they will make the university, but if they don't then I would prefer that, rather than use their elbows, they go innocent into the world like Muishkin, or the good soldier Schweik.

4

The Self-Inflicted Wound

by 'A. N. OTHER'

ABOVE THE Confessional should hang these words of Benjamin Constant: 'What is more, I hate the fatuity of a mind which fancies it excuses what it explains; I hate the vanity which is only concerned with itself when recounting the evil it has done, which seeks to inspire pity in describing itself and which, being indestructible, hovers over the ruins only to analyse itself instead of to repent.' And let some god add an impatient admonishment and sign it.

Fellow songsters, with overtones of underdog and undertones of overdog, with whom perhaps I shall be kennelled between these covers, greetings! How ashamed we shall be to be seen in each other's company! To have crouched in our little barrels like the Rector of Stiffkey at Blackpool, and proclaimed our woes for pelf!

Up here, there is a sword-sheen on the windblown rushes, and the young river wells out of the bog dark and bubbling like a sudden staunchless wound. My world is not peopled by men and women. My realities are the weather, the possession or lack of a bottle of paraffin, the impending demise of a shirt, the level of the stream, the direction of the wind, the existence of a leak in my fishing-waders. Nor are my friends exultations and agonies: chiefly they are a squat cottage, a dun and boggy moor, an acid stream of small, lank trout. With all these I have a deep uneasy relationship, and I must speak of them with propitiary euphemisms, as the Greeks spoke of the Eumenides, or as Lapps say 'our friend in the woods' when they mean the bear: for if any of them turn on me I am lost, and none are tame. I have had four cottages shot under me.

The sounds to which I am accustomed are these: the com-
minations of the grouse, cackling like drunken Beldames on
the peat and heather: a wind that at 1,500 ft. always soughs
and rattles my doors and screams thinly in my rod-top when
I pursue the ritual with the trout: the ticking of an alarm clock
that will only function lying on its face, that gains or loses
according to eccentric whim, its sound now lethargic, now
quickened into clanking like a squadron of Uhlans crossing a
frozen bridge: the susurrus of trout frying, their eyes turned
to clear white beads, and the whin-n-g-g of sniping fat,
like a ricochet from a rock: the eructations of the coffee
pot: the rustling of a basket chair minutes after I have sat
in it.

I have a portable wireless. When the battery died I contrived
to wire a torch battery to it, and by rationing my listening time
to a few minutes a day I gleaned something about a royal baby
and a royal engagement which seemed a strange gloss on a
world grown unfamiliar. The last phrase that the instrument
uttered was easily memorized. 'It means above all that Britain
and America are marching hand in hand into Space.' After
that, not even a death-rattle.

Early last autumn, I had been fishing: the stream was low
and the trout morose: I had been wearing Polaroid glasses,
staring all day at running water and walking on yielding,
shuddering tussocks for hours. On my way back to the cottage
I remembered that I had a letter to be posted: it is six miles to
the nearest pillar box. I was light-headed, the solid ground
rippled, I had that disembodied feeling. I stopped one of the
infrequent cars to pass and asked the driver to post the letter.
The man angrily quoited the envelope on to the road and drove
off with a crashing of gears. Had I seemed peremptory? Even,
perhaps, alarming? There was a girl in the car, they had looked
tense as though in the throes of a quarrel. But the odd thing
was that such behaviour did not appear in the least odd to me
but rather as though with the same dark yet lucid purpose the
man had come that way expressly commissioned to repudiate
my request. Had the wireless announced that the royal baby
was indigo or that a upas tree had been planted at Kew, I

should probably have accepted it without question. So, imperceptibly, one loses one's bearings.

Perhaps sitting and thinking is the penultimate stage merely. The end is just sitting.

Conversation with a friend:

'You imagine I just sit up there and brood endlessly and unprofitably about Life. Shall I tell you what in point of fact I do?'

'By all means.'

'I just sit up there and brood endlessly and unprofitably about Life.'

As, for instance, that 25,000 Americans move home every day . . . that unproductive cow-whales are inseminated with torpedoes of sperm. And, more pleasurably, that a man navigating between Timor and Sourabaya kept alive for 3 months, after he had fried his wallet in sump oil and eaten it, by using wood from the structure of the boat to cook the barnacles on his keel. Or that many of the secrets of the salmon's life cycle are still inviolate.

Farson and Williamson, Crusoe and Thoreau, handymen all. Fishermen too. I cannot make a gate or sew a button. If Friday came it would be he who would have to teach me. I am morbidly averse to threading a needle—through the eye I see the long parched vistas of celibacy. And it is of a piece with the whole hilarious pattern of self-sabotage that I have almost, if not utterly, placed myself beyond reach of what is nearest to my needs and longings. The aroma of cooked goose is fatal in the air.

My assets are briefly enumerated: the knack of catching trout in small troubled waters; the grace to thrill to the silver-gold inkling as I do; a handful of friends and enemies on whom I inflict a rasping tongue and a marshmallow heart. Copy-book maxims, loaded with dum-dum. A habit of gnomic, almost vatic, utterance from a brain stuffed hugger-mugger with literature. A skull full of rubble and a pen full of tropes.

But no peace. The rats would eat my nine bean rows. The combs would drip gall.

A contemporary of mine at Rugby told me recently that

he recalled me for something toughly independent in my bearing. The *Noli-Me-Tangere* of a flayed squirrel, I suspect with hindsight. Lord, behold us with Thy blessing, once again dissembling here. Heaven lies about us in our infancy and continues to misrepresent us to the grave and beyond.

Stupendously unique and at the same time cliché-ridden as life is, I leave to my frivolous mainstream friends the intellectual frothing about behaviour-patterns and the chain of causality. The Tao that can be expressed is not the Eternal Tao.

It is not decorous for a man in his forties to be uninvolved in the cash nexus, to clutter friends' vistas like a *Clochard,* to snare mallard and have fixations on piscine Lolitas.

Gatsby dreamed and dug clams before his dream was wrecked on those exclusive lawns and he died of it. I am mithridatic to dreams, I ride my nightmare on the curb.

If I need fish, I fish the rise: if I want experience of a mystery I fish the stream: that moment when life strikes upward from the unfathomed holds in it something of the ineffable lottery, the thunderclap of hope that is experienced in our relationships with women. When I net a good fish I have a primitive instinct to hurry back with it to the cottage, the mother-ship that lies rolling in a trough of the high moors, battened down. But we ship no dreams. The crew are hardened cases, you can tell it in their faces. I say to my friends, 'F—— me, Jack, you're all right'.

To a lonely child the seducers are Mole, Rat and Otter, Huck, Quartermain, Bevis, the Coral Islanders, the young Tarka chasing the moon across the meadows away from the black-and-silver-sliding Taw: their territory is nebulously sited between Thule and Cloud Kukuanaland, and once you sign with that mob, if you think you can ever pull out, you'd better get wise to yourself. They'll follow you wherever you go and sooner or later put the finger on you, lisping the low and delicious word 'Nuts'. Throw in some Lawrence, a pinch of Rilke, a whiff of Proust and you're a gone gosling, however long it takes.

I too used to think I had a beautiful talent once, baby, but

I was too secretive to do anything except play with it in the dark and let it nibble my fingers. I was afraid it would sneak away and someone would put a collar on it. It was going to stay on MY island, and like it. My friends will not let me starve —quite. Nor will I allow them to—quite. At one time, it appeared, they cordoned me off and sought to ostracize me back into conformity. Now from time to time I visit them and they appear glad to see me. Walking great distances and arrayed in a variety of their donated garments, I appear in their midst and camp among them in the mice-delighting cottages of summer migrants, attending their functions like an Eleventh Day Brahmin, and gratefully drinking their beer, letting off a few verbal pyrotechnics and loosing the odd shaft of paranoid bitterness to maintain the character they have conferred on me. Their wives tend to bunch protectively in my presence, to exact kitchen labour, and to prod me with small insults, discreetly. It is no time at all before someone volunteers to run me back to the reservation.

I eat hecatombs of trout. But the winter is less benign. Occasionally I have a windfall, such as the rabbit I picked up on the road last year, not flattened to any great degree: I remember the quizzical look it gave me after I had skinned it, the tufts of fur adhering round its awful bald brows. Happily it had not been poisoned. Once during a period when the policy was not to feed me I ate cattle-cake.

People are fascinated by certain questions. How does the pole-squatter dispose of faeces? Is the young mother breast-feeding? What precisely do Lesbians *do*? Do the lonely talk to themselves? In my case, the answer to the last query is in the negative. I occasionally address the sheep: 'I want three volunteers, ewe, ewe and ewe.' Or to the gravel-voiced autochthonous grouse: 'Wotcher, cock! It's no bleeding good saying "Go back!" all the time.' And to the little birds on the moor: 'Hi! Pipit: where's the penny world we bought?' But to myself, no. I have said it all long ago in a clearing in Malaya, the nearest European fifty miles away, the pineapple brandy depositing a lead precipitate on my entrails, and the knowledge that I had murdered my marriage spreading like a stain on the night, while the gibbons ululated and the rattan slats creaked. Almost like Sapper. Almost like hell.

I displayed early several unpropitious characteristics to a marked degree. Tergiversation, the retreat from attainment, the element of *nolo episcopari,* almost literally so in my case since my mother, dear deluded pietist, prayed for nothing so ardently as that I should add another to a long and stately line of bishops. Bible and Daily Light were always placed by my bedside: doors on Sunday were always left open for the sacred strains on the wireless to wash from cellar to attic. My father posted Latin examinations to me from India. He was a man either incapable or ashamed of any expression of affection for or solidarity with his children: the old India of *koi hais* and shibboleth had seized, shaken and, I surmise, stunted him: he was cruelly self-conscious: appointed young to a coveted position, he resigned in dudgeon after a small difference with a delegation from Whitehall: insisted on discharging in his spare time, and in an honorary capacity, duties that carried a large salary: was the only passionate Mason of whom I have ever heard: could not after forty years in India easily refuse a beggar. And at home the gypsies would pick the daffodils along the drive and sell them to my mother at the door.

Two incidents throw some light on my father. When I was a baby he gave me, in error, a spoonful of Hair Restorer: immediately he drank the contents of the bottle. When one of my sisters who was a turbulent child was in trouble at school and her headmistress wished to arrange an interview with my father, he contrived a cable from India recalling him a fortnight early so that he could avoid the meeting.

Then, too, the High Toby approach to people: 'Acceptance, or your life.' I could ever only relax and court a woman after she had capitulated.

Also a great secretiveness regarding my deepest wishes, and much volubility on most other matters: the duck trailing a broken wing to draw off the pursuit.

At Hide and Seek the primal thrill of panic when the voice called 'Coming'. Adam among the leafage crouching from the growl of God.

'There are those who desire a certain thing with such ardour and determination that, for fear of missing it, they omit none of those things that will ensure their missing it.'

Defiance and apprehension, I now translate, hardening into a fatal amalgam of pride and *culte de moi*. Tell the child not to stick peas up his nose, and he does so immediately. We do not need the Vedas to tell us that the shadow of a cloud, the love of the malicious, intimacy with another man's wife, youth, and opulence are the five equally transitory things in the world. But some must prove the truth of every warning with their heart's blood. They may not be able to meet the bright eyes of danger, but cannot resist the veiled glance of risk. Old gnomic Anon. still in there bitching!

So I did not write to a young wife for nearly three years when posted overseas. Plunged into the military cauldron, I became a fairly efficient officer, suddenly aged about six. If I wrote, my wordless longing would be revealed—and letters were censored. No news is good news. Share this in secrecy and silence, another bond. Johnny will sleep again in his own little room once more. And don't tell Johnny he will be sleeping alone, he's a bit short on understanding about now, and tends to write letters from Malaya to wife now in India describing the snub contours of his Malay girl's breasts: his own love is axiomatic, hers must be tried by ordeal. Not certifiable—quite. Perhaps tromometric presages informed me of impending loss and I determined to incur it by my own agency and not another's.

So we lay in our narrow mosquito-netted beds, night after night, week after week in the Transit Camp, close enough to have reached out a hand to the other, and never uttered a word, while India changed hands ponderously, and the guns and daggers were stored up in the thatch.

Sometimes in the silence, memories of India possess me, Horla-like. Perhaps when the buzzards are wheeling over the moors. It may be some small detail, a magpie's windmill flight recalling minahs: or a shot pigeon's feet, pink and shrivelled like dried chillies: or the nictitating glow of burning bracken at dusk waking memories of Diwali: or when, waiting for a market bus, the lilting Welsh voices poise between joviality and self-pity: when I see Snowdon, as I used to see the great ranges, Nanda Devi, Badrinath, Trisul convoluted like a narwhal's horn, touched with rose and floating free, more insubstantial than the clouds themselves: when water seeps across the road from a rock face leaving a zigzag trail, like the urine of the humped bullocks on the mud tracks as they shogged to the villages in the cow-dust hour. Or even, sometimes, when one tries to obtain a straight answer to a direct question. Old splendours and stenches insinuate, a *sitar* plays in the mist, and one has that longing, like Rat fevered for the sea.

Instant coffee is excellent if not confused with coffee: Kipling, too, if not mistaken for poetry. And the lines that stick are these:

> But Himalaya heavenward heading huge and vast, huge and vast,
> In a million summits bedding on the last world's past—
> A certain sacred mountain where the scented cedars climb,
> And — the feet of my Beloved hurrying back through time.

One of my last acts was to visit an Indian prison with an officer from a British regiment. Three of his men had been sentenced to fifteen years' imprisonment: they had been returning to barracks one night, drunk, had stumbled over some Indians sleeping on *charpoys* in the open, and had beaten two of them to death. It was the beer, they said, and the country, they had not known what they were doing, it was all over in an instant. We could only assure them of their chances of remission, and offer the probability of serving their sentence in England now that the transfer of power was certain.

And so I came back, to stand at last on these sobering hills.

Halfway, and I flag already. I have to go to a friend and beg him to assure me that it is worth continuing. He reassures me, tactfully suggesting that I simplify my language.

But words are what I have, I have lived with them too long: we torture one another and practise small perversions to salt the darkness, partners in a marriage gone stale.

Disaster-prone, and supine, in my heartland, and after untold provocation offered by me, it seems that I retain a few dear friends that I would wish, and have not sought. Through them I am alive. In terms of soft cash I have had perhaps ten shillings a week over the past year. I cannot deal with money except to disburse it. All the false trails in a paper-chase of banknotes indicate that I cannot understand it.

If I bite the hands that feed me, it is because I am hungry for more than friends can spare: lost bread, the *pain perdu* of a love that does not survey my acts or make concessions, but loves me as I love myself, irrefutably and without end. In friendship no bread is better than the half-loaf usually afforded: but they have given me wine as well. And if there is nothing further to be done, and nowhere left to go, I shall say that they have left me thriftily to die in my own dung.

Time that was the dog at my heels is now the wolf at my throat.

But I have a kind of dulled belief that I am being battered into the shape of a writer: Mussolini confident of the Parolini Column hurrying to his relief, Hitler in the bunker pinning his hopes on General Wenck advancing from the south. I have extricated myself so far at many eleventh hours and perhaps there is some hope in this. At Rugby the sixth form were allowed to work for half an hour after Lights Out by the light of candles in sconces. Mine burned late into the night always, because I never started to work till then. The knowledge that friends see me inextricably caught in the patterns of failure provides me not only with the necessary material of grievance, but also with the only stimulus to which by fits and starts I can respond. I succumb from time to time to the comforting theory of the Last Laugh. For my favourite incident in history is that of the siege of Sphacteria, when, after months of unsuccessful assaults by conventionally-minded generals, Cleon, who had infuriated the archons with his vapourings, bragged that with 500 archers and himself in command he could reduce it in a fortnight, was scornfully offered what he asked and made good his boast.

One cannot precisely define the point of no return. Regrets are fruitless if one cannot act otherwise. The bookmaker who complained that he was thousands of pounds out of pocket for the current year and more for the preceding, was asked why he did not give up bookmaking. 'What?' he expostulated, 'Give up my means of livelihood?'

If life is an *affaire* that has come to grief, words are the means of expressing sour grapes for the defecting partner.

La parole n'est qu'un bruit et les livres ne sont que du papier. Il n'y a personne que moi ici.

The last and loveliest with whom I shared my life left me eighteen months ago, accompanied by what is technically known as the Duly Authorized Officer. It lasted five years, and those who had known for years that she was a paranoid schizophrenic but had not thought to mention it, did not concede it a chance to endure six months. I shall not write of her here. She is dowered as few can hope to be, and flawed beyond despair. When love seemed a relevant word, we lived a life of hermetic seclusion. When I woke to the truth of her condition, I had the fatuity to believe that I could oppose myself to it and succeed. There are no witnesses. Even at those moments which we believe to be the most intimate I came no closer than the rescue squad who hear the faint rapping of the entombed and know that the fall must be sealed off.

To be the paramour of one held to be a maniac is not precisely to live in society, more especially if she is related to illustrious men. At best it fascinates morbidly those who can fancy themselves pitying the plumage, yet walk wide of the dying bird. But live on. There will not be a time when I shall not remember you.

I am fed selected scraps of news about her. It is as though I am no longer to assume that that period of my life in reality occurred or was mine. But it is very real to me although, or perhaps because, I am no longer quite a real person.

To have known something incapable of vulgarity is no small privilege. 'Body thicker, clumsier-looking, specially so about the tail', reads the legend on the backs of fishing licences, differentiating the young trout from the salmon parr. So too the mind. The others will wash around in their little pools, rising to the same flies, sinking to the same caddis grubs as their sister-fish. But when the peal and grilse are running, silver ingots in the dusk, I shall think of you already far out on your mysterious journey in steep Atlantic gulfs beyond the trawl.

Suddenly I find myself sick of this, and wish to break it off on a note of aposiopesis. I have camped on the perimeter of a friend's life while writing it, and it is time to go. *Lusisti satis, edisti satis, atque bibisti, tempus abire tibi est.*

How will I end this piece, I am asked, and what do I think will be the outcome of my affairs? I will leave it open, but the prognosis is not good, it cannot be when the wax is reduced to screaming at the stylus, the forme to bickering with the hare.

To endure the winter I have a project to smoke trout like *bückling* if I can lay my hand on some oak shavings, so it seems I plod on. Also I try to write, but the erosion of my own identity, and the slow loss of fact, may rule out fiction.

The exasperated concern of others will reach its term. The therapy of the kick up the backside will soon be tried again, though it is doubtful whether it can be effective with a person who has been kicked by a heavier boot in a more vital spot.

I have been passed from hand to hand like a calumet at a pow-wow, and also like a red-hot rivet. Friends and enemies have done their best and worst. A man like a rock, a man like an empty éclair-case, have diagnosed and prescribed. A spring ago a person of no great fastidiousness unpacked herself for me in an idle moment, but all that I found in that community chest was a heart like a parched pea.

I have still the temerity to hope to drift along, unless I choke on a metaphor or founder in my own bile.

So?

5

Homosexual

by 'JUDE FAWLEY'

ON THURSDAY I shall appear in court again. They will have
dug up a good deal more. More questions, more hints, more
hopes that the enquiries may be splendidly 'complete', every
single incident a separate charge, every charge productive of a
separate statement with my signature below the caution and
the 'facts' that may put me in prison for years. It began with
one 'isolated incident' (nothing to worry about, said the close-
cropped friendly detective constable who came to S—— to
fetch me here) but further enquiries were interesting and would
take time—a week, that would be enough, so away I went to
prison. Only for a week: I got bail today.

Years ago I knew it would happen one day. The gaiety, the
cynicism, the wit—they could not hide it from me. For a long
time I have feared arrest and yet invited it—planning to escape
from the pressure by asking the world to take note—Look I
am queer, so that the burden might be shared. Eleven and a
half years—that was my time on the tightrope, and fantastic
were the contortions that kept me there. But there was no
other side, no goal or refuge. Only the wire swung between
nowhere and nowhere.

But of course there were other I's—and these constructed
selves, along with one or two postponements of ill-fortune
provided me with—what? Some popularity with colleagues,
a love of the music of Mozart, shelves of books, invitations
to people's houses, a fair income which I spent without thought,
and a few moments that will return when the cell door clangs
to on Friday week. But never, during the whole time, has
there been that fluid solidity of character which I have longed

for. By this silly-sounding phrase I mean a character that is still and yet moves, that reaches out and yet resides in its own inviolate centre, that knows itself and is yet not afraid of that knowledge. I lack definition. Men have said that of great men however: Boswell, for example, has been likened to an onion. But with genius it does not matter. Boswell managed to write the Life of Johnson. Without genius, or at least some outstanding and valuable talent this vagueness of being, this continual bewilderment at what one is doing, this skidding apprehension of things, can lead to this: a man of thirty-three, jobless, almost homeless, on a charge of gross indecency with another male person (whom, in a way, he does not know) in the borough of N—— between March 1st, 1959 and April 1st, 1960.

Like blind Oedipus I can ask: What paths have led me to this place?

The outstanding and simple answer may be phrased in a word of sinister import: brinkmanship—or the state of being almost. At birth I almost died—and so did my mother, but skilful hands in the early hours saved us both—she at forty-three a tired and longing woman; I a creature with hands like a turkey's claws when the gravy is a-making on Christmas Day.

At school I was almost clever—but when the entrance exam for grammar school came along I needed a good deal of coaching in arithmetic and so, when the results were announced, I was commended for my English only. At grammar school I was almost brilliant for a short time—but when it came to open awards at Cambridge I got a mere Exhibition, not the Major Schol. I longed for. In Higher School Cert I almost got a State—but in French I merely passed. At Cambridge I almost did well—but in Part Two of the Tripos I got a mere Two-One. And so on. Marriage was hell. Being alone was hell. Living at home was hell. Living in digs was hell.

The worst hell (in those days) was the army. I was terrified. After two months they discharged me. I remember saying to myself as I boarded the train at L—— 'And now I can begin living.' To prove this I bought a piano score of the Brahms B flat Concerto on the way home—but it wasn't home, it was my wife's home. She was pregnant and embarrassed by my presence. I was a weakling, back, shamefully back from the army—while some people who lived quite near had got commissions.

We were never close. The intimacy departed and she prepared for the motherhood that had precipitated the marriage. We began to hate each other. And the child was to prove a barrier, not a link. That was my fault.

I longed for schooldays and the friend who had taught me so much about books and the body. I almost cried for those week-ends we had spent together in all the corruption of innocence. I needed to regain what I had never possessed—a golden age of youth, energy, achievement, and joy. The quest began: at first in the mind, only, remembering that schoolfriend and the long summers.

In January 1948 I began teaching at a grammar school in the Midlands. I left the finding of digs to the school secretary and found myself in a large, still house in the care of Miss W——, tall, angular, throaty, who removed the lumps of coal from the grate when I went out in the evenings. There was cocoa for supper—the like of which I was to meet again twelve years later in prison. At week-ends I returned to S—— where my wife was loving the child.

I grew friendly with a sixth-former. I visited his home and shared his records, books and suppers by the fireside. In the school holidays we wrote letters: there was nothing that would interest my close-cropped detective constable who told me that the world soon forgets.

And so the double life began: by day, clause analysis, set books, mark sheets, an occasional successful lesson, difficulties with discipline; by night, the longing, the isolation, visits to cinemas and homes, the hope of meeting someone in lavatory or pub who would love me. All this, with increasing complexity for eleven and a half years: the hurried embrace, broken appointments, a month or so of regular meetings, resolutions to write a book, to stay in and do more marking, to learn the clarinet. And behind it all the passionate conviction of doom; the iron-filing jerking towards the magnet of public disgrace;

the pattern of despair. My favourite authors bore their testi-mony: Hardy, Crabbe, Gissing, Johnson:

> Time hovers o'er, impatient to destroy,
> And shuts up all the passages of joy.

Some nights I could not stay in my room after seven—not even with the long-playing records which were consuming a large part of each month's salary. I would just go out, searching, longing, occasionally drinking heavily. Friends were there to welcome me, but I rarely called anywhere. On a lucky night I would take someone back to my room for the illusion of love.

Eleven and a half years of this. Then I applied for a Training College Lectureship. The boy with whom I was in love told me I could easily get a better job. 'Do you want to spend your whole life teaching C and D Forms?' he asked. Surprisingly I was appointed. At once I feared for what I had done and the first three nights after the appointment were sleepless and feverish. 'I shall be starting again,' I said: 'I shall be away from every-thing and everybody I know.'

I moved into college and consoled myself: "This is my home, at last I have a home.' It was a small flat, cleanly furnished and my own. I arranged my books, records and photographs, bought a dish-cloth to keep the bath clean and set about the new work of teaching teachers. For two weeks I lectured, marked, read, and tried to fit in.

One afternoon I was looking through some scripts when the Porter knocked. 'Could you be at the Principal's Office at half past three, please?'

'Yes, certainly.'

At half past three I found a puzzled Principal. 'Someone from the Clerk's Office is coming from C—— and wants to see you. That's the Legal Department. Got any idea what it's about? Been killing anyone on that scooter of yours?'

'I've no idea,' I lied.

This was it. The moment towards which all moments had tended. Every book read, every drink and body enjoyed, every relaxed or tense moment had led to this. I knew.

We waited. The official came at a quarter to four. Five

minutes alone with the Principal and then he called me in. He sat uneasily with a dossier of grey (prison colour, I later remembered). He did not want to begin. Neither did the Principal.

'Well, I think it's up to you. . . .'

The official moved a little and half regarded me.

'I'm afraid I've come with bad news. . . .'

I knew.

'We have been informed that you have homosexual tendencies;' (he pronounced a long 'o' in the first syllable) 'is that true?'

I was aware of the brass inkstand and paper-knife. I looked down at the desk and tapped it.

'Yes.'

Of course no authority could employ such a person, I must resign and then I should receive my salary until Christmas. A form of resignation was typed and I signed. I could leave my things at the college until I could arrange something. The Principal asked me to carry on as usual for a day or two. I refused. No one was charging me with any act. Only get out of the College!

During the months that followed my states of mind changed so often and so fast that memory is bound to deceive in reconstruction. First, anger: I could have done this job, why couldn't they leave me alone? No one need have known. How stupid it all is! Fear: What will become of me? Am I to be an outcast for ever, never teach again—and what else can I do? Is this the very end? Contempt: They will not let me work. Very well. I shall be paid until Christmas and until then I'll enjoy the fruits of my non-labours.

But there could be no enjoyment. Every waking moment was tinged with guilt. To be reading a life of Savonarola in the morning was very disturbing. That morning should have been a time of struggle, of gritted teeth against the imprecision of a Grammar School. I should have been trying to convince the Fifth that clarity and firmness mattered, or hoping that at least one Lower Sixth boy would be able to share, in some modern, drain-pipe-trousered, Jazz-on-Friday-nights way,

Wordsworth's dark sense of alarm as the cliff reared itself. It was wrong to be alone, reading, worrying, dreading. Reading should be earned by a day of combat.

The lost boys meant life itself. But I had been a danger to those boys: for eleven and a half years the breath of corruption had been upon them. Now, it would appear, even the best of what I had to give was tainted by the giver. And I had loved to see the fine shocks of hair in the afternoon sun, the firm shoulders poised above the exercise book, the clean radiance of faces. And now it was all dirty: even the jokes and fooleries with 1c could be sinister hints that when one got a little higher up the school. . . .

And I remembered the grousing, the resentment, the longing to give up teaching. Mere defence mechanisms. I had never meant it: tomorrow the boys would still be there, and at one moment perhaps there would be glory in it.

One morning I walked down to the local police station. This was to be a move in my vague and desperate rehabilitation game. I would face them: tell them what had happened.

The Superintendent was in court: the Chief somebody or other would see me. A neat, large man, so much a uniform and a baton that I cannot remember his face.

'Good morning. I've come to enquire if you could help me. It's about something that happened last summer.'

'We'll try. Sit down, won't you?'

'Well . . . it's like this. Last August I was brought here and questioned. During the questions I admitted that I was a homosexual. I had been reported by someone at the park, loitering about . . . waiting for someone.'

He said nothing. I wanted him to stop me, to caution me, to put me right about the correct manner of confessing crimes.

'On that occasion I made no statement. I signed nothing. No charge was made. The plain-clothes man wrote a lot down but I signed nothing.'

It was as though this signing nothing might get me my job back. I hammered at it.

He spoke. 'Oh yes, I remember now. I had nothing to do

with it at the time but I was told you had been interviewed. We interview a lot of people you know.'

Then I told my story. The grammar school; the resignation; the fortnight at A——; the dismissal; the new job at T——; the breakdown; the fear and uncertainty; the interview with the MP who said he would go into it. The story told itself mechanically even the joke got in.

'They dismissed me for having homosexual tendencies. It was a mixed college. I wonder if they would have dismissed me for heterosexual tendencies—after all I was unmarried.'

'Well, you know, we get to know a lot about people. But I'm sure nothing went from here. You were frank with us and we've been fair with you.'

He could not think how it had happened. He could understand that I was sorry to lose a new job. He could assure me that no action had been taken by them.

'I've seen the MP and he said——'

'The MP here?'

'Yes, and he seemed interested and said he would make enquiries.'

'Yes, well, I expect we shall be hearing from him in due course. But it takes time you know.'

I agreed that it took time. That was it. The interview had been useless. I felt that this man was regarding me as the sort of person who might rush in to confess to the latest murder. The police are troubled by scores of them, we are told. He shook hands and wished me luck.

The previous summer played itself through in my mind as I returned to mother, the Nescafé and the *Guardian*. I could not escape the images. The pattern was dominated by one person—whom I shall call Stephen. I carry his photograph; perhaps the police found it.

Stephen, in any event, has been interviewed by the police. Or did he go to them? He threatened to in his last letter to me, but I can't be sure. And even if he did, I can't work up any real hatred. He had to do and be what he did and was, and so did I. At the heart of the summer was Stephen.

He was brilliant, lively and good looking. I did not teach

him—his sort of form rarely fell to me. But we came together and it's very difficult for me to remember any one day of meeting or first interchange of word. I think it was near the time of the staff play that I first walked up the road with him. Certainly we walked up together after one of the performances; there were other boys too, but Stephen was the boy I talked to.

After this I was aware of Stephen every day. In the staff room his name was often on the lips of those who wished we had 600 more like him. In exams he wrote at enormous length and always to the point. I would pass him in the corridor between periods. No word was exchanged but I felt warm inside and no longer alone. At four o'clock he would be at the bus stop a few yards from the gate, awaiting not the bus, but me. One day he asked me to identify a line of verse. I knew it and was able to complete the couplet. He was very pleased and I felt very proud and scholarly. There was a bridge between us: English literature.

Stephen was enjoying *Sons and Lovers* and more of Lawrence. Not until later did I realize that the mining background was a personal concern of his. Not until much later did I realize why the book took a sudden possession of him, expelling Shakespeare and Pope.

I suddenly thought of a plan. (No doubt the police have this as the first move towards seduction: but I'm not sure whether Stephen mentioned it.) We would go to Eastwood for the day and visit Lawrence's birthplace. I had read of the plaque recently placed on the lintel. We would have a glorious day of literary pilgrimage, guided by the map in the back of '*The Intelligent Heart*'. Stephen was enthusiastic. The date was fixed: the Wednesday in Whit week which was half-term. Each year I keep the anniversary, silently in my mind (perhaps in prison this year)—May 28.

It was a perfect success. In my diary I wrote: 'A flawless day with a perfect companion.' That one day was simple direct happiness. Looking back now, I see it as akin to that wonderful moment in Britten's '*The Turn of the Screw*' when the governess apostrophizes Bly with 'How beautiful it is. Each day it seems more beautiful to me,' and then, at once, the icy stab of

66

Quint's theme is heard. At the end of the day Stephen drank a shandy outside a pub in N—— while I drank beer inside. He was fourteen. It seemed splendidly reckless.

And then followed a period of companionship and delight, of book borrowing and lending, of cinema going, of walks up the road every day at four, of meetings down the road before morning school, and finally an invitation to Saturday tea at his home.

I was accepted. There was a splendid meal, a long walk with Stephen during which we discussed philosophy; on our return bottled beer and cheese and pickled onions, and the pang of separation when the last bus was nearly missed.

Then I fell in love with him. Here was what I might have been years ago—intellectual brilliance, beauty, gaiety, to set against my mediocrity, my large ears and gangling awkwardness, my gloom and melancholy. Someone has said that homosexuals seek to duplicate the self, not complete it. Perhaps that was what I was seeking then—a lost mode of being that I had never had, the ideal self I never was.

My love was genuine, silent, and controlled. I resisted the temptation of even laying my hand on his shoulder. It should be enough to hear him talk, to make sure he knew the world's greatest literature—I remember a parcel of *World's Classics* Tolstoy posted to him at Easter, when I knew his address only because he had written it in a book lent to me—to meditate on those eyes that could argue, persuade, rage and mourn, and perhaps one day to possess a photograph that would lift this passage of life above the ravages of time.

Another day shall stand for scores. There was a Friday afternoon's holiday to compensate for the Founders' Day Service on the following morning. It was hot, do-nothing weather. Without conscious design we found ourselves in N—— at lunch time.

'What about something to eat?' I asked.

'What about fish and chips?' said Stephen.

'That's much better than something to eat,' I said.

We queued up at Stephen's favourite shop and came away bravely equipped. Then to the Prince's Gardens (a kind of small park set back from the main road) where we got superbly greasy as we devoured the fish and chips and read the wrappings. When our hands were as clean as grubby handkerchiefs could make them Stephen read me his English Literature Exam papers which had earned him first place.

'You'll never hear better literature than this,' he said.

And so on through the summer. He came to S——, my crummy hometown as Holden Caulfield would have said. From there we went to Cambridge, saw the sights, climbed St Mary's tower, stayed overnight but did not sleep together. (The police believed me on this: Stephen had claimed no act of indecency at the hotel.)

One afternoon at S—— Stephen said:

'There's one part of your life you've never mentioned. Your marriage.'

At once I collapsed into autobiography, told him everything and knelt at his feet as I admitted my love for him.

'I wish I could change,' said Stephen. 'I'd do anything to please you. You're the best friend I have in the world.'

We returned to M——, his home, and I stayed there, on and off, for the rest of the holidays. There was a tension between us. The ceremony of innocence was drowned. The act of gross indecency lasted about ten seconds. As my statement to the close-cropped Detective Constable has it: I did not masturbate him.

Stephen grew in stature and in favour with headmaster and most other people too. I went on trying to deceive myself that as things had been they would remain. But by Christmas I knew that this brief and strange biological function of mine was at an end. The tides of life were carrying us opposite ways.

We quarrelled. There was verbal savagery, harsh callous inconsiderateness on both sides and a weariness where once energy and delight had reigned.

By the time last summer had arrived we were each locked in our separate world; however, I could not forget him, and in anger he often thought of me.

I spent most of the holidays hanging about parks and lavatories, trying to forget him in the arms of anyone who might be interested. I let myself drift, regretting the school I had left, fearing the job I was taking up and smiling grimly inside when I thought that Stephen had been the *fons et origo* of my move. At least I should not ache each day when he took his place in the hall at prayers or passed me unconcerned in the corridor.

Then the police picked me up. I had been to Oxford for the day on 'Toad'—my new moped, so called after the most famous terror of the highway, that remarkable animal whose history I had been reading with first formers each Christmas term for the past eleven years. I got back to S—— shortly before eight. I almost went straight home: there was no urgency in my blood to find someone that night. It was just routine to go to the park lavatory and hang about.

There was nothing doing. By eight-twenty I'd had enough of the day. 'Toad' was across the road. I was unlocking him when someone was suddenly there.

'I'm a police officer. Perhaps you could explain . . .'

But there was no arrest, no written statement, no charges.

'That's all from us . . .'

Even after this I hung about. Years before a kindly policeman in B—— (our neighbouring monster of a city) had watched me enter a urinal three times in twenty minutes, and, after warning me that it could be serious to a man in my position, had sent me on my way. This, even this, taught me nothing. I still hoped by some miracle to find someone, to love someone, to belong to someone. The books weren't enough; the music wasn't enough. Visits to friends and intellectual discussions weren't enough. Always the incompleteness and the fear. Always the knowledge that life couldn't be genuine. And worst of all, memories.

I got bail quite easily on Thursday. The close-cropped detective constable (I believe he'd had another haircut) greeted me with a polite 'Good Morning' rather like the Inquisitor's opening words to Joan in Shaw's play. There was to be one charge only—but I must sign documents to have the incident with Stephen taken into account. He smiled as though he understood. 'But you won't be charged with it.'

'What about the bus conductor?' I asked.

'Nothing about that,' he answered, as though I had mentioned sodomy in the presence of Mrs Grundy herself. The previous week they had been most interested in the bus conductor from T——. They wanted his name, which I honestly did not know. They wanted the make of his car, which I honestly did not know. Now they were quite indifferent.

My solicitor was cheerful. 'It's going very well at the moment, nothing to worry about.' And then we went in—numbers 51 and 52, the youth from the shop in W—— aged seventeen years and I, unemployed, aged thirty-three years.

H——'s statement was read out. His mother gasped at the climax. I am the seducer. The local paper has made its headlines out of me alone—'Teacher gets bail', 'Teacher for trial', and H—— gets mentioned in the text. His defence will be my wickedness. His statement says: 'I agreed.' But I should not have asked him to agree.

The incident was absurd enough and fitted that Frenchman's definition of love as the friction of two skins.

'Do you often do this?' I asked him as we walked to my room. (We had met in a lavatory: I had been out for a drink.)

'Sometimes. I suppose it's natural,' he answered quietly. 'They used to call me "Mouse" at school.'

He struck me as being one of the insulted and injured. Perhaps he was as isolated as I, perhaps this mouse was to be the loyal friend, seeing me again and again, and not only for this. I asked him if he liked his job.

'It's just a job. It's all right.'

It was all too calm, too trivial. I should have sent him packing. It was not shyness. Just another job. His face never changed: no smile, no rhetorical eyes like Stephen's. It was absurd to expect passion. Yet I longed to be wanted.

He sat on the bed, the expression still a neutral tone. He was waiting for me to begin.

'What are you thinking?' I asked.

'I was wondering if we shall be out in the van tomorrow.'

Even now I could have thrown him out. There had been no contact. Why the hell were we there?

We went through the motions. It was raining. I gave him sixpence to get to N—— on the bus. He went: I was no more alone when he had gone.

Some months later the police picked him up for soliciting in N——. He remembered me and told the story. Perhaps in that moment he was paying back a world that had rejected him—the school where I taught and from which he was expelled. I never taught him at school. He must have been a sad misfit—nicknamed 'Mouse', quiet, sleek, cornered. And so the two misfits came together, merely by chance, one lonely night. But really they never came together at all.

Why, I wonder, did he tell the police that we talked about records and played some? What could I have played him? Mozart? Bartok? Or would the second act of '*Tristan*' have enriched our encounter? I can't understand this mis-statement. For the most part, however, he was accurate enough. He could remember who came first; I had forgotten.

So much for 'Mouse' who merely triggered the bomb. In court he is still neutral, poker-faced—but that is too self-conscious a phrase for it: to 'Mouse' all this is just something else.

And then of course the police at S—— were asked in to investigate. It was the same detective constable who had said 'That's all from us' last summer when Stephen was at the heart of the matter. A young man with a solid countenance, a no-nonsense person who would never let go when he (or his superior) had made up his mind to get to the bottom of something. Obviously, sheer hard work was getting him on; thoroughness and efficiency were his attendant spirits. There was nothing sinister, nothing to make even the angriest suspect rage 'This bloody place is like a police state', but rather the steady, here-a-little, there-a-little devotion to his calling that you find in Conrad's Captain MacWhirr or Dickens' Inspector Bucket.

Dinner was almost ready. I answered the door. There he was. Last summer continued.

'If you've come to arrest me, let's get it over this time. I've had enough.'

But he had not come to arrest me. There was an enquiry from N—— and it was thought I could perhaps help . . .

'Give us about half an hour,' he requested mother, who was not yet sure what was afoot. We walked to the police station.

He related H——'s statement. Suddenly, without the preparation necessary for such a desperate venture, I decided to lie and brave it out. I denied everything, angrily, almost believing myself that it had never happened. Quietly and according to rules he cautioned me, deliberately freezing himself in my heat. I concocted a story; he wrote it down, with the infinite patience of one who knows that however deep the well of truth, buckets can reach down if the chain is long enough. (Hence Inspector Bucket? I wonder.) I finished with a defiant 'And that's all.' He said nothing and looked down at the laboriously written sheet (his pen was the only slightly inefficient feature: and I don't think he enjoyed writing), sadly reading through this folly of mine.

'You don't believe me, do you?'

'You've made your statement.'

'But you don't believe me, do you?'

'It's hardly a matter of what I believe.'

'Look. . . .'

'Why should this youth make all this up?'

'Perhaps he knew I was queer. I've told you I've spoken to him three or four times. Perhaps I should have paid him off. He's in a spot . . .'

'Blackmail?' A glint of official interest flashed in his eye.

I was not ready for this. 'I don't know, I don't know.'

'Well, is there anything else you'd like to add?'

'Look. Since last summer when you brought me down here I've lost a home, two jobs and have been ill. I've been trying to get back, start again, belong somewhere. For over eleven years I was a teacher—it's all I know, all I can do. Occasionally even I was a good teacher. This is the end of my teaching life and you know it. Some two-bit kid drags me into this, I can't prove I didn't do it, and you don't believe me. Of course it's always the young who are innocent, of course the accuser's in the stronger position. What the hell can I do? I'm queer, queer as they come—you know that, I told you last summer. So now there's this. What do people want? What do you want to do with me? Can't I even try to get a job, to start again without all this? I sometimes think society gets the criminals it deserves. If I'd not been naturally lazy I could have become the sort of person who'd declare war against the whole bloody set-up. They threw me out of the college. I'd done nothing there. Then I just crack up. Doctors, clinics, tablets, talk. And now this. I've had enough, I tell you, I've had enough.'

'He was able to describe your room.'

'Of course he was. Lots of people knew I had a bed-sitting-room. You could see the record player through the window.'

'But why should he make it up?'

'You don't believe me, do you?'

'It's not a matter of what I believe. I don't understand why some people are like you. I don't think anybody does. I just want the facts. I'll have to send in a report.'

I began to tremble slightly. The desk looked huge—it was the Principal's office all over again. The paper lay before him with my signature to complete it. We had been much longer over this than half an hour.

I reached for it, crumpled it in my hand and threw it across the room.

'There, you've got what you want. It was all lies. Are you satisfied?'

'You wish to make another statement? You don't have to.'

'Oh yes, I'll make another statement. Much shorter. Just write this: the alleged incident took place.'

With the unco-operative pen he rewrote the caution on a new sheet. The lies lay on the floor near the grate. He wrote slowly, time being no object in the pursuit of truth.

My one sentence was signed. He would send in his report. In about a fortnight I should know if there was to be a prosecution. He wanted to help me. Yes, he had known I was lying. I wasn't the same man who had been so honest with them last summer. He believed me now. I could go.

Mother said my face was ashen. Emphasized perhaps above the turtle-neck pullover which I had knitted years before at W——, a brilliant red then (the Head forbade me to wear it) but now prophetically and recently dyed black.

73

I felt numb and indifferent. The job I hadn't got in the place I longed to be, the breakdown, the failure to get a home, the disastrous conclusion with Stephen—what did these things matter now? This was it: the untutored incident that actually occurred. Now the law would take its course. Just another queer arrested, just another corrupter of youth to enliven Sunday breakfast tables.

I took a good look at our room. There were my records, the new library book begun the day before, the brass clock that had marked the passing of time as 'Mouse' and I had failed to connect on the bed at W——. And soon I should be in prison. That was the only truth that mattered. And there I should find no Mozartian perfection, no unputdownable books, no leisurely breakfasts with the *Guardian*.

Why and how had it come about?

I can't find an answer to satisfy myself. Not even a multiplicity of separate answers. Sometimes the only child of an elderly mother . . . but then my cousin, similarly placed, is married and perhaps happy. Mother longed for a daughter. Perhaps that's it. But I am not in appearance or behaviour effeminate. I am not a homosexual for the sake of fashion or for the purpose of experiments in living. I only know that I could never marry, or even love a woman as others do. But I am aware of a strange and terrible beauty in the world—the oblique vision of a queer.

When Mother had understood what had happened and was a bit calmer, I played '*Acis and Galatea*' on the gramophone and tried to prepare myself. A fortnight would give me time to tidy up the wreckage.

Next morning, about the same time, the patient detective constable returned. A warrant had been issued at N——. I rushed for a neighbour to tend mother, put two pounds in my wallet, packed a few things (I didn't know the futility of this at that time) and walked once again to the police station. The patient one did not speak.

An afternoon in the cell; a walk round the caged yard at four. Cigarettes and pipe were allowed. Then at 5.10 the car bearing the close-cropped detective constable arrived from N——. He

74

read the warrant to me; my belongings were handed over to him. We journeyed to N——. There were no handcuffs.

Why the hurry? What had happened to the promised fortnight? The close-cropped one told me later. The statement from S—— contained the patient one's report: there it stated that I had said something wild about 'not being there' and 'it's the end for me.'

They were worried about razor-blades, gas ovens and sleeping tablets. At N—— my shoes and belt were taken away. Through the night, at half-hourly intervals, there was a mighty unlocking of doors and someone would come in to see if I was all right. The electric light could not be switched off. I must not cover my face with the blanket.

Bail was refused. I was to go on remand to L—— Prison for one week. There I could apply to a Judge in Chambers for bail if I wished.

A friend visited me in the cells at N——. Later he wrote to me at L—— and got me a solicitor. I shall not forget speaking to him through the bars at N——; to him at least I was not a moral leper.

Another friend gallantly hitch-hiked from the Midlands to L—— and was allowed to see me for 15 minutes. He had been at the college and on the night of dismissal I had broken down and explained my departure. He was in the room next to my flat; we had similar tastes in music so the papery walls did not matter. He was sorry and did not hold it against me. He helped me string up my books.

He is only nineteen. His mother knows too. When I appeared in court the second time he was there. One officer, while completing the enquiries, asked how long I had known him. The implication was obvious. If you're young and you know me there's dirt in the air. I told his mother about it. She was not surprised. 'They'll think anything: it's their job.'

Bail was allowed. I must stay in N—— but might visit mother if my host would accompany me. The local paper reported the alleged suicide threat.

And here I am, with two days to go. Bail was renewed as I have said. One charge; admit the offence with Stephen. One charge. One incident. But it's a lifetime that will be on trial. A lifetime of failure and muddle. Ovid's five words fit once again: *Video meliora proboque; deteriora sequor.* For I have longed for excellence and perfection. I wanted perfection in knowlege, my own being, and personal relationships. The greatest failure was with Stephen; the next greatest the Two-One at Cambridge. After a time I spat at perfection and took my pleasures where I could. I hoped to fix the casual into the permanent; to begin with some hurried, furtive embrace and find the person, man or youth, returning to meet me again and again. But it has not happened.

And what does 'Society' want? To lock me up, I suppose, for months or years and leave it at that. If this happens I hope I may be granted the supreme strength of scorn, finding it possible to pare my nails in prison, aloof like a true outsider. What matters is the judgment of the self on the self. I do not feel ashamed of having slept with members of my own sex; I do feel ashamed of the weakness in my mind when I thought it possible to enter into a relationship with 'Mouse' and others like him. But it is stupid to expect 'Society' to understand. Society has its own business, such as it is. And 'Mouse' is trapped.

When I taught boys I entered their world—in some measure, imaginatively, perhaps not accurately. I was close to them, finding again the world I had never possessed. I conclude that I have never grown up—that sanctified word 'maturity' is a concept I meditate on with a cock-eyed mind, not a concrete reality I share with other mature men.

Finally, what images will people my cell? Stephen, now learning Greek and going to Rome for Easter; piano duets with P—— who is now on the way to pianistic distinction; fish and chips devoured along the street with J—— who is now reading History somewhere; the cut and thrust of debate with the Sixth form; introducing 5c to the Eatanswill election when contemporary events made it real to them; the desperate hours when so-and-so did not turn up; the great body of Mozart's music which I have in my head; the splendours of Johnson's prose; the searing beauty of Stephen's eyes.

Other things should be mentioned at this point; they have all contributed something. A very early memory: I am sitting in the wicker chair; it is early morning and I am in my night-shirt. I am whimpering and I mutter to myself, 'If I only have a dream it's wrong.' The years of uncertainty for my parents: keep him there or let him leave? The misery of being ninth in the form. The sense of disaster which became an adolescent metaphysic. I saw the world as a great error, and if there were a God he had committed an error so gigantic that no heaven could atone. Love was man's answer. Love could make it all tolerable. I remember laying down the law about it to the girl I imagined myself in love with: 'Exams like Higher School test so little—facts, opinions. There ought to be an exam to test our capacity for loving.' I felt I should get a distinction.

And the ideal?—An 'I' with the certainty of touch that would have led me to a partner with whom I might have shared my fragmentary insights. An 'I' with such powers of mind that the wretched unreality of the incident with 'Mouse' would have been impossible. An 'I' centred on this northern midland region which I once described as 'the Utopia of the heart'.

When Stephen and I were waiting for a bus in Eastwood I said something which sounds sense after nearly two years: 'Be good, be excellent, be first class. Have nothing to do with mediocrity. Be pitiful to the weaknesses and failings of others, but merciless to your own.'

Two more days. I can read G. E. Moore's *Autobiography* to clear my mind; I can listen to the G minor Quintet to fortify my mind with the tragedy that dissolves into ironic joy.

For the rest I can discern no meaningful pattern. I cannot say: Good will come of it, or: The whole thing is tragically absurd. I simply do not know. But one thing I have realized: if my close-cropped, melodiously-voiced, kindly detective constable were making a statement in court about Tristan and Isolde it would go something like this: 'Intimacy took place. Both guilty parties are deceased.'

From the outside even 'normal love' looks queer. What can a queer expect?

6

Pederast

by 'JOHN DAVIS'

For I am every dead thing,
In whom love wrought new alchemy.
For his art did express
A quintessence even from nothingness,
From dull privations, and lean emptiness:
He ruin'd me, and I am re-begot
Of absence, darkness, death; things which are not.

John Donne

IF I HAVE got to uncurl my toes I had better say, 'Can I kiss Johnathan's mum?' There, it's done: compression of toes by painful association. Newton's law of opposite and equal reaction has already contrived to relax them. I can write. But Johnathan's mum, Sylvia, was far more than the recipient of this mumbled and circumspect inanity. She was the first adult woman I'd really known, and as such I endeavoured to explain my real self to her; it was a test-case for sympathy. My indulgence was facilitated by the aura I had conceived, and flaunted, about this woman and her son as Madonna and Child. For not only was she the first woman I had really known, but Johnathan was the first creature I had seen as someone's *child*, as opposed to either the globe-eyed infants whom, in my capacity as prep schoolmaster, I regarded with distaste and tenderness as inevitable 'embryology', or the *boys* who are, who can be, a highly specialized animal, whose uniqueness I shall hope to demonstrate.

The occasion of my shame, and my quote-line, was of my own engineering. The east-coast prep school, like many others, maintained sleepy holiday economy with a skeletal staff, and dispossessed black boys looking oddly incongruous in Harrods flared flannel shorts and powder-pink sock-tops, their powder-pink belts weighted with gigantic knives which were concessions to holiday captivity. Sylvia was 'holiday matron'; a last-minute emergency model, divorced and just returned from the tropics, she gave the impression of having stepped out of an Indian army mess on ladies night all oddly hot and hungry with her sabre-slash mouth still awash with pink gin. Her exotic sophistication confused my nineteen years, but was not incompatible with the Madonna conception, which time, anyway, was to prove little more than a face-saving device. One night I got strangely built up on words, the effect was precisely like alcohol, talking as only a foolish young man may about Art, Love and Beauty, capitalized, and being in effect no more than an oblique, heightened though wary exposition of self. An act; but one so passionately played that she misinterpreted its intent. I was too intoxicated by my own lyric to panic when she resignedly proposed the wretched youth's seduction. We ascended a clock-tower, while I took such possession of her meaningless wood arm as I supposed was expected of me. She wiped my face with the sabre-slash and my person with her body. Cold and disinterested as if I'd just clambered out of an arctic pond, I was anxious only to flee, whilst somehow maintaining face. And so, 'Can I kiss Johnathan's mum?' How after all could I molest a virgin mother. Bored and floppy, rather than angry, she stroked my hair, 'Poor John!'

I awaited reprisals with a fevered apprehension which was constantly on the defensive, and shooting at shadows. Shove ha'penny. 'John, you play with Sylvia.' 'We've tried,' I said, hoping by means of the plural pronoun to baffle any rumour by implying some failure on her part as well as mine. And then the reprisals, with an apparent idleness that covered a deadly precision. After a film with a boy star, in a car full of my regular colleagues, 'Oh, wasn't he pretty!', accompanied by a public smear from the sabre-slash. A cigarette offered to a non-smoker in my presence, '*John* doesn't have any *vices*!' So, fine; any ordinary day. But this happened to be the day the Wolfenden Report was published, and the popular papers that littered the staff-room all carried the word *vice* in one context or another as their headline. Most priceless, though, was the picture of myself. We idly turned over some newly arrived B.B.C. wall charts portraying the evolution of man. The penultimate picture was of a rather bewildered ape with a reluctant cognition dawning in its eyes. Perhaps it had just bitten the apple and didn't like the taste much, but the point was the caption, *Near Man*. Yes, of course, dear, cruelly insulted Sylvia 'knew some near men'.

Strangely perhaps my association with Sylvia was not a traumatic experience in my life. I mention her as the first person whose hostility I aroused by openly, if obliquely, owning to the fact that I love boys. It is for her then, whom I was unable to involve in the hot struggle of her hopes in the dust of that tower, as much as for those with less cause to be angered, that this apology is written. I am neither convict nor practitioner, and so do not propose justification of homosexual acts involving small boys. I would simply present the facts concerning my own affections and desires, and suggest that they are neither vicious nor diseased in an attempt to demonstrate something of the quiet and reality of a predicament where there is seldom any audible truth. Pomp? Maybe. And this raises another introductory reservation. As the most misrepresented type of homosexual I live not only constantly reflected in the trick-mirror of my own self-conscious sense, but also with the knowledge, equally ever present, that what I love, and so value infinitely, is to many other people either unutterably disgusting or absurd. Consequently much of my dealing with the world is conducted, as it were, in an antechamber of the mind. I do not easily admit of alienation. When I must, as this article demands, my instinct is to retreat up an Olympus of fantasy there to forge words, endless words, in the terrible machinery of wildness and hurl them with Jovian pride at your hypocritical heads. . . . Again, if I am to baffle pride behind anonymity, and endeavour to sketch 'what it is like to love the boy impossible', the difficulty is still not ended. Some people may, in sincerity, be unable to believe that you can love a boy: 'I mean, an *educated* bloke? That stands rounds and plays darts?' To them I can only answer rhetorically. Where would you begin were I to suddenly let my jaw sag incredulously through two inches of space and say, 'Yes, but *why* do you like girls?' It is exactly the same question. And whether you leered and said, 'Curves!', or drew yourself upright and said, 'Young man, St Paul . . .' my answer must be only as confused, and as inadequate, as yours.

My observations here are general and current: I am not concerned at all with the phenomena of my own adolescence. However, an autobiographical note of sexual development is imperative both as dispelling charges of effeminacy, insanity, etc., as may well arise where few conceptions of homosexuality are accurate, and also in the interest of the truth I am seeking here.

Yes, I loved a girl when twelve: a wide-eyed child in a yellow dance frock who still wanders in the shadows of my peripheral vision. Before the annual ball when I would see her I scraped my spots with the scalpel I used for making model aircraft. Then, naturally, my sex and my love were as the poles apart. No, I was not seduced at my public school, nor (to crying regret) did I have any sexual connection with other boys there. I entertained myself; secretly borrowed certain articles of clothing from younger boys who were pretty. When seventeen I fell in love with a beautiful boy of thirteen. In a second, at a glance, some chemical change took place in my brain that four years were to prove irreparable. The incomparable power and beauty of this love turned inwards: I left school early solely because I was unable to sustain its terror. My passion ran on, and we met many times, whilst, uncannily, he defied puberty till well past sixteen: he accepted only kisses, and then with anger or reluctance. I then learnt of my boy's having spent a bewildered week-end in a middle-aged man's bed in London: scream liar if you will, but this had *paternal sanction*. Mysteriously the shock to myself was delayed until I saw the man in question when, having the guts to kill neither him nor myself, something popped in my head and for some time I became a psychiatric out-patient. Adolescence is only another word for melodrama. No grudge now. . . . A rugger injury rejected me for National Service. (For the cartoonist of the homosexual, I am a county sprint champion.) I taught for two years at a prep school. Sense ebbed and flowed fairly secure from the terror of love I never wanted to experience again. One or two beauties of twelve or thereabouts sat (dressed) on my (dressed) knee. Ashamed only of secrecy I drearily changed my underclothes. Such performance sounds callous: it was not. Am now twenty-four, and at what I must describe as 'one of our oldest universities': a youthful but boy-less place.

'You deny carnal knowledge, then?'

'In grey England, your honour.'

'You've assaulted innocent foreign children?'

'He just clambered in, your honour. They do sometimes. I couldn't refuse—he was a Count. He had a silver wire on his teeth. When I felt his smile spreading over my lips in the darkness I licked the wire. He was like one of those bears that breathe. But I was ashamed.'

'Ah!'

'I was ashamed because holding the naked breathing I felt secure for the first time in my life; because I couldn't do anything else but cry.'

Of the few articles about homosexuality that appear in the press, and which are as often as not followed by eager correspondence peremptorily declared closed by editorial footnote, many fail to define their terms and so read rather like a description of arithmetic without any numerical consideration. It is further surprising that one can read the several thousand pages of the complete Havelock Ellis without discovering any simple statement that *there are three distinct types of homosexual.* Of such unscientific definitions as have been formulated that of the novelist Gide is, I think, best. 'I call a *pederast* the man who, as the word indicates, falls in love with young boys. I call a *sodomite* the man whose desire is addressed to mature men. I call an *invert* the man who assumes the rôle of a woman and desires to be possessed.' It can I think safely be said that the existence of these different types of homosexual, and the contempt with which they regard each other, has done quite as much to misrepresent themselves in the regard of 'normal' persons as has the canon of convention. M. Gide goes on to describe this. 'The difference amongst them is such that they experience a profound disgust for one another, a disgust accompanied by a reprobation that in no way yields to that which you (heterosexuals) fiercely show toward all three.' (*Journals*. English edition 1948, p. 246).

It is tempting to follow M. Gide further, however it must here suffice to say that he goes on to depict pederasty as natural, and the other two only as deserving of moral and social censure.

If these definitions be accepted as true (though in this subject no response is calculable) it will be understood that scoutmaster jokes are alien to the sodomite; that to the pederast the loose term 'homosexual', with its most usual suggestion of adult males, must cause more pain by far than the eruption of very large black men at a Little Rock ladies' tea-party. These facts simply are not known.

Instances of the hatred rampant between these types might be multiplied indefinitely, but is outside my purpose here. One example I may cite. In a recent, and wholly sincere book, a young man convicted of adult homosexuality expresses horror at the pederast. No one, however, might read the book without at once remarking a certain irony, for whilst the man in question speaks of desiring to be possessed when a boy, and was later convicted for (allegedly) being possessed as a man, he condemns men who 'chase' boys. How, one might ask, can the man who wants to be possessed like a boy legitimately deny his lover the real thing. I don't want to pursue this further. I raise it only because the explanation of this hatred is simple and vitally important. The love of all homosexuals is, precisely as that of heterosexuals, a thing infinitely personal and infinitely beautiful. Can one then wonder at their being reluctant to have it compared with *anything*, let alone a phenomenon receiving perhaps even more public condemnation than their own particular love?

Inevitably the censure of society, as much as of the sodomite and the invert, falls most heavily upon the pederast. This is understandable if unjust. The reason for it may be simplified as threefold. 1. Small boys are innocent. 2. They must not be

diverted in, or from, their natural development. 3. Most of us
associate the dawn of sexual awareness with some disturbance
and unhappiness, greater or less, and from this we want to
keep our children as long as may be.

This is society's argument against the pederast. I will not
contest it as I want only to present such persons' loves and
desires as unvicious. Their acts, and possible consequences of
their acts, inevitably involve morality and psychology and
precise definition of circumstance beyond any present pre-
sumption of mine. However in an age when the denial of God
is repeated, even encouraged, upon the West End stage,
morality must, logically at least, reside between the brackets of
hurt, whose definition would seem here to rest with the
scientist.—Incidentally he does not believe, Mam, that my
occasional hug, my awed look, at your twelve or thirteen-year-
old will 'pervert him for life'. Nor, quite honestly, do I. But
the *facts* of such odd desires in a grown man. . . .

The truth here is best built upon the obvious. At some stage
of adolescence the vast majority of healthy males experience
at least passing sensuality for younger boys. No one, I think,
will deny that a young boy may be lineally, plastically beautiful;
many, however, only hide from themselves that he is desirable.
Oddly the boy knows it, and may supplement the effect instinctively, often to an astonishing degree. Many parents
neither know, nor believe this. Just how often it is the master
who nearly seduces the boy, and just how often it is the boy
(yes, nice, like yours) who nearly seduces the master, only
someone who has taught at a prep school can tell you. Incidentally, the statement that Nero was not a god resulted in the
claimant being eaten by lions. Digestion did not invalidate the
fact: Nero was not a god.

It would be idle to attempt a definition of the sexually
attractive. If we take the criterion of pretty as a basis, may not
further definition best be said to rest with the attitude and
consequent deportment of the object? Look at the boy:
probably you don't know what one is. Physically he is beautiful; technically he is 'sexually undifferentiated'. How does he
behave? But first let it be remembered that we are not question-

ing the normality of that behaviour, or suggesting that any advantage be taken of it. The first technical and physical manifestation of puberty, if uninitiated by himself or others occurs spontaneously. Before, and for a long time afterwards, his attitude is well summed-up by the caption of a photograph of a much younger child I recently saw which was, 'When I grow up will I be a girl or a boy?' The feeling is of course entirely unformulated; but just how strong it is I shall shortly illustrate. It might be as well to remark here that this may often be a time of extreme physical beauty: the boy has lost the prominent tummy and seeming outsize head of childhood, but not yet gained the unbalanced proportions of adolescence: he appears to be in a timeless drift. This, I think, is a commonly observed fact whose formulation does not pre-suppose prejudice. This is the period of curious animal games (so well concealed from parents that many do not believe them): tumbling games of Coastguards and Smugglers, when the latter will conceal the contraband down the front of their shorts in the hope of ruthless search. Like all young animals he enjoys all physical contacts, but he is, too, constantly seeking to draw affection from whatever quarter he can.

My conception of love (in so far as I have practised it with a boy) does not involve his crude excitation. Nor, obviously, does the boy invite the familiarity of his master as he does his fellows. But he does, or rather may invite it nevertheless, and then with a subtlety which is the more devastating in its circuitous approach, its tenderness and bewilderment. This is when the animal is dangerous: this, simply, where you fall in love.

I can demonstrate the animal only fractionally; but as typical. Of some five subtle assaults upon myself during two years' teaching there was one which I did not automatically endeavour to discourage. Initially I was unable to do so from sheer fascination, innocent, and akin to bird-watching. Later I fell in love. Tony was just thirteen and bore himself with a superb, solitary aloofness that completely disdained law and order. He commenced his courtship of myself I know not why, though probably as a result of a smile, and in the added knowledge that I was but an amateur pedagogue of twenty-one about to go up to the university. He was a weedy kid in many ways, a snob-boy through and through with *two* furry black hunting helmets. He skied all winter and sat in the Mediterranean all summer, and was solid gold in aspect as well as circumstance. In addition he was ravishingly beautiful. However my point here is the approach of this child. To Tony all the instincts of the 'femme fatale' were first nature, and seemed to flow from deep inside him. By turns I suffered cruelty, the soft-pedallings of retreat, streaks of an astonishing tenderness (quite years, I would have thought, beyond his age), and shattering tantrums of bitchiness. The whole was made the more compelling by a precision of timing that concealed all this from my colleagues, and I followed, limp captive.—It can doubtless be said that I encouraged the undifferentiated animal in a secret game and that my imagination supplied the rest. I do not think so. What I do know is that compared to Tony's technique Sylvia's was that of a frigid child; so much vestigial coeleocanth. Tony was no prudish boy. One of his more engaging habits was to hurl himself on to my knee whenever he found me in a chair. Once established he would snuggle down, and being Tony, would take and give a running commentary on the rate and significance of my pulse. I buried my nose hopelessly in his hair. Home.

At the moment I live in a virtually boy-less environment: a barren place made tolerable by my own, often silly, invention. I have Tony to write to, sparingly as one must; to worry about, for somewhere he is out of my control curiously following his young animal senses: somehow, though, I've learnt to hide myself a little from jealousy, as a result of the seduction of the boy who ruled my adolescence. I have some 150 photos of Tony, and some of other boys, But above all I have time to think; albeit in circles. I am now in the unattached and, as it were, self-sufficient state in which presumably I am expected to live for good. The first part of my article sought to demonstrate what a boy is, and to suggest that it is possible to fall in love with him, precisely as, and with the same emotions with which one falls in love with a girl. In this second part I shall try to list some of the effects which a virtual proscription of my emotions has upon me at the present time, and also such effects as result from the impossibility of consummation, and are so relevant in any environment.

The chief effect, obviously, must spring from the knowledge that what you love the majority of society considers wrong. In practice this condemnation is of no account at all. When you or I move a smile or a hand in love we simply do not stop to consider its significance within Whitehall or the diocese of Canterbury. At other times this ever present censure works very differently. The results of this trapped nervous energy, its turmoil, might be listed indefinitely. Perhaps it is sufficient to offer only the confused indecision, embarrassment and resultant chaos in a normally competent journalist. All my succeeding paragraphs will be concerned with the results of this mental inversion, and enforced furtiveness. I raise and worship my gods in fantasy where you can never despoil or discredit them. How *dare* you say what I shall love and what I shall not love!

In face of real criminal proceedings retreat is no less inevitable; identification no less impossible. The other day I cut, from one of the top person's gargantuan Sunday tomes as it happens, a judge's summing-up of some wretched man's conviction. In addition to publicly expressing the hope (surely irregular?) that parents might get him into their 'own hands' and deal with him 'as they thought he deserved', the (admittedly extreme) offence was dismissed with the redundancy that only hatred engenders, 'This is filthy, disgusting, immoral, and beastly behaviour', etc. How do I reconcile another's reprimand such as this with my own affection, which is love, nothing less, and whose beauty I cannot deny and remain human? What intellectual compromise do I evolve where integrity, or if you like perverse pride, forbids that I should make any divorce between an owned and ownable tenderness for boys and its acknowledgment as a basically sexual phenomenon?

I have the utmost respect for those few good, usually elderly, schoolmasters who have been able to sublimate their affection for boys into a selfless concern at once for the plain as the pretty, and into much else besides. I would regard them more highly were one of them once to own to a secret though unconditional passion for little Y. way back in '33.

I could not deny J, A, C, or T. if you came round with a pistol tomorrow. You may say, 'Homos always flaunt themselves like that; that's why they wear yellow bowties and giggle ecstatic soprano'. No, mine is the empirical romantic belief in the insoluble link between beauty and truth. I may flaunt beliefs badly, with incredible stupidity as on the night when I was disgraced before Sylvia, but the human instinct to seek identification with another through self-revelation cannot be hidden for long. I cannot present a false face to a friend. And the struggle is absurd because all I must say is, 'Sometimes I fall in love with boys about thirteen. See?' Usually I take a coward obliqueness, and say, 'I can understand a bloke falling in love with a boy'. It is enough.

Since the fiasco with Sylvia my defence of the faith has tended to silence. In fact I have only been involved in two clashes up here. One was an argument with a venerable don who likes undergraduates. *Men!* I patted his white hair because I was drunk and called him a sad gardener of over-blown roses. When a boy goes to seed his bloom withers. The other occasion was when a neighbour, a youth of eighteen straight from school for whom I had no particular liking, happened to come into my room. I imagine he had previously overheard some conversation of mine with a friend, for he suddenly stopped before a photo of Tony on my mantelpiece, and with a compulsion that would have astounded even Pavlov said, 'God! Are you really as *queer* as that?' Indulging what I afterwards realized to have been a lifelong curiosity, though quite on impulse, I let out one of those punches you see in westerns —but missed. Tony, needless to say, remained. What I could not rid from my mind was the hatred of a tone that was utterly convincing in its sincerity.

Choirboys. Oxbridge (now I've contributed to that dreadful term) swarms with them. I've adopted ours as a strange corporate love, not because a few of them sing in candlelight, but because they represent an emotional focus or orientation whose development, like any elaborate fantasy, has little logical basis, and that largely inexpressible. Because, if it be an indication of sanity or otherwise, their grey flannel suits do not contain ten per cent of nylon, and they march about in a woollen crocodile which is a terrible soft silver in the sunshine. Because they are there. Because, carried off a rugger field with a broken collar-bone in my first term the last thing I heard before dropping into unconsciousness was one of those who happened to be watching say to his companion, soiling a tiny top person intonation, 'That bloody man's *killed* one of *our* men!' I was not killed. In fact I was subsequently told that I had passed out with an idiotic grin on my face. *Our* men. And I offer this particular reminiscence in full awareness of its adolescent flavour. Crudely, where one cannot bed the object of one's choice one is liable to all manner of hyper-aesthesia, where sentimentality, even mawkishness, has both a real and respectable place sometimes. Whether there is an ultimate choice between premature senility and residence in Istanbul I cannot say. Meanwhile I regard these boys with numbed awe. They are the outward manifestation at least of a freak emotional security, and their every aspect is loved because inextricably familiar. I will certainly write to *The Times* should that drab and greasy god Terylene ever come amongst them.

Incidentally, if you are one of those people who occasionally make jokes of the choirboy–scoutmaster variety this surely reflects only one thing: a sinister aspect of your own semi-unconscious which you daren't face. Some spotty little excitement way back, probably.

A circumscribed sexuality inevitably exaggerates erotic fantasy, channels energy into extraordinarily trivial obsessions, and produces all manner of hyper-sensitivity. I can suggest only a fraction of such phenomena, and must refuse to invoke the power of sexual desire, though less out of deference for your sensibilities than because I am not prepared to break myself in the attempt. Of desire I will only say that I have vomited physically, in the street with shame and confusion, simply at the sight of a boy. That sometimes, as when once I saw Palestrina, a technicolor child at our choir school whom I have raised in loneliness on to a remote pedestal, I have had to retire to bed with a dose of barbiturates of a proportion more usually administered to wild stallions about to be transported by air. Palestrina, sartorially a walking advertisement for Daniel Neal's, with some eight woolly grey suits, seemingly for ever new, appeared on this occasion to have had a four-ounce bottle of ink emptied over the front of his clothes. In addition his nose was bleeding, but neither disturbed the pride and midget self-assurance of his customary progression up the road, his forgotten satchel bumping rhythmically against his flank. . . . But no demonstration of desire. It must suffice to list a few of the phenomena that result from its bafflement. They will be jumbled. One may not, alas, detach one's own mind and dissect it dispassionately at a remove.

Whether he owns to it or not a man's behaviour, and his thought, are constantly determined by his subjective conception of what other people may be thinking about him. In my case this psychological law sometimes has the effect of making me regard boys as teddy-bears; as small warm animals, and of hiding from myself the sex which lies beneath the sentiment. It is as if I wanted you to say, 'He thinks of his boys as teddy-bears: we can accept him'. One comes to live in this world; a world of softly clothed dolls. If one is lucky enough to emerge from it, meet a real boy, the artificiality which is usually so compelling falls away: one's puppets, my Palestrina and others, become suddenly paper-thin and about as colourless. To meet with reality is to emerge like a prisoner from a dark cell and walk for a moment in the sunshine; to be suffused in a forgotten warmth, and filled with unspeakable tenderness. So I saw Tony again after nearly two years.—Only afterwards does one begin to face the futility of retaining the object of love. Then one returns to the darkness, to the fantasy and the artificiality. Odd skills and consolations.

I can pick out the word 'boy' from an encyclopaedia page in one second flat. I have a dialogue-ear of demoniac persistence whose development I attribute largely to *boy*; a nonsense-rhyming machine which it is he again who gleefully flicks into motion. I have a passion for boy photography; a bastard art, but an art nevertheless, and one with all art's agonies. I am prey to knitting-pattern boys and advertisement boys; to Palestrina and his pages Vittoria and little Nasco, who are projections of reality, and also to boys who are solely my own creations. There is no end to incidental sublimation.

Privation produces secret cults, and cults have their mysteries. I imagine it is for this reason, as much as because any man endeavours to define the uniqueness of his love, that I am obsessed with exact terminology. To me a *boy* is an animal completely different from either a *child* or a *youth*. I should like to go further and say that *boy* is a word rightly applicable only to the statistically inevitable three per cent of beauties in any given collection of males between the ages of eleven and fifteen. Again, if you want to hurt me, you have in your condescension only to refer to the bricklayer's mate as a 'boy'. Should you wish to anger me beyond endurance, just call a real boy 'handsome' where you mean either 'pretty' or 'beautiful'. I'll writhe all right then. There is one curious respect in which the pederast has an advantage over the heterosexual. His mind may more readily be pure. Since the mass media do not prostitute the object of his love twenty-four hours a day; since no one pastes brown boys in one-piece bikinis in tube trains and there are no strip-boys in *Reveille*, he is as free of the more dubious erotic inheritance as the prelapsarian Adam. Quite what would be my reaction to Palestrina performing the 'two lip test' nightly on telly, Nasco being repeatedly tumbled on to Cinemascope beds and so on, I don't know. Probably I should need to be carried about on a litter in a state of total exhaustion. The thought, anyway, is a profitless and dangerously obsessive one. Like wondering how long the rods of candy are before they are chopped up into mint lumps. But what does this prove? Assuming that you are not incited to promiscuity, and are a better man than I should be in your place, then what is all this synthetic erotica *for*? Is it a necessary insurance against impotence? Are you unable to maintain heterosexual direction without it? You are naked lovers with a licence. Your love, though, is often farther from nature than mine. I wonder, when you do find real union, as sometimes you must, doesn't the existence of this dreary propaganda machinery pinken your ears just a little? Or can you comfortably accommodate the cinema hoarding and yellow Sunday papers in bed with your wife? I have an excuse for a pin-up mentality, as and when I may want it. You have none.

This university is a boy-less place. There hasn't been a boy here since 1700 or thereabouts. Consequently my present life is sometimes a mockery anticipation of old age, and there descends a deep spiritual loneliness which social concourse serves only to emphasize. There have been freak consolations, as when once, by a quite extraordinary coincidence, I tumbled out of a doorway to bowl over no less than Palestrina. It was on its way to its trumpet lesson. The trumpet fell out of the box with an indignant clang. Feeling foolish, and after a furtive glance at the empty street, I straightened its cap and whisked a finger down its nose. It dropped its eyelids, peach blossom came out of the sky, and I set course for the barbiturate jar. Now I slink past the crocodile, for once afterwards it smiled and waved with more warmth than summer. But mostly, like the old man, my mind is thronged with hollow voices and the myriad, technicolor pools of past memory. David, with the light on his hair, his features drawn, waxed facets like a Ribston pippin, lips of the cliché chiselled. Peter, with tight round buttocks like a cleft champagne cork, eyes blue as Omo and skin like a strawberry-ice, whose habit it was to wiggle out of his shorts at bed-time without undoing so much as the snake-clasp of his belt. The voice of white Tony at tennis, his lips sprung wide, playing with myself in no single sense. Bawls over the net, 'You'll never beat us!' Then aside, with the smile that broke Troy, 'We're a bound pair'. Schoolgirl remark striking another schoolgirl's heart, maybe. Dedication of another half-bottle of whisky. Yes Tony, perhaps the only boy who could call a master he'd singled out for destruction by his Christian name *and* leave the staff-room in the headmaster's presence by walking two steps over a sofa simply because he felt like it. Hot memories that tauten the stomach or the breast. Palestrina again, the wind plucking idly at the hem of his shorts at the number eight bus stop, his head cocked sideways, his teeth bared breathing puzzlement into the rain; or after his fight his intolerable newness in the agony of scragged disarray. —The old man dribbles on to his page. But then he has little left to him but fantasy, and glimpses of Palestrina—silver glass child in the roar of the black traffic.

My love-letters are like any other man's. Only I carbon them, both because sometimes they have to be ends in themselves and also because they might at any moment prove vital to a solicitor. I mean mine. Rules go to their writing, some of which impose absurd technical problems. Words must be monosyllabic, sentences limited to ten words, and the whole never longer than four-hundred words. Sentiments must be equally simple, and with allusions to only such things as one may mutually share, yes, with a child, Their object? Simply to draw a grubby card, or half-page of blotchy inconsequence, for the reliquary in scarlet ribbon: to discover whether the boy is all right; to say I'm still there. The whole problem is sometimes heart-breaking because, obviously, the boy to whom I write has moved into a new and baffling school, and is still an animal whose sole concern is with his immediate environment. Parents who don't get letters on Monday mornings from small sons at boarding school know the cruelty of this lore. Nevertheless a letter occasionally comes (though in my case I've known a broken hip, total immobilization and boredom necessary to effect its despatch). When it does spiritual restitution is astonishing. Nothing can blanket the sun. But all the waiting.

Whatever philosophy one may evolve one cannot repeatedly engage and break the higher emotions without some consequence. Boys such as Tony, whose beauty alone is not readily found in the plural, are not often dropped at one's feet. To find, far more be accepted and even loved by such a creature, only to have him wrested from one, may jar the system intolerably. Parting, though, is only human destiny. It's when the process has been repeated not once but several times that there is a danger of an unutterable despair. In my place one must not think in terms of the permanent physical possession which is the mistaken ambition of love. Of loss, too, one must not think at all.

I have endeavoured to show that men can, and do, fall in love with young boys, and suggested that this phenomenon is not vicious, if only by virtue of the tenderness inherent in so many such relationships. Further, I have instanced a few of the effects which both actual and imagined oppression have wrought in myself. I have no intention of soliciting for either the approval or indulgence of an active pederasty involving crude physical excitation. I would however plead the *attraction* of pederasty as a phenomenon that is both human and very far from diseased. Lastly, I would demand that it is no sane peg for jokes. It is disgusting, though true, that many people regard the dismissal and subsequent ruin of a schoolmaster, curate or whatever, as exceedingly funny. Often, incidentally, an ill-timed caress, or even a rumour is enough. Few of these jesters reflect that this may well be the double of the man, and the identical love (nothing less) that taught their grubby selves the multiplication table and won them scholarships, to ignore God knows what other ministrations in their bloodiest years. For how long can you deny responsible and intelligent recognition of a phenomenon inherent, albeit minutely, and probably disguised, in all of us. And even if your own unconscious desires are buried beyond reproach are you so selfish, such a gaping puppet of conditioned-reflex, as to believe that there can *be* no other love but yours?

For my own fear, I am afraid not so much of any likelihood of ruin as of myself. The human sense of isolation should need no explication here. My fear, like any other's, is only that when it matters I may fail to find the sympathetic identification without which no man can last long. Were I to shut you in a black box and ceaselessly decry what *you* value most, then I suggest that something in your head might go pop. I don't intend to enter any black box. I remain free; but a lead-boot man that gropes the extension of his arms for a star.

Finally, I am afraid lest deprivation, or imagined deprivation, should harden me against my fellow men. Bloodiness I can, and will, meet with bloodiness. God forbid, though, that I should turn my back on any human failing, as some others have turned, and presumably will continue to turn their backs on mine. But is any love a failing?

7

Seduced as a Girl

by 'MARY LOVELL DEAN'

'YOUR LOVE is like a coin that has passed through so many hands it has become worthless.' So runs the translation of an old Spanish song. And as I listen to the peerless beauty of Victoria de los Angeles singing this trite little quip I reflect that, after all, my story is age old, and, I suspect, as little understood now as it was when the Spanish poet penned his little reproach. I reflect also, and with pride, that worthless though I may appear to some, I am yet able to take hold of this exquisite singing and listening know that the moment is justification in itself and the arid desert of worthless memories does not matter.

At least, I know that I cannot allow it to matter too much, for if I did, just to live would be impossible and as a cloak for guilt I can plead a miserable childhood.

As a child I was ruthlessly and brutally oppressed, both physically and mentally. In wild and silly moments I have felt as if all the world were against me. Deliberately persecuted. Sought out like a doormat for other people's dirty feet, but a doormat passivity I never could feel. If I now echo, like a strutting spiritual peacock, 'but, look, I have come through'— but come through to what? What does a doormat do when it gets up and walks about? Surely, first of all, it must shake off some of the dust and mud.

Since I am not exactly a doormat, I can only hope that an attempt to shake off some of the shackles of the past will help to bring home yet more strongly the fact that the unwanted child is a menace both to itself and the rest of society. From my observation, most people seem to know this well enough but know it only as an observed clinical fact. For the unwanted are usually silent: their lack of trust, both in them-selves and the outside world, like high walls, forever closes them in. If I now have the courage to admit that it was sheer luck that kept me out of a home for unmarried mothers during my teens and early twenties, it is because I have in recent years, against a background of security, had a chance to indulge in introspection, digging back painfully into the past for some self-understanding. Pity, I neither want nor need, unless it is pity for the child and young woman I was. If you are tempted to dismiss this as self-pity then think again, for it is only because I have swallowed my pride and pitied the child I was that I have learned some tolerance, both of myself and others.

And I have certainly had to swallow some pride, for as I re-read the incidents I have described I can only think 'What a poor little fool', but I realize that I was too angry to think and too lonely to care. The first little story is important to me only because it was an occasion when it was again, just luck, that prevented me from wrecking the desire for the vengeance of a lifetime, on one poor fool of a man who presumed just a little too much. It would have been a pity if he had taken the punishment for all the others as well as for himself!

The place was Germany, not long after the war.

Together with a red-headed girl friend and two Control Commission officers, I spent an evening dancing and drinking in a leave-club. The evening came to an end rather early so all four of us went to the rooms of one of the men. We two girls, I was about twenty-one and my friend a little older, believed that there was safety in a foursome. We did not know that they had two rooms.

It soon became obvious that the evening's climax was to be rather more than we had bargained for. The men were insistent, we reluctant. The more dominant of the two, a stocky, pugnacious fellow, finally flew into a towering rage, locked the door and pocketed the key. He was intent on my friend, a richly curved plum of a girl who was a sweet and innocent virgin. I thought so anyway! Had I been alone I do not think I would have cared greatly how the evening had ended. I was too lonely and gullible to have much resistance. What would one more promiscuous adventure among so many others have mattered?

The powerful pug with the key in his pocket was not exactly drunk but his self-control was wearing a bit thin. The red-head, pale, flaccid and stupid, seemed to be looking at me for protection.

My self-control split right open. I wrenched at the door handle. The wood about the screws must have been rotten, for it came away in my hand. I had a weapon. A strong jabbing stick of steel with a handle on which I could get a good grip.

'Give me the key, or I'll strike you.'

Even in those days I hated violence, or thought I did, but not at that moment. I wanted to stab him, to tear at the flesh on his face. His eyes just above my own, just within my reach, hard and bright with anger, floated with memories. It would have been very satisfying to have jabbed the steel in one eye socket and to have wrenched it down his cheek.

I am not very big, nor very strong, but he must have realized that I was prepared to use every scrap of my strength and would have stopped at nothing.

He drew back, murmured something conciliatory, and gave the key to the still stupefied and tearful red-head. She unlocked the door and fled. I followed, still clutching the dangerous door knob, feeling a mixture of relief and disappointment. On the way down the stairs I heard him shout. 'You bloody little wild-cat bitch.'

Outside in the street I just caught a glimpse of my friend disappearing at top speed; she seemed to be running away from me as much as from the seducing pug. On reflection, I cannot blame her.

The men were watching us from their lighted square of window. I flung the door handle into the road and watched it skim across the hard-packed snow, then turned to find my way back to my hotel room.

The little German village lay cradled between mountains. I could see distant peaks and feel the presence of tall conifers.

The sharp purity of the air and the absorbed silence of the snow caught me in a panic of isolation. Humanity stank and I stank with it. I wanted to become part of the snow, to fold its freezing blanket over my head.

I had been called a bitch. Well, it was just. No doubt the men were righteously indignant. We were all degraded and our only maxim 'If you can't be good, be careful'. If we were bitches, then the men were no more than penial notch-gatherers: all of us, following the example of our parents, regarding sexual union as little more than an extension of masturbation. The greater the promiscuity the greater the need, for there was no real easement either of body or mind. In those days I was caught on a roundabout. To me the act of sex was no more than a few moments of illusive warmth and sense of belonging that afterwards left me more alone and afraid than before.

I first set foot on this miserable roundabout at the age of fourteen.

I was at that time already working, having left grammar school as soon as my guardian had the legal right to take me away. London was being heavily bombed and the firm that employed me bought up a large hotel and annexe in North Wales.

The annexe, a musty mausoleum set uncompromisingly oblong on the side of an awe-inspiring mountain, housed my cousin, the managing director's secretary, who was supposed to be responsible for me; two other secretaries, a hearty-mouthed telephonist, the chief accountant—the villain of the piece whom I shall call Mr Hawker—and his wife, who acted as housekeeper.

We each had our own rooms. Mine, quite naturally, was the smallest, a bare little room constantly filled with the shadow of the great grey-black stretch of mountainside, and at night the stealthy rustling of cockroaches that crawled from beneath the wainscoting to die by the dozen in the thick yellow powder I used to spread under my bed.

It was my job to keep the office stamp book. But I never could add up. Following a rush of work I found that the wretched book, with its inky smudges and scrawled entries just would not balance. After hours of tortured calculations I finally had to give in and show my cousin. She set mouth and eyebrows in a long-suffering sigh and sent me to Mr Hawker.

With a cry in my heart that nobody loved me, I crawled into Mr Hawker's office. He sat impressively at his large desk. I had watched him on many occasions and envied his remarkable ability with figures. He could simply run a pen-tip down a column and put in a total. A feat which I envy still. I glanced over his shoulder at the account and ledger books with their inhumanly neat figures and felt ashamed.

He looked briefly at my blotchy stamp book. The tale of agonized woe must have been obvious. I remember how steadily and unsmiling he looked at me. For the first time I was aware that he had warm brown eyes. I wanted to look away, but because he was a man I accepted his gaze as a challenge and stared back.

'I am busy at the moment. Leave it with me—my dear.'

The last two words were balm to a sore spirit and I felt them in my memory all the rest of the day.

The cloying sense of warmth that reached me from Mr Hawker was a completely new and disturbing experience and one which I hugged to myself with my usual secrecy.

The events of the evening of the same day are still vivid and perhaps worth recording in some detail.

My cousin and her colleagues sat round the fire after our evening meal gossiping. Mrs Hawker's dreary efforts as housekeeper and cook were a constant source of resentful comment and the Hawkers themselves lively gossip material.

'Isn't Mrs Hawker queer? She can be very nice sometimes but she seems all tight in the middle, especially when he is around.'

'I wonder why those two got married? Did you hear them rowing at one another the other night?'

'Well, it's not surprising. Hawker was in the bar all evening, hanging around the Bulldozer for what he could get.'

'He's a crawler.'

The Bulldozer—our nickname for the managing director—indulged occasional mad fits of drinking. Success had gone to his head. When he was drunk he was known to bring out wads of pound notes and hand them around. I had once taken him a message. The room seemed to be full of empty champagne bottles and he gave me a handful of crumpled notes—twenty pounds—but my cousin gave them back next morning.

'Anyway, I'm sick to death of sardines on toast. If she is screwed up in the middle because of Hawker, then I'm screwed up in the middle with indigestion.'

My young presence was probably a damper on the conversation. I was not encouraged to join in and would, in any case, have been too shy, certainly with my cousin present. Before the move to North Wales I had spent all my leisure time reading. Books were an escape and I read everything and anything that came to hand. The annexe was bookless so I spent the long evenings monotonously knitting and inwardly fretting—mostly about the estrangement with my cousin. I had always worshipped and adored her and I fancy she was puzzled at the lack of my former doglike devotion. I resented her forthcoming marriage and distrusted her smooth, smug, successful fiancé. I did not recognize my feelings as jealousy.

A recurring dream that had haunted my childhood had come again to trouble me, a dream that never seemed to end but to drift with me into wakefulness. My cousin would be running away from me along a narrow pathway that ran through a meadow. I could never catch up. Another figure followed with a heavy dragging tread that seemed to pull me back. But it was the meadow that haunted me. It was thick with wild flowers and strange moving grasses, humming with brilliant, iridescent insects and winged creatures, alive with glowing colours, vivid and more real than life. If only my cousin would stop and look. But she ran as if she was afraid and I could do nothing to persuade her.

This helpless inability to communicate was strong with me that evening. I listened to their gossip and hated its shallow cruelty.

Mrs Hawker entered the room. There was something almost

gypsy-like about her dark hair and hard glittering eyes that were nearly black. She wore harsh colours, bright reds and greens. She was unusually talkative and friendly, and asked us if we had heard the story of the old woman who swallowed a bullet.

At the chorused 'No', she picked up the poker and turned to face us, her back to the fire.

'She bent down to poke the fire and shot the cat.'

With a high laugh she turned to jab at the burning coals. Jane, the telephonist, guffawed. My cousin and her co-secretaries tittered with embarrassment. I hugged my blushes close to my knitting pattern and tried to pretend I had not heard.

Long ago when I had been quite small, perhaps seven or eight, I remembered being alone with my aunt. I had been set to polish the floor.

'Go on,' she had urged. 'Polish it in the corner'. 'Go on, Polly,' Her voice became a mocking sneer, 'Polly shit in the corner.'

She repeated it several times, varying the emphasis and baiting me for a reaction.

I rubbed harder and harder at the floor, trying to hide my hot red face and trying not to choke on the painful lump that had risen in my throat. Of course I understood, but nothing would have made me admit it. My aunt finally gave up and echoed her face-saving laughter away down the stairs, leaving me to smear my tears over the polished floor.

I felt a similar sense of tightening pain at fourteen and Mrs Hawker had become hideous. I was absurdly sensitive but I really felt as though the nasty little joke had been a personal taunt and set for me alone, like a trap. There was a moment of silence. I felt that all eyes were upon me, waiting for a reaction, but I could not look up.

My cousin covered the silence.

'Let's all go across to the hotel.'

As soon as they had all gone, I threw down my knitting and sat down at the ancient wall piano. Many of the keys were stuck and had sounded their last notes long ago. I could not play but

SEDUCED AS A GIRL

tried to every time I was alone in the house. With the help of
a faded copy of 'First Piano Lessons' that had been left behind
by some former tenant, I picked my way, note by note, through
the pieces and wondered if I was too old to take lessons. I
became so absorbed that I was very startled when Mr Hawker
entered the shabby sitting-room. More cause for blushes.

'I didn't know you played the piano.' He moved close to me.
'I've been looking at your stamp book. You know you are
about two pounds short?'

Two pounds! For me that was a fortune. I earned ten and
sixpence a week.

'Never mind, my dear. I don't suppose it will matter.' He put
his arm around my shoulders.

The affectionate arm was a deep shock. I do not think I had
realized until that moment just how lonely I was. Here was
badly needed warmth and comfort. I was afraid to move closer
and equally afraid that he would turn away and leave me.

'Where is your cousin? And the others?'

'They've gone over to the hotel.'

It did not occur to me then that he must have slipped out of
the bar when his wife and the girls arrived, and had come back
to the house in the hope of finding me alone.

'And they have left you here, all by yourself?'

Hawker was a fleshy, obviously sensual man, and his
marriage must have been a gnawing frustration. I have learned
since that he was habitually unfaithful and yet his wife held him
stubbornly. They had been married many years. He had evidently fallen into the habit of taking his sensuality where he
could find it. And it had probably not been difficult for he was
handsome in a rich masculine way, even featured, full-lipped,
his eyes a soft, enticing brown. Although at forty, perhaps
something of the maudlin old roué was sometimes apparent.

The office girls were wary of him. His wife was in constant
attendance, ever watchful. For Hawker the frustration must
have been unbearable. I doubt if it had occurred to Mrs
Hawker that he would be so foolish, so dissolute, as to turn his
attention to a junior, a mere child.

'You are a lovely girl. Much nicer than all those others.'

He pulled me a little closer. He must have considered 'the others' each in turn and sized up his chances.

'You mean my cousin.' I was ready to defend.

'Oh, she's a nice girl, but not as lovely as you. She is flat-chested!'

He dropped his eyes to my firm, rounded breasts but did not dare to touch.

'I must go now. Don't worry about that stamp book.'

Later that evening when we were all preparing for bed, I went to my cousin's room to say my customary goodnight. I had seen my cousin undressed many times, but this time I observed her carefully. When I returned to my own room, I undressed to the waist and gazed at myself in the mirror. A few months before my development had filled me with horror and I had gone to school with a chiffon scarf tied tightly around my chest as a flattener! I was fully developed but emotionally completely unready. My cousin had fitted me with a brassière and this, together with the ridgy waves of a permanent at the local hairdressers, I had accepted as part of the equipment for starting work. My idealized cousin was my model but one I did not hope to equal. But if breasts were significant then my cousin was sagging and flat with unusually large ugly nipples.

I went to bed full of a new happiness and pride in possession.

Next day, my cousin called me. She held the stamp book.

'This is very serious. You are two pounds short. You will have to re-pay it.'

I was completely taken aback and protested. After all, I had not stolen the money.

My cousin was adamant and sent me to the secretary's office for a reprimand. He talked to me from a great distance across a desk that seemed enormous.

'The office is like a great machine. Each member of the staff is like a cog in that machine. If one cog breaks down it affects all the others. Your work is important. You must pull your weight with the rest. We depend on you.'

I crawled away miserably devastated, but once outside the office my sense of injustice returned. As for being a cog, I would have preferred the rôle of spanner.

From twelve-thirty to one-thirty I was in sole charge of the office whilst the rest of the staff were at lunch. Signal for the comforting Mr Hawker.

I told him about the stamp book.

'I have to pay a pound now because that is all I have saved up, and you have to deduct the rest, half a crown each week.'

I could not keep back the tears. Hawker's arms were around me again, his suit lapel against my cheek. The essential warmth and comfort. He tried to give me a pound towards the debt but I refused to accept it.

'Tomorrow is Saturday. Come into my office in the afternoon, as soon after lunch as you can. I will show you how to keep the stamp book so that it won't get into such a mess.'

When the pay packets were brought round later that day I found my usual money intact. No half-crown deduction.

I met Hawker in the corridor.

'It's all right,' he whispered. 'I have taken it out of petty cash. Don't tell anyone.'

My gratitude was as boundless as my naïvety.

Next day, after lunch, I set off for the office.

'Where are you going?' My cousin stopped me at the front door.

'I've left something in the office. A book.'

'We are all going for a walk. Are you coming?'

There was not much suggestion of a real invitation and I shook my head.

'I have some odd jobs to do'.

My cousin shrugged and turned away.

Hawker was waiting in his office. He totalled up the latest pages in the stamp book, running a pencil once down each column. Half an hour's struggling calculation for me was completed within a few seconds. I could not hide my admiration.

He pushed back his chair from the desk and stood up. His arms were around me. He kissed my hair, my face, and sought for my mouth. I was alarmed and tried to wriggle away.

'Don't push me away. Little darling! I love you.'

Love! It was too much. I had cried out in vain for someone's love. For my aunt's. For my cousin's. But they had all rejected me, all pushed me aside and I felt I was worth nothing.

'I must kiss you. I love you.'

Hawker, perhaps without realizing it, had hit on the magic formula for seducing unwanted little girls.

I was completely innocent, or perhaps, ignorant, would be a more apt word. I believe that the childhood shock of losing my parents and the years of emotional frustration that followed had blunted my normal development. I knew the basic details of childbirth but nothing of the act of sex, and was not—consciously—curious. Emotionally I was still a five-year-old crying out in the night for mother or father. Particularly for father. The father who had sat hunched in my aunt's kitchen shortly after the death of my mother when I was five and had blubbered.

'You'll take her, won't you? Don't say as you won't take her. I don't know what to do.'

I saw very little of my father after that. I almost forgot him and when he did come to see me he was like a stranger—one I disliked intensely.

If Hawker wanted to kiss me and undo the buttons of my blouse to feel more closely, why should I stop him? I wanted love, affection, and knew of no subtle distinctions between its various qualities.

For Hawker it was all too easy. He would not have had the courage to insist if I had resisted. He grew more bold, more confident.

He kept his eyes close to mine, watching, waiting for the slightest sign that he should draw back. An hypnotic gaze, willing me to relax. One arm firmly about me, his free hand, careful, deliberate, seeking the genital cleft. I was utterly unresisting, caught and held. Also curious. It was an extraordinary revelation. And soon away in a strange, silent ecstasy, drugged by the absorbed brown eyes.

There was no climax. The hypnosis lost its power and gave way to boredom. Hawker fell to kissing me again, told me how much he loved me, how happy I had made him.

'Will you let me love you again? But we mustn't let anyone know. It must be our secret.'

I left him, stamp book in hand. It was a heavy secret. Somehow I knew it was all wrong and that if my cousin found out she would be angry. I was uneasy, but whispered to myself, 'But he loves me,' and that seemed a good enough excuse for anything. 'And,' I asserted, with a sudden realization that it ought to be necessary, 'I love him.'

During the weeks that followed, Hawker laid a hand on my arm, or sought a brief embrace, at every possible opportunity but he was careful not to take unnecessary risks. There was no sign of any outward change. Perhaps I was even more withdrawn and even more stubborn with my cousin, but it was all put down to stamp book sulks. I was careful to hide the fact that the half-crown was never deducted from my pay packet. The bathroom mirror and my nakedness were a new rich delight and I took greater care with my appearance.

Hawker was becoming impatient. The occasions when he dared to seek me out alone for any satisfying length of time were rare. My part was always the same, silent, passive, unresisting. Hawker was restrained and careful and seemed to be quite without misgivings. I was quite unaware that he might have other needs to be met and remained virgin. The dreamy, hypnotic ecstasy never completely aroused me, and I did not think that loving held any further secrets.

Hawker took his wife to the hotel bar several evenings each week. They were the only outings they knew how to enjoy together. He chose an occasion when several members of the staff from outlying sites were staying in the hotel for the weekend. There was quite a gathering and must have been quite a party atmosphere.

That night I awakened to find Hawker standing beside my bed. The room was flooded with the cold impersonal light of a full moon.

I jumped out of bed and sought a dressing-gown. Hawker quietly shut the window.

'We mustn't make any noise.' His voice was thick and low. For the first time I felt really uneasy.

He was different. There was an urgency about him and he swayed slightly as if drunk. He pulled at my dressing-gown and could restrain himself no longer. All the careful gentleness that I had come to trust had gone. His exploring hand was fumbling and feverish, he pushed me backwards onto my bed and suddenly thrust deeply.

I struggled away from him and stood up, backing against the wall. He had become a monster who only wanted to hurt me and I was ready to defend myself in every way I could, ready to bite, kick and scratch.

Hawker cursed himself for an impatient fool. He pleaded forgiveness, hoarsely whispering his contrition. He gazed at me as he had done so many times before and tried to draw me close, but I was badly frightened and the eerie moonlight was not to his advantage.

There was a little, soft sound from the door handle. The door opened and Mrs Hawker entered. She had evidently not been as drunk as Hawker imagined. She stood for a moment inside the room, glittering with anger. The three of us stood as if frozen, incapable of movement. A few seconds that stand in my memory and seem longer than years. Suddenly, abruptly, she crossed the room and struck me across the cheek. It was no more than a light glancing sweep of her hand that hardly moved my head. Like the brief touch of a bat's wing—more fraught with evil than any of the thumpings and clouts I had received as a child.

Mrs Hawker turned to her husband who had not moved and trundled him out of the room like an old sack.

Hardly a sound had been made. The rest of the house remained heavy and silent with sleep.

I slowly recovered and crawled back into my bed. From downstairs I could hear the Hawkers' voices, high tone, low tone, briefly loud and then hushed, eventually the sound of sobbing.

I was cold, but made no attempt to warm myself, and lay fully outstretched. As if still listening I drifted slowly into sleep.

Throughout the days that followed, Mrs Hawker, her face

stonily set in a mask, moved about her duties as housekeeper with harsh abrupt movements. Hawker kept his eyes averted and only slowly recovered his bounce and self-esteem.

I lived on dully from day to day, occasionally looking at Hawker with contempt, but mostly avoiding him. My loneliness became an armour and contact with others more superficial and brief than before. As the weather improved I explored the mountains alone and was glad to be alone.

The secret was closely guarded. The Hawkers must have lived in terror that I would break down and tell my cousin. As the days went by the surface tension eased. I maintained my placid, aloof mask, played my part in the office and lived within a wall of silence.

Not long afterwards the London office was opened again. Some of the staff had to return and I was granted permission to return with them.

I slipped quietly back to London, hardly saying goodbye to anyone. I was setting a pattern for the future that would be constantly repeated.

Even now, my most powerful memory of North Wales is the stoney mask of the suffering Mrs Hawker.

It is difficult to say what effect this Hawker incident had upon me, but it must have been at least partly responsible for the confusion of my subsequent years of adolescence.

I was barely seventeen when I began to fend for myself in London. At that time, 1943, with the wartime labour shortage, it was possible for a girl of my age to earn quite well. With about £3 per week I had just about enough to keep myself in a bed-sitter, making my own sketchy meals over a gas-ring. My job and my new friends were Fleet Street fringe—a perfect setting for a Bohemian free for all and I went straight into it without misgivings. Truly, a lamb to the slaughter.

Sex was still largely a mystery. There had been one or two boy friends near my own age, but they had seemed like children. I found their tentative, hesitant efforts at love-making extremely irritating. Hawker had left me impatient of anything less than the mature approach of an experienced man. This, and no doubt the unconscious search for a father, constantly drew me to older men.

Shaun, a journalist, was a compromise. Young enough to be attractive but still many years my senior. He had helped me find a room and knew that I had run away from home. I can still recall his incredulous expression when I told him I was a virgin, that I did not think I would remain one long, and was curious! If Shaun was in any way gifted it was as an opportunist—he did not waste much time in incredulity!

Looking back I am torn between a desire to laugh at what was no more than absurd youthful brashness and an intense self-pity for the callous disregard with which I used myself. I was partly like a small child intent on finding out, and partly trying to buy my way out of a lonely insecurity.

My feelings during the first few weeks of independence had alternated between a proud exhilaration at my ability to stand alone and an abject terror of the future. I was very much aware that there was not a living soul who cared what became of me. The world seemed to consist entirely of people who lived in tight, self-sufficient groups. Each little group like a circle of joined hands that excluded me. Shaun seemed to offer a break through. Naturally, he was more than willing to allay my sexual curiosity—in a way that was gratifying to him alone—but nothing more. My sense of isolation increased. Fortunately, this miserable affair was brief. It ended in fiasco.

I had comfortably supposed Shaun to be an atheistic co-traveller. When he asked me to go to Church with him I thought he was joking, and still thinking it was just a prank, suddenly found myself inside a Catholic Church amidst the full ceremonial of an Easter service. As Shaun went to the altar to take communion I slipped away to nurse what I took to be an insult. So I was nothing but a sin and had, no doubt, been 'confessed'. I was already regretful and disappointed but now I felt cheated and ashamed.

Shortly after this I became close friends with a young woman who had been recently widowed. The memory of Freddie—as I will call her now—is still a little bewildering. Her husband had become a bed-ridden invalid a few days after their marriage.

She, no longer a wife, had been a devoted nurse for about ten years. I realize now that I was a perfect foil for Freddie. With me she had a chance to loose off ten years of frustration. She was twice my age. In the conventional view of a kindly world she should have been a helpful influence. It must be true that 'abstinence sews sand all over'. In Freddie's company I learned to know the inside of several London bars and to enjoy the conversational limits of the uniformed Armed Services on leave and in search of diversion. My tiny room was frequently a haven for late-night foursomes. Freddie was having her long-needed fling.

The rare occasions when I visited her home were like journeys into another world. She shared a suburban house with a married sister. Again I found myself among Catholics. The house had something of the tiptoe atmosphere of a sacred shrine, with a crucifix and holy pictures in every room.

Eventually Freddie came to me tearful and worried. It seemed that her restraint had on one occasion subsided altogether. She was terrified she might be pregnant, and that the responsible young Australian might not marry her. She had confessed to her priest and accepted a penance.

I thought of Hawker, Shaun, and by this time one or two others and wondered that anyone could make such a fuss.

I was slowly becoming revolted by the facile simplicity of Freddie's outlook and by the shallow, casual company we were keeping. My stifled longing for music had long since found an outlet in books and poetry, a need that was incomprehensible to Freddie.

At the office I was surrounded by writers and journalists but I was too timid to strike up the friendships I really wanted. I had been engaged as a shorthand-typist and looked after the correspondence of a director. I discovered that my boss had a sentimental weakness for aspiring youngsters, so I told him I longed for a chance on the reporting staff. He agreed. For instruction he told me to watch the work of one or two of his favourites.

One of these was a bearded young graduate from Oxford.

To me, with his cultured family background and growing reputation for intellectual brilliance, he seemed completely unapproachable. His articles were as erudite as *The Times.* I would not have admitted to anyone that I barely understood a word.

The other man whose work I had been instructed to admire was equally terrifying. He was tall, grey-haired, an austere presence. He was said to have had some success as a playwright, certainly he enjoyed the respect and admiration of the staff. On one or two occasions he edited some of my news stories and pointed out with his usual quiet courtesy how I could improve the writing. I felt flattered that he should even have bothered to speak to me.

I was very conscious of my lack of education. I read a great deal, moving from trash to classics with little discrimination.

One day, the austere playwright—I may as well call him A.P.—invited me to coffee. The invitation alone was enough to undermine my reserve. Poor little goose—I told him how much I needed guidance if I was to make good my brief schooling. He offered to act as tutor. In exchange, as coolly detached as ever, he proposed that I should become his mistress. And, of course, I must have time to think it over!

During the next few days A.P. was away. I was in a fever of indecision. He was so urbane and aloof. I remembered his hands, their cool, still whiteness. I remembered him as he walked through the office. He always seemed to be curiously divorced from the nervous bustle around him. He was not very popular—but then, he could make even laughter seem vulgar. Uselessly, I tried to draw advice from Freddie. But beyond tut tutting at the awfulness of the suggestion, she was soon away on her own problems.

The world is full of Freddies. They are insensitive to fear in others until it has reached breaking point and is screaming for attention.

When A.P. returned I agreed blindly. It was arranged that we should meet in a Marlow hotel the following Saturday. But first I should meet his wife.

This last was mumbled indistinctly. I could not believe

I had heard correctly. But I did meet his wife. She was a beautiful woman. She had a rich glow about her like dark honey but her voice was flat and toneless. The three of us walked along the Chelsea Embankment in the darkness of late evening. I do not remember what we said except that our words were unconnected with our feelings. I was tense with embarrassment. The meeting was mercifully brief. A.P. called a taxi for his wife, and they spoke a few words aside. It seemed that she nodded agreement before she was driven away alone.

He called another taxi. As soon as we were on our way, I said, "Your wife is very beautiful. . . ."

It was more of a question than a statement. I wanted an explanation. A.P. hedged and quickly veered the conversation away. He said he would not come to my room that night and probably would not come at all until he had found me somewhere nicer to live. Perhaps a little flat. It was all rather vague, but there was nothing vague about the return ticket to Marlow he put in my hand.

I slept little that night. Every fibre of body and instinct told me not to go, the next day, to Marlow. What did this man want of me? He was so cold and detached. He had kissed me once, but without warmth, almost as if he had done so out of duty. And why should I have been shown to his wife as if for approval?

Sleep finally came on the decision not to go. Somehow I would explain and get out of it as best I could. It was the suggestion to rent a flat for me that was most frightening. I was to be kept. The word prostitute flared up in my mind. As for the offer to help me with my work, it was just a blind, he was kidding me that I had potential ability.

The next morning I awoke late. In the rush to make up for lost time I suddenly decided to pack a few things for the journey to Marlow—just in case. I wanted time to reconsider.

As lunch time drew near, Freddie breezed in to say good-bye till Monday. Her fears of a pregnancy had proved groundless. My various colleagues were each, in their own way, intent on the week-end to come, cheerily bidding goodbye, anxious to get back to the closed circle of their own family groups. I had a choice between my dreary, silent room or the train to Marlow. I thought of him waiting to meet me at the station.

The journey to Marlow was leaden with hopelessness. I told myself angrily that I was absurd and ridiculous. Was I really going all that way just to tell him I had changed my mind? As soon as I saw him I knew that the decision would not be mine. I had little strength of will, and in his presence, none at all.

We spent the rest of the afternoon walking by the river. There seemed to be gaiety all around us with little boats bobbing on the river and dancing reflections. I wanted to be young and gay too, not walking, stolid and apprehensive, beside this pale grey-haired man.

Dinner that evening was comical with embarrassment. The hotel seemed to me as grand as the Savoy, and I felt conspicuous in my cheap and shabby clothes. A confusing, overlarge menu was placed before me. I glanced across at A.P. but knew that there was no help forthcoming. A sudden rash determination to make the best of things coincided with the word 'lobster'. Lobster was luxury class to me and I had never had the chance to try it.

When the monster arrived it looked distressingly different to A.P.'s more homely dish. Even worse, I was given a queer elongated fork, which I thought safer to ignore. If you have ever tried eating a lobster without taking the claws and legs between your fingers, you will understand why I went to bed hungry that night.

Hungry in more senses than one. I was supposed, as far as the hotel was concerned to be A.P.'s secretary. We had separate rooms. I retired to mine soon after dinner. A.P. decided to stay in the lounge a little longer to make the whole thing look authentic.

Alone in my room I dithered uncertainly, wondering what I should do. Should I be undressed, already in bed and anonymous in the dark? Should I wait for him as I was? When he did come I was sitting on the edge of the bed in faded, schoolgirl pyjamas. I must have looked like an orphan waif. He was resplendent in a dark, rich, silky dressing-gown.

My awestruck fear of him soon gave way to a mixture of contempt and pity. He was almost completely impotent. Once again I was overwhelmed with the impression that he kissed and fondled me without desire, without need, but as if to do so was a pre-arranged plan, a duty.

He stayed with me only a few moments. He left me bewildered—was that all he wanted? I was certain of only one thing. He had used me—or attempted to—as if I had been devoid of feelings. No more than a dog that could be pushed around at will.

I have often wondered what explanation lay behind this incident. I am sure that it was arranged with the connivance of his wife. Perhaps I was to be used as a cure for impotence. There may have been other, possibly more sinister, reasons. Who knows?

A.P. was again mercifully absent from the office for several days. During that time I met Simon and with him a temporary safety. In no time at all we had vowed ourselves into a lasting, if doubtful, alliance. With Simon to run to for protection it was not too difficult to tell A.P. that I could not meet him again. He was angry, perhaps a little hurt. I neither knew nor cared and scuttled back to my new anchorage.

Simon was a conscientious objector. I lapped up his naïve idealism. It was just what I wanted and I felt at home in the mess of high-flown pacifist and World Government pamphlets that cluttered every spare space of his room.

One would expect a man who had a wife and two mistresses to be abundantly and assertively male. Not so Simon. He was gentle and clinging. He managed to keep all three of us safely at his heels with persuasive adoration. If emotions threatened to boil over he would flood into tears. For some inexplicable reason none of us could bear to hurt him.

In spite of what seemed a genuine, all-absorbed love for me, he continued to keep a desultory contact with his other two 'wives', one that continued throughout the three years of our attachment. We were all supposed to be highly civilized, superior beings even, to whom Art and Idealism were the only things that really mattered. Jealousy was not admitted. It is not easy to equate jealousy with free-love, so it was pushed underground where it was powerful and continuous.

We lived in a homely disorder of paint brushes, floating scraps of John Donne and Scheherazade on an antique gramophone. For me it was, at least, a harbour against intolerable loneliness. Our sexual desires, if haphazardly satisfied, were given a clean and wholesome place, far preferable to the sneaky, hole in the corner attitude I had known before.

The four of us could have gone on living together for the rest of our lives if it had not been for my inability to accept that I could not have Simon entirely to myself. I might have accepted it willingly enough if I had been able to live for something else. Simon's wife, for instance, was an artist and not unsuccessful. The other girl seemed to find her work as a librarian more absorbing than Simon. I was constantly nagged by the thought that my own efforts were hopeless, though in fact, I probably did not do too badly, bearing in mind my educational handicap. I still tended to look upon everyone else as being more clever and complete than myself. Still largely the cowed and frightened child, eternally waiting for the next blow.

My job was not considered essential in wartime, so at eighteen I came under the jurisdiction of the Ministry of Labour. I had to decide whether or not I should register as a conscientious objector. Finally, but without real conviction, I followed the example of the only person who had given me real affection. I felt pacifism to be right and the argument for it a good one and had great admiration for the many I knew who had courageously stuck to their convictions, even to the extent of accepting imprisonment, yet measured against Hitler's war, with its concentration camps and Jewish massacre, it seemed futile and unrealistic.

I was too young to be brought before a Tribunal. In the meantime, I was directed first to one unacceptable job, then to another. My earnings dropped by nearly half and I was often penniless.

Simon gradually sickened me. I began to suspect that his brave adherence to pacifism was, even if unconsciously, really a choice of a lesser terror. He could never have faced the rough and ready camaraderie of the forces. He had been a molly-coddled little boy and had, I gathered, a rather rough time at school.

His sexual demands were constant and unflagging. For me it had become no more than a wearisome routine. I was occasionally unfaithful which upset him a great deal. Like a parasite tired of its host, I was really looking for a more satisfactory successor to Simon, rather than for sensual experience. Not surprisingly, I was soon shaken off—after I had given the little I had. It may not seem credible, but in spite of so much experience, I remained sexually dormant. I was, in fact, becoming almost frigid.

It required tremendous effort to finally break away from Simon. I had sufficient intelligence and objectiveness to see exactly what my life had become, but felt too ill-equipped to start out afresh. My health too, had long since broken down, largely because of insufficient food.

Most powerful of memories was a day when I bought a few pears from a London barrow. They were surprisingly cheap and I could not believe my good luck. When I arrived home, I found that though they looked good on the outside, the flesh beneath was brown and rotten. That night I dreamt that I was in the back of a taxi with Simon. He seemed normal enough, but when I touched him my fingers sank through into a pulpy mess of decay. I knew that I had to get rid of him before the rottenness spread all over me. I opened the door of the taxi and bundled him out.

It was this dream image—what does its real interpretation, if any, matter—that gave me the impetus to finally leave him. I joined the Control Commission and went to Germany. Simon continued to write, letter after letter, but I did not reply. I made a sacrificial burning of each of his letters and the accompanying reams of embryonic free verse, as they arrived.

And gloating over the flames reflected with black humour that I had refuted my father and all my relatives by quoting Simon as the only next of kin, on one of the official forms.

Poor Simon. I regret my harshness. He collected women the way another might collect paintings, books, even bric-a-brac, loved them all and could not bear to part with a single one. On his own eccentric terms he was genuine and steadfast in his love for me and certainly had an equal capacity for suffering. We were both emotionally immature. Surely, no one expects children to be merciful with the feelings of others.

As for my eighteen months in Germany I think I have said enough in the first few pages to give a fair indication. I managed to run away from Simon but not from myself.

In anticipation of a possible question, what became of me in the end? We are brought up on stories that conclude 'and so she was married and lived happily ever after. . . .' We usually greet such an ending with a sneer, but frankly, I am grateful.

8

Wife of an Impotent Husband

by 'VERA VAUGHAN'

FIFTEEN YEARS ago, after a wedding which was quiet for
various family reasons but which seemed satisfactory to all
concerned, we went off on honeymoon. I am still unable to
think of the little hotel in Cornwall looking over the sea, of
the indulgent kindness of the other visitors and the perfect
spring weather without pain and embarrassment. For this
wedding which seemed so normal and happy led to nothing
physical between us. My new husband liked having me around
and enjoyed my company but was quite incapable of the act of
love and completely uninterested in me as a man interested in
a woman. Through the long nights of that fortnight, I lay
awake contemplating this fact that became clearer to me as
the holiday wore slowly on. But I tried to assure myself
that either it would work itself out or that something could be
done about it.

We came back to London and set up house. I got to know
my new neighbours and made friends in our part of London
and behaved as carefully as I could to fit the rôle of a new wife,
settling in to a middle-class way of life. Occasionally people
took us for brother and sister, or even father and daughter, as
my husband is fifteen years older than I am, or expressed surprise that we had only been married for such a little time—we
appeared as if we had been married for years. On the whole, my
play-acting must have come off quite well as we were regarded
as a happy newly-married couple.

For the best part of three years, I stayed in a state of suspended judgment on the situation. I lived with an unformulated
hope that the nightmare would vanish and we would start on

our married life proper. From time to time, I would wonder what other people made of this sort of situation. I was inclined to think that such a thing had happened to very few others in known history as there was so little evidence to be found. In later years, I have come to the conclusion that it is a much more common misfortune than any of us would imagine but that it is aired so seldom that there is little evidence as to how people react to it.

I took to hunting through the dark corner in my local library where books on sex and psychology were kept, glancing somewhat furtively over my shoulder and, on the occasions when someone I knew bore down on me, hastily snatching a book from a nearby shelf and becoming immersed in cooking or mountain climbing. The index of a book on sex would give something like this:

IMPOTENCE. 45, 192.

Page 45 would usually set out the causes of impotence. Re-lations with parents in childhood had caused a deep-rooted fear of the whole business and this would need to be cleared out of the way before normal marriage could follow. But I could never recognise either of us in the neat case-book histories that were given. My mother-in-law had far too much of a sense of humour to be like the dominating mother-figures; my husband was far too balanced and sane in all things save this one particular, and I may have been inept and clumsy, but I felt I had more intelligence than these cipher-like creatures.

Page 192 would be at the end of a chapter on Difficulties. If, I would be told, this happened, it was best to tell your doctor and he would send you to a specialist. But my doctor, an old doctor who had been a G.P. for many years, had been told and had shown no interest at all and had certainly not moved heaven and earth to send us to a specialist. We were both reluctant to force his hand, as we felt, perhaps mistakenly, that the happiness we were trying to make in finding a *modus vivendi* could be very quickly destroyed by starting an endless round of specialists without there being any guarantee that we would find anything better to put in its place.

Other shelves in the library occasionally yielded a novel or play on this sort of problem. There were very few, as literature on the theme of sex seemed to be about people who had sexual relationship all too easily. The question was usually who the characters had relations with, how often and whether they were normal or what kind of abnormal. It seemed that on the rare occasions when impotence came up as the subject of a work of fiction, there were only two things to be done. The first was that the wife should have an affair with the first possible man she met. This was much more effective if she taunted her husband the while by pursuing the affair under his nose. The second course was for the woman to descend slowly into neurotic gloom and end up in some sort of violent frenzy.

Neither course appealed to me as practical. For the first, even if I had wanted to, it is not all that easy for a middle-class woman of very average looks, with limited income and fairly quiet habits, to start up a love affair with one of the friends who came to see her husband and herself. I am also very fond of my husband and, although I may privately have entertained bitter feelings, I regret it if I ever make them too obvious to him and could certainly not embark on a protracted scheme for humiliating and hurting him. As for descending into neurotic gloom, I showed no signs of it. I may have been very miserable from time to time and have wept into my pillow some nights, but nothing made me lose my appetite, I had a strenuous and demanding job and a host of other interests and my reason seemed to stay as usual.

All this time, I was aware of the tide of erotic philosophy flowing on around me. On all levels, it was assumed that sexual relations are of great importance. This made it difficult for me to arrive at the scale of values which it was becoming clear was necessary if I was to face a life-time of my situation. Physical relations between men and women were not, I must come to see, of the first and only significance. In novel after highly-praised novel, men and women fell in and out of bed in various combinations. Films and plays led up to the sexual intercourse which I imagined others would carry on when they got home. This tendency showed up most unexpectedly in the context of theology. I had become interested in the Church's approach to marriage. We had married in church as believers and I wondered whether the Church regarded us as married irretrievably because our marriage had not been consummated. I plunged into a labyrinth of two traditions stemming from the early Fathers—those who held that marriage was made by the free consent of both parties and those who held that there must be consummation for it to be a real marriage. On the way to arriving at the conclusion that my marriage was, in technical terms, voidable but not void, I read a fair amount of modern theological writing about marriage. I found here the same emphasis on the enormous importance of successful and satisfying intercourse. This seemed to me as unbalanced in its way as the rigorous denunciation of sexual pleasure by the Desert Fathers.

Most difficult of all were the women's magazines which I affected to despise but which held a horrid fascination for me. They are immensely proper and moral, but they assume that a woman's whole purpose in life is to attract her man, and having once got him, to keep him hard at it. This fed my growing sense of inferiority as a woman. No one could have set out consciously to give me this feeling as no one knew about this thing. Nor did my friends discuss sexual matters except to tell the occasional funny story. The tone of voice sometimes used to refer to spinsters would shock me, as I felt I was cheating by in fact being in the state which married people looked at askance, while having the apparent status of a married woman. I also felt somewhat dishonest with my unmarried woman friends who did not talk about these matters but eyed me with some curiosity and envy for having an experience which I did not in fact enjoy. Perhaps I was more aware of sex as a background fact than most of the people I met; this stage of my consciousness was a throw-back to the time when I was seventeen and vastly interested in sexual experience without being able to do very much about it. The practical result of these feelings was that I deliberately cultivated a carelessness in my dress and appearance. I had never been very successful at either, but I now equated caring about such things with sex and attempted to spurn it all as being beneath my notice. I became prickly and egg-head; I remember speaking at a quite important women's meeting wearing a badly home-made, mud-coloured cardigan which I attempted to flaunt in the face of charming, attractive women as a symbol of my superiority in what mattered.

I was cured of this after eight years of marriage by being physically attracted to a man who became a friend of us both. I found myself looking as good as I could when I was likely to see him. There was never anything between us except a close friendship which still goes on, but I moved on from a concern about my looks to please him to being interested in clothes and appearance for their own sake. I discovered that most women dressed for other women most of their lives. I now take a moderate interest in what I wear and how I look, with moderate success, but I enjoy contemplating other women who are more successful.

Some three years after marriage, I found myself going to a woman specialist as I had had internal troubles for some time. She was charming and helpful, though inclined to take the line that, if nothing could be done with my marriage, I should take steps to extricate myself from the situation. She arranged for us to see another sort of specialist. We went for many long weeks, sometimes one of us and sometimes the other. We paid a lot for this privilege. I suppose he was well-meaning; he was certainly not at all charming or helpful to us. He showed us how to make love; he explained the paramount importance of sex in life and he gave us practical sessions on love-making. Both of us suddenly decided that we could not stand any more of it, and we retreated to lick our wounds. In a way, this helped. It threw up so sharply the inanity of the completely erotic approach to life that I was encouraged to push my own absorption with sex into a healthier, less important place. This is a continuous battle. I am still apt to be swamped by a burning desire, probably physical in origin, to experience love-making, which lands me in a swamp of self-pity or in vapid dreams of encounters either with a man met casually or with an imaginary male-figure. Both these leave me with a bad taste and a great lassitude, but I can often snap out of them by the memory of the little man posturing and pawing in his expensively-fitted consulting rooms.

Some years after this experience, we changed our GP and found an intelligent, kind, younger man who very quickly became a friend of ours as he does with most of his patients. He had a different approach to our problem. He is immensely interested in families and children and is obviously sorry that we are denied so much that he thinks worthwhile in life. He is sure that nothing can be done about this sort of impotence. As the effect of the deprivation falls more obviously on me, he suggests that I should fill my life with plenty of interests so that I am kept amused and not allowed to brood.

This, in a way, makes sense to me, but it is really bad advice for someone of my temperament. For this in fact is what I had done instinctively when it was clear that the situation was likely to go on. I plunged into doing things; I gave hours to the job I was doing, above and beyond what was expected of me; I filled the rest of my time with good works and political ploys as well as insisting on doing all my own housework. I have a natural tendency to keeping on doing things, inculcated by a stern Yorkshire upbringing when it would have been a crime to sit and read a book before the late evening, if at all. Add to this an abundance of nervous energy which comes from a well-sexed woman having no physical outlet for her sexual energy. Top it with a desire never to sit and think how wretched I was and was likely to go on being, and it will be seen that I rapidly got to the stage when I worked one way and another for sixteen hours every day, and flopped into bed so exhausted that I fell into a deep sleep immediately. This seemed a splendid way of arranging my life, as the intolerable time was lying awake next to my husband who was in a deep and happy sleep.

It even affected the sort of holidays we took. I encouraged my husband to walk all day in all weathers over rough mountain country. I would maintain to the death that such holidays are far superior to sight-seeing trips to Rome or to lying on sun-warmed beaches in Spain. But when we started doing this, I was unconsciously influenced by the need to avoid arriving at bedtime wide-awake and full of sexual desire.

Sufficient years have passed for me to regret the habit of always doing something. Not only have I collected too many commitments to let me sit back, but I have lived at a tough pace for so long that I cannot stop working at something so long as I am awake. I can only hope that increasing age will enable me to ease up and become old without stridency or frustration, but I would be happier now, and very possibly later, if I had grasped at the beginning the nettle of a life without fulfilment, as it is commonly called, and not imagined that I could find fulfilment instead in forever doing this ploy or that. I have somewhat late come to realize that being a woman is important in itself even if no one is using me as a woman, and that I do not need to justify my existence or to prove how successful I am by endless activities.

A few years after my marriage, it became evident to my friends and acquaintances that I was showing no signs of producing children. Some of them became openly curious about it. I found that my close friends had been well chosen, as they accepted it without comment as one of the things about me which they took as bravely as they took the way I looked or talked. My husband is not given to making close friends, though on the whole he accepts mine equably. Judging from the little he seems to know about the families of men he works with, I should imagine that to them the fact that he has no children, if they ever come to know about it, is as marginal and incidental as the colour of his eyes or whether he owns a television set. The men we meet at home with their families usually drift off into masculine discussions with him about trains, the weather, gardening, company law or the government. He seems to avoid easily any subjective discussions with anyone. On the isolated occasion when I was set on about my childless state in his presence by a woman in a train, he was immobilized by astonishment. I had told him that it happened but he had never seen it in action. He rescued me efficiently when he recovered from the shock, though I sensed a slight regret that he would never know what she would have said next.

These attacks on me come from women mostly met casually who are proud of their own status as mothers of a family, even if they have produced only one ewe lamb. They pretend, to themselves as well as to me, that they are impelled by an urge to help me to achieve this same felicity. They will begin fairly early after meeting me by saying: 'What family have you?' 'None,' I say. Then they will begin probing and I will try to change the conversation. But they can almost always get through the weak place in my armour by suggesting that I have a better or easier life because I have no family to worry about. I protest that I would rather have had children and that anything I might be doing is second-best to that.

At this point, the most staggering things can happen. Women you have met only five minutes before will hitch up their chairs and will pour out questions and suggestions. Methods for improving the chances of conception in sexual intercourse will vary from old wives' tales which probably have some basis of commonsense to startling excesses which one might expect in an anthropological handbook about backward tribes in the bush. This would be fascinating and diverting were it not for the persistent chorus: 'Have you tried that?'—expecting an answer.

Then we might move on to operations, tests, specimens and sub-fertility clinics. The interrogator is usually a lady whose knowledge of these is bound to be hearsay. Extraordinary things would seem to go on behind the closed doors of hospitals and surgeries, or perhaps it is that I do not understand the *ad hoc* vocabulary which such women have evolved to describe the physical functions and organs. My escape to safer ground is usually by way of case histories. 'You know, I knew a woman who . . .' With luck, I can play that game too. 'Yes, I had a friend who . . .'

Trivial stuff, perhaps. But it is surprising how it can continue to hurt. The more convinced is my questioner of the importance of motherhood and its possibility for every woman today, the more inadequate I feel. I have suffered from examinations and probings from specialists and I will not open these sores to a casual acquaintance. Not only does this make it difficult to answer these direct questions, but I find that the sores have been opened for me to deal with in private. I dislike the gleam that comes into some of these women's eyes which may be a deep concern for my happiness but which looks uncomfortably like a morbid salaciousness. Most important, this matter is one that concerns two people. I have on occasion yielded to the temptation to pour out the cause of my childless condition, but I have bitterly regretted it immediately, as I seem to have betrayed my husband's trust in my loyalty and discretion. Moreover, such confidences are always a flop as the recipient is incapable of comprehending that sexual intercourse might not be possible for some people and hastily brings the conversation to an abrupt end with embarrassed incredulity. I can imagine that she will have a good story to tell her husband that night in bed, and I am left dissatisfied and questioning about what had, before this encounter, been proving a satisfying and developing relationship with my husband.

It is difficult to assess how much of the feelings of discontent and restlessness that come over me are due to sheer physical frustration and how much to the general expectation that women have today from marriage. The current ideal is that women should have as much physical pleasure as men from intercourse and should have an equal part in it, while prettily paying lip service to the dominant role of the man. I suppose that, when women find it does not work out like this, they are inclined to keep it very quiet to save face, as they might be thought to have failed in skill or to be deficient in feminine allure.

The impotent male is traditionally a figure of fun which probably means that anyone in this situation will keep quiet about it. The woman in the case, if she is not prepared to join in the laughter against her husband, may add to her feeling of personal deprivation, a grudge at being put at the wrong end of a funny story. I suppose some deprivations are tragic, some lead to heroism as in overcoming physical disabilities, but this deprivation when it comes under discussion is comic, and this makes it a difficult burden which must be borne secretly and unheroically.

I think it is this fact which has led me sometimes to an unreasonable resentment that I am dragging about with me a burden which is almost entirely secret. Even if it were known, it seems, I should gain no respect for having gone on carrying it. I cannot, alas, claim that I have carried it very cheerfully or intelligently, but I am inclined to feel that I should be given the credit for having gone on with the situation. I find myself stupidly and nastily irritated when friends congratulate me on my nice husband. 'So charming, so kind, so intelligent.' Instead of rejoicing in this, I nearly always want to turn on them. 'If you knew what I have had to put up with all these years. . . .' Of course, thank goodness, I cannot say anything of the sort. In the end, I would rather have what I have than not have had marriage to him at all. I suppose my reaction is much more an egotistical desire to be considered a heroine than anything else.

The picture is not one of unrelieved loss and I am coming to a stage in my story when I can begin to see this in my sane moments. It is good to establish a close and affectionate friendship with a man and it is good whether there is a sexual relationship or not. The very limitations and frustrations in our situation have played a part in knitting us together. Perhaps we have been able to learn greater tolerance; because we have not been able to make up violent quarrels very satisfactorily, we have avoided the violent quarrels. Because our marriage has had to find its way without physical pleasure, we may have come to value some of the good things that pass other couples by or which they take for granted.

I would place as an immense gain the special friendships I have enjoyed with other men. I have already mentioned that, after about eight years of marriage, I went through the process of what is known as 'falling in love' with a man. I use the phrase in inverted commas in my mind, as my experience has shown that love between men and women does not depend on physical attraction. If I were asked if I loved my husband, I should have no hesitation in saying that I do and that I love him far more than I could love any other man. The physical act of love is an expression of something that can exist without it, though it is obviously an easier relationship to keep going where it is practised than where it is not. Any other attitude to love would, if logically pursued, lead to every man deserting his wife for a younger woman when she has reached an age when sexual intercourse means less to her than it did before.

It would be better then to say that I was sexually attracted by a man. When I became aware of what was happening, I was alarmed. A small part of me whispered that here might be the chance to find out what it was all about, to experience at last the heights of passion, to be carressed and cherished in the way I had a right to expect. But, apart from the moral issue which loomed large in my mind (in the circumstances, it would have been a mean trick as well as wrong), I did not at all relish embarking on the whole business of clandestine meetings, making sure that we should not be caught in the act and having to make love because the chance presented itself rather than because we wanted to. My instinct was to run away from it, even if it meant dramatic speeches about never seeing the man again, though this would in fact have been very difficult to arrange.

I had chosen fortunately as it turned out, for it would have been impossible to strike such a pose with this man. I do not suppose I shall ever know whether he was aware of what had happened. I am fairly certain that he had no more than a casual interest in me as a woman. But he liked both of us and we were thrown together with him a good deal. He has quietly hung on to my friendship unperturbed by the storminess of my love-hate relationship with him.

Since then, I have been granted one or two more friendships with men which have a special intensity because I am more aware of their masculinity than a sexually satisfied woman would be. It is almost as if I have energy left over to enjoy being with men and to make them enjoy being men when I am there.

The dangers are not as great as might be supposed, for constant companionship with my husband has given me no taste for friendship with a man who would make love to a woman because he happened to have the opportunity. These

E
129

men enjoy any chance of meeting my husband and I make great friends with their wives. I have often felt sorry that women who have normal relationships with their husbands so often seem unable to form innocent friendships with other men. It probably took my more abnormal circumstances to prove to me that this is possible.

In the end, however, it must be said that while great good has flowed out of the situation for me, it is not an advantage for a woman to embark on a marriage without sexual relationship with her husband, especially in this day and age. I have never found any sort of proof as to how often it occurs, though I am aware that many cases of impotence are being cured by psychiatric treatment. There remains the problem of the incurable and there are, it seems to me looking back on my own experience, a few things which might have helped me to avoid such desperate unhappiness.

First, although I am outwardly sophisticated about sex (one has to be these days to enter polite society at all), I could have done with a far more informed and intelligent picture of what the whole business was about. The facts of life include not only biological information, but such things as decency to another human being. In a case like mine, a woman who realises this can probably do a good deal to help a man who must be feeling miserably inadequate and helpless. At any rate, she can avoid wounding him mortally by giving the impression that she considers that the whole business of marriage is designed to keep her stimulated frequently and then sexually satisfied.

Secondly, I had to learn to grow a protective armour to the pattern of advertising and art forms which can seem to exhort their victims to bigger and better sex. It is, of course, necessary that artists should express as clearly and forcefully as they can their insight into the age-long business of sex, but it can seem that one is being bullied and titillated and encouraged into an absorption with this one aspect of human activity. It may enter into most of life in one way or another, but it is not its only *raison d'être*.

Then, there seem to be very few people who are able to see this sort of thing straight and this has been a trouble to me.

Several times, I have come to a stage where I knew I wanted to go on with my marriage, but I longed to talk it out with a wise listener or, at any rate, with someone who would let me blow off steam. Even though I hope I would have chosen such a person with the greatest care, as I did not want to wash my husband's linen before any sort of public, I have only once felt able to discuss it as freely and objectively as I would like. Of course, it has had to come out very occasionally to people who know us well. Even with them, it has been a matter I do not on the whole mind their having to know, but I do not want to discuss it at all or even to have to mention it. My one blessed and necessary safety-valve is an unmarried woman friend who happens to have a cool, sane mind and a rare ability to like everybody as they are. With the rest, I have a fear that they would think of my husband as less of a man because of it, though they would take great pains to be nice to him.

Perhaps in the end what is most surprising is how little difference this whole thing makes unless we let it. It is as easy to be immersed in the lack of sexual relationships as it is in the practice of sexual relationships. The major issues of the day are not sexual. My husband and I work together, as much of a team as many another couple, for what we feel is the right approach in religion, in politics and in social causes. We can enjoy music, books and natural beauty together. We can laugh together. Perhaps it all means a bit more to us because . . . but I see that I am falling over into a sense of superiority over lesser mortals which is only the other aspect of a sense of inferiority.

9

Unemployed Diabetic

by 'A RELUCTANT PENSIONER'

To MANY people my disability may seem of a comparatively trivial nature; for unfortunately (and I use the adverb with a full sense of responsibility) it is not one of the currently fashionable Big Four—that is, religious, racial, political or sexual.

My religion is of the same well-established brand as Dr Fisher's; my complexion is of an acceptably Nordic pink; my politics are as impeccably blue as Mr Butler's (though not, perhaps, as Mr Thorneycroft's) and my sex life could not possibly interest the editor of the *News of the World;* and yet, in spite of this altogether unexceptional background, I am unquestionably a lame duck, and there is at least one thing I have in common with most lame ducks: I belong to a minority. In an era of full employment, I am without employment. In a land of opportunity, in a society that pays lip service to the Napoleonic conception of *une carrière ouverte aux talents*, my groping foot has never been able to find even the first rung of the ladder; and consequently, in the midst of a community that is undeniably prosperous, my line of march lies along the frontiers of poverty, as near to actual indigence as the Welfare State allows a man to tread.

The basic diagnosis then—if we must put a name to the malady—is unemployment, a disease prevalent enough at one time, we are told, but nowadays virtually unknown. And it is this latter aspect of the situation that renders it so damnably bloody; for if it is a tragedy to be unemployed in an army of upwards of two millions of unemployed, one feels infinitely more wretched to be condemned to idleness when the rest of the world is a hive of productive (and liberally bank-noted) activity. In the Big Battalions one may always seek consolation in the misfortunes of others; but when we are going it alone even this dubious satisfaction is denied to us.

To understand why I am unemployed, you must permit me a brief excursion into the art—or science—of autobiography. As a child I was a sickly little brat, and because of this my education was limited to four years at an elementary school (the face-saving, upper working-class euphemism 'secondary modern' had not then been coined). I was well advanced in my ninth year before I began to walk in the valley of the shadow of the Pedagogue, and at thirteen it was all but over. At the time I did not much regret what I had lost, but now I regret it bitterly. The thing I wanted to do most during my schooldays was to get into the Royal Navy, for I have always been in love with ships of war, and a better than average knowledge of naval history is almost my only claim to academic distinction. But with my myopic eyes and phthisis-threatened lungs this was clearly impossible, and when my father invited me to join him in his small bakery business I thought it might as well be that as anything.

And so I became—and for far too long remained—a baker. For the greater part of my day I was considerably underemployed; I was not able to pull my weight and I knew it, and this was in itself a source of serious dissatisfaction. But having made my choice, I decided that I must abide by it, which I continued to do until my ever-worsening health, coupled with my parents' impending retirement, at last provided me with a legitimate excuse for seeking a change. I was then thirty years of age, and I should mention that by this time I had contracted yet another disease. I was now severely diabetic, my life dependent upon regular injections of insulin which I had to take in enormous doses every four hours.

Que faire? I was manifestly unfitted for anything other than clerical work, but here I found myself confronted with another difficulty: not the obvious one, lack of suitable experience—for I could keep books of double entry as far as the final accounts, and I could also handle correspondence—but my age. The phrase 'too old at forty' is familiar to everybody, but by this time of day it has become rather a bad joke. Nowadays the age limit for industrial employment is frequently as low as thirty-five, and for office labour, other than the executive grades, even lower: thirty, twenty-five—even at twenty-two or twenty-three one is sometimes too old. There is a perfectly good reason for this, and presently we shall have a closer look at it.

My prospects, then, were not bright. If I was a competent bookkeeper at thirty, there were men six or seven years my junior who were equally competent, and on most occasions the younger man would get the job even though his qualifications might be inferior. I perceived, therefore, that I should have to compete in a more restricted field, learn to do something that most people could not do, or did not want to do, and a paragraph in a commercial encylcopaedia turned my thoughts in the direction of languages.

'Today a knowledge of languages sets the worker on a separate plane, for the man who can speak or write two or three foreign languages is a specially valuable member of the staff of many businesses . . . and should always find substantial remuneration for his efforts.'

Substantial remuneration! Here, I thought, was my opportunity. I would become a commercial translator—and I saw unfolding before me a glorious vision of future prosperity: neckties, watches and chains (and a round, well-filled belly to support them), regularly-paid bills, fawning bank managers, Bentley motor-cars . . .

Accordingly, I enrolled in evening classes, and within eighteen months I had carried my studies as far as 'O' level. From this point I began to specialize in commercial work with a view to taking good-class commercial examinations at advanced level, and a year later I passed the first of these. Other successes followed and in the course of time I amassed a collection of no fewer than seven certificates. And I should like to say here that I succeeded in passing all my examinations—and invariably with high marks (on one occasion, in a romp with a German examiner, I obtained 93 per cent). The English, and the French also, apparently, make heavy going of languages; but really there is very little to it—once you have reconciled your-

self to the unpalatable necessity of taking off your coat and
working like hell.

Having mastered my subject, acquired my qualifications,
I now took energetic steps to secure employment. I visited the
local employment exchange—armed, of course, with my scraps
of paper—and was placed on the professional and executive
register. I also enrolled with five private agencies, and at the
same time I inserted an advertisement in a widely read commercial journal. And all the while I was closely watching the
employers' advertisements in the daily press. But I soon discovered that employers were not at all anxious to utilize my
services. There were no replies to my advertisement and in two
years I have not had a single offer from either the labour
exchange or any of the private agencies. And this is not because
there is any superabundance of good translators—at least, not
with documentary evidence in the shape of examination
certificates to support their pretensions. When I took French
at advanced level there was only one other candidate, and this
in an area that probably constitutes the second greatest concentration of population in Britain.

Of course there are in these days any number of people
who profess to know French, and not a few of them with 'O'
level certificates; but this latter examination is, after all, only
a children's examination, geared to the curriculum; and
success in it by no means implies any great degree of com-
petence in the language, much less a complete mastery of it.
Again, many people get through by picking up the majority
of their marks in the French to English paper. Most candidates
seem to put up a good performance here, but while it is one
thing to be able to read French, it is something altogether
different—and infinitely more difficult—to be able to express
yourself in it, and countless persons who pride themselves on
having 'kept up' their French by reading might be disagreeably
surprised if they were to open an English book at random and
attempt to translate a few sentences into the foreign tongue.
I know such a one, an ex-public schoolboy. Last summer he
postcarded me in French. The result: half a dozen words, three
serious and elementary grammatical mistakes. Here we have

been discussing French—to an Englishman, the first foreign language. Languages other than French—German, for example —are, as we know, not widely understood in this country.

And yet, this paucity of linguists notwithstanding, I still could not sell my labour. The reason I learned from the principal of one of the private employment agencies. It seems that the number of firms with a volume of foreign correspondence sufficiently heavy to justify their employing a full-time translator is a small one. The rest usually have someone on the staff, a person engaged on other duties, who can read the occasional French letter; and outgoing mail, which presents a more serious problem, can always be handled by the translation agencies— as also can letters in other languages. I was told that there are even instances of firms writing to foreign customers in English, which is surely not merely bad manners but also bad business. Commerce, then, has indeed some use for the translator, but all too often is either unwilling or unable to pay for him. Not that my own demands in this latter particular have been exorbitant. In fact I have never set any price on my services.

It was about this time that I became aware of another and even more serious difficulty. From a radio programme about diabetes I learned that diabetics often experience trouble in finding work on account of superannuation schemes. So far as I have been able to ascertain, these schemes may be divided broadly into two main groups. In the case of the larger firms, the entire personnel, or a certain sub-section of it (e.g. staff as opposed to work people, or male employees as opposed to women), is covered by a single premium: and from most schemes of this kind persons suffering from certain diseases, including diabetes, are specifically excluded. There is also an upper age limit—hence the cry 'too old at thirty', or whatever it may be. Small employers, on the other hand, insure their workers individually, and here each case is considered on its merits. But for the diabetic there is always a substantially increased premium, and this the employer is naturally reluctant to pay. In practice he never does; for even in the extreme instance of a diabetic being the only suitable candidate for the post, he would still not get it. The employer would simply re-advertise the position, and sooner or later he would find what he wanted. In view of the fierce competition prevailing in the commercial jungle, and the slender profit margins obtaining in some types of business, we can hardly blame him for doing this.

Of course, most of us who find ourselves in this predicament, irrespective of whether it be through age or sickness, would be only too willing to accept employment on almost any conditions. If we are not eligible for a pension scheme, so be it; but at least give us work. Unfortunately this is not possible, for where a superannuation scheme is in operation the employer, under the terms of his agreement, is not allowed to employ anyone outside it. Every day, I spend the best part of an hour searching through hundreds of advertisments in the 'Situations Vacant' columns and the words 'Appointment subject to the candidate's successfully passing a medical examination' (i.e. for superannuation purposes) occur constantly.

I have encountered the problem at first hand. A large engineering firm in my neighbourhood (though in fact situated at about twenty miles distant from my home) advertised for a copy writer to help in the production of catalogues and instruction manuals. It was stated that no specialized experience of the engineering industry or of advertising work was necessary (and I must emphasize this); all that was required was the ability to write clear, concise and grammatically correct English. They did not even ask for an arts degree! I applied for the job and sent them a specimen of my writing. They would find very little wrong with this, for it was a copy of an article which I had sold for five guineas to the editor of an evening newspaper. I also spoke of my attainments in languages. They probably already employed a translator, but it is always useful to have somebody in the background who can deputize. I thought that on the whole my candidature was a tolerably strong one; but remembering my disability, and not wishing to squander time and money travelling to a fruitless interview, I told them frankly that I was not eligible for most superannuation schemes. My application was unsuccessful. In their reply, the advertisers thanked me for letting them see my work, but regretted that, in view of the difficulty I had mentioned, they could not invite me to an interview.

Now, there are many people who regard the attitude of the insurance companies in this matter as flagrantly injust. Insurance is a straightforward commercial transaction, freely entered into by both parties, and if an insurance company considers a person a bad risk, then clearly it has a right to refuse him. But has it a right to prevent an employer from employing a man outside a pension scheme—to prevent that man from earning his livelihood, which is what its veto in fact amounts to? Morally, it has not; but the remedy is by no means a simple one. It would be utterly wrong to picture the insurance companies as grasping, unfeeling tyrants, standing between a man and his bread merely to avoid the loss of business that would inevitably ensue once they had admitted the employer's right to avail himself of that considerable body of people who would be willing to work outside the protective umbrella of superannuation. No, the difficulties are rather of a technical nature; and although the problem is far from being an insoluble one, it must be remembered that while the number of victims is not small, we do, nevertheless, constitute a minority. Most work people, the fortunate ones who are sheltered by the 'umbrella', are eminently satisfied with existing arrangements, and the companies, therefore, have no very compelling motive to alter them. There are some who look to a political solution; but political action, I think, is neither practical nor desirable.

It may be noted in passing that many firms (mostly small ones) who are not thus hampered by the provisions of a superannuation agreement do not hesitate to exploit the situation to their own advantage by actively seeking workers among these unhappy classes, offering salaries and conditions of employment that no person with any freedom of choice would even so much as dream of accepting. I heard recently about the case of a middle-aged man (he described himself as an accountant) who was convicted of embezzling several hundred pounds of his firm's money. It was revealed, during the trial, that although his responsibilities were heavy, and that each year many thousands of pounds passed through his hands, his salary was only £250. This fact does not excuse his felony, but it does, I submit, serve to extenuate it.

That, then, is my problem. At thirty-six I am unemployed and probably unemployable—not because of my indifferent health, for by now that has improved sufficiently to enable me to perform any sort of clerical work, but simply because the only firms who have any use for my particular abilities are the larger ones where there is invariably a superannuation scheme in operation. I am not eligible for membership of the scheme, and therefore I am not eligible for employment. I can write business letters in three languages; I could at one time keep a full set of financial books (in these days my bookkeeping is a little rusty); I have learnt, over the years, how to handle tactfully both customers and suppliers; I am in all respects desperately anxious to please, and I should be content with a modest salary; and yet, in an age of full employment, when your labouring man can command his thousand a year and his office counterpart at least half that sum, I am still unemployed —and this despite the fact that I live within twenty miles of two of the greatest commercial cities of the Empire and am prepared to travel daily to either!

And yet I am still unemployed! Whenever I hear of anything that is in the smallest degree discreditable to the working population—a shop assistant stealing his master's half-crowns, a wildcat strike or a drunken labourer blackening the eye of a policeman—those words come crashing back into my thoughts like the reintroduction of the haunting major theme into a great symphony. These are the indolent, incompetent rascals who have never had it so good! And yet I . . .

In the evening classes I attended I have measured myself against these mediocrities. I have seen them struggling for the best part of a month to grasp the difference between the nominative case and a direct accusative object (they never succeed in unravelling the mysteries of the indirect object), and having failed to do so, as most of them did, abandoning the class in swarms, scuttling back to their more congenial haunts and occupations, their pubs and their dance halls, their drinking and their wenching, like beetles before a pursuing foot! I have heard the ripple of embarrassed sniggers that ran round the room when the meaning of the word 'gender' was explained to them. I have seen five and thirty adults gaping vacantly at such a baby sentence as 'the boy was in the garden', and not one among them able to identify the preposition. I have watched them perspiring for more than half an hour over the relatively simple task of translating a hundred and fifty words of not very difficult English prose into French, laboriously looking up every other word in the vocabulary at the back of the book, and with the business still unfinished at the end of that time! Even the ex-grammar school types in my second-year class (they were staging a 'come back' after having been mauled by the examiner in the examinations of the previous summer) were utterly incapable of understanding the correct use of the inflected form of the relative pronoun. In my first-year French class there were at the beginning of the session thirty-five of us present; on the last evening, there were only five, and of these I was the only one to enroll for the second year. Of the thirty-three students who began to learn German with me, there were only two of us present at the end of the two years' course. And yet, despite my 100 per cent attendance record, my high marks and my examination successes, it was I who was the failure; for totally devoid as these people were both of brains and of energy, they were in comfortable and well-paid jobs, whereas I, with all my ability and industry, was—and still am—unemployed.

Observe what a corrosive effect adversity can produce upon character! Nothing, neither wild horses nor a regiment of soldiers, would induce me to admit that I am by nature an envious man. When I hear of the good fortune of another, I am usually the first to congratulate him—even when his felicity stems from something as fortuitous as a win on the football pools. In particular I have always been generous in my appraisements of those who have got right to the top of their tree—the men of altogether exceptional talent; and I should like to see people of this calibre even more liberally rewarded. But when I contemplate my fellows, that is, the chaps of only moderate ability and, reflecting that I have at least as much to offer as the rest of them, contrast their arrogant prosperity with my own seedy poverty, then I am veritably consumed with envy and, as the above outburst shows, inclined to treat them with something less than civility.

So far I have not said anything about the disadvantages of my situation; and to be perfectly truthful, there is very little to be said on this score. Certainly, there has never been anything even remotely resembling persecution or intolerance, anything worthy of being ranked with the severe disabilities experienced by certain racial or religious groups—to mention only two categories of sufferers; but there have been a few minor inconveniences, and at the head of the list I must place poverty. At the moment, my sole income (apart from an occasional— a very occasional—guinea that I pick up from free-lance journalism) is fifty shillings a week sickness pay. Presumably I could obtain further financial assistance if I chose to apply for it; but I do not choose to apply for it; my fifty shillings suffices; it keeps me afloat and that is all that matters. Besides, national assistance in any shape or form is not the answer to my problem. It is not merely additional cash I want, but the opportunity to earn it. At present I am not earning anything, I am living on a state subsidy provided out of the earnings of others; and that is what I find so damned humiliating.

Yes, my fifty shillings suffices. But although it is enough for my own subsistence, it does not, unfortunately, enable me to discharge my obligations towards others—towards my parents, that is. When they retired from business their modest savings, principally the fruits of abstinence, an old-fashioned lower middle class frugality, were just sufficient to buy the small terraced house in which we now live. After the purchase had been completed there was very little left; and, as in my own case, they have to live exclusively on the state pension. Their plight could be worse. They have a roof over their heads, and they are not on the breadline; but when one has said that, one has said all. There is definitely no money for luxuries, for those hundred and one desirable little items that are in some measure the consolations of old age—many of them, incidentally, things which our affluent proletariat has long since ceased to regard as anything but essentials. I am not, of course, directly responsible for this state of affairs, but that does not prevent me from regretting my inability to remedy it.

For myself I have but few complaints. My tastes are in all things extremely simple, and it does not cost much to satisfy them. Indeed, the only time I was ever seriously embarrassed on my own account by the emptiness of my purse was when I was learning my languages. School and examination fees, dictionaries and textbooks made a hell of a hole in my pocket money; and as one would expect, I have never been able to visit those countries whose tongues I have learned. This latter circumstance has imposed a very real handicap on my work, for while I have been able thoroughly to master grammar and vocabulary, and can translate into the foreign language at the speed of careful English, I have never been really competent in conversation.

And of course there have been the humorous interludes. For example, my poverty, as manifested in my shabby appearance, has on three occasions brought me under the surveillance of the police. I have one good suit and naturally wishing to preserve this, I used formerly to go about dressed like a more than usually disreputable-looking tramp. Inevitably the day had to come when I should be taken for one, and sure enough it did. They were searching, I remember, for someone who had set fire to a dutch barn and they apparently found it difficult to believe that I was not the man they were seeking. I fancy that even after I had satisfied them that I was not, they still suspected that I might be regularly sleeping out. I must say, however, that the representatives of the law were always very nice to me during these interviews, and I attach little credence to the tales of those scoundrels who would have us believe that the police officers are bullies and brutes. On the contrary, I found them not only exceptionally courteous and good-humoured, but also, when I had told them something of my story, downright sympathetic. Happily, I was able eventually to scrape together seventy shillings and buy a tolerably presentable ready-made suit, whereupon, I am delighted to record, I was immediately readmitted to the best society. *Ainsi va le monde!*

I must confess, though, that I really was seriously annoyed when the police mistook me for the murderer Christie; for at the time I was nearly twenty-five years younger than that gentleman—and not nearly so bald. I am always willing to help our friends in the police force, but in this instance their attention—for the reasons mentioned—was something less than flattering. By the bye, he was an amusing fellow that Christie. His reply, when asked why he had killed one of his victims, was the wholly delightful: 'Oh, she had such thick ankles.' There, I think, he caught an echo of Oscar Wilde.

And nor was I at all pleased when, after performing a trifling service for a man, he wanted to reward me with a 'Pourboire'—to tip me like a bloody porter, blast his eyes! But enough of whining. Even in this prosperous age there are still plenty of people who are acquainted with poverty and unemployment, and the following letter, which I saw in an evening newspaper, and which I make no apology for quoting *in extenso*, sums up the tragedy in far better words than any I can command:

'I state my own case, not in any moaning spirit, but as a typical one of a group which seems to need special consideration as regards employment.

'Only one job has been offered me through official channels in a year (that job being far beyond my strength).

'I have been denied friendships, and even religion [*sic*] because of shabby clothes and lack of spending money. I live alone in a room with a greedy gas meter and life seems hopeless at this time of year (Christmas).

'We haunt the public libraries for their free warmth and walk the streets conscious of our ever-growing shabbiness and of other people's good, warm clothes. Our shopping, too, brands us as sub-human, as we ask for the cheapest foods in the smallest quantities.

'Our slowly increasing debts tie us to shops where credit is offered, and so we are denied freedom of choice and price.

'Give us a break, employers! We are not work-shys. We really do want work—and without asking for the earth'.

One of my own pet grouses—and here envy rears its ugly head again—is the extraordinary efforts made by well-meaning people on behalf of certain other unfortunate minorities—the blind, the spastics, the war-disabled, the refugees, the epileptics, even discharged criminals—all have their champions who are prepared to move heaven and earth to get them into employment, to place them above charity; but no one has ever raised a finger to help me! Perhaps it is because I have never succeeded in attaching an eye-catching label to myself, for the label, as the chap who puts salmon into tins could tell you, is everything. I am not pretending, of course, that my own vulgar little disability is as severe as those of some of the groups I have mentioned—as that of blind persons, for example; manifestly it is not; but when it is a question of finding work my difficulties are at least as great as theirs. The British Diabetic Association, I admit, is doing a really excellent job for its members, but even this energetic and enterprising body cannot actually compel an employer to engage us.

And if I have received no help from others, what have I done to help myself? Well, as I have explained, I have learned languages—and I have also told you to what purpose. In fact, the only practical fruits of my studies to date are a couple of letters written (*gratuitement, bien entendu*) on behalf of one of my friends; the first, *en français* to the directrice of a village pension; the other, *auf Deutsch*, to an eminent missionary. The story of this last episode is rather worth the telling.

Years ago, this friend of mine, who is an Anglican priest, met the great man while the latter was on a visit to England. Shortly after the distinguished visitor had returned to Africa, my friend wrote to him upon some pretext (in English, as that doyen of radio comedians, Mr Gillie Potter, used to say) and back came a letter bearing the internationally famous signature. Throughout the years that letter, with its signature, was treasured; but in the autumn of fifty-seven its possessor entertained a brother clergyman in his home for a few days, and at the end of the visit the letter was missing. Now, fantastic as it may seem, my friend swore that his guest had swiped it; but realizing that it could be recovered only at the expense of a scandal, he decided he must replace it from source, and so at Christmas that year he sent the missionary a greetings card, counting upon receiving a card or a letter in reply. When it was obvious that a reply was not forthcoming, he indited a long letter to his celebrated correspondent, but there was still no reply, and it was now that he sought my aid. If an English letter would not do the trick, perhaps a German letter might, and would I write it for him? I would and I did, and the device worked. A few weeks later my friend had the ineffable pleasure of receiving a signed photograph which, suitably framed, is now kept in his deed-box, in his safe. Moral: I should probably be just as successful in extracting a remittance from a procrastinating debtor, but no one will give me the chance. *N'importe.*

Oh yes; there was one other occasion when I managed to put my knowledge of languages to some practical use. Once, when my father had missed the BBC news bulletin, I was able to obtain the result of a football match, in which he was interested, from the German radio. The score—*null zu null*—pleased him, and as I am genuinely fond of the old boy, I was equally delighted, and inclined to think that perhaps my hours in the classroom had not been wasted after all.

I have already made a brief reference to the odd guinea which I pick up from free-lance journalism, but this activity is more in the nature of an outlet for surplus and frustrated energy than a regular source of income. My initial effort, an article about the German corsair cruiser *Seeadler*, was bought by the first editor who saw it, but then followed a series of rejections, a common enough experience, surely; but as the workmanship and finish in these other stories was just as good as—and in at least one instance even better than—in the first, I wondered why. I received my answer from a friendly professional whom I used to know. Success in journalism, he told me, depends not only upon the ability to write competently, but equally upon the knowledge of what to write about; in other words, upon a capacity for distinguishing the potentially saleable from the definitely unsaleable. Thus, my yarn about the gallant Von Lückner and his leaky old *Sea Eagle* possessed that eminently vendible quality, novelty; whereas my article on the Royal

Navy's operations against SMS *Königsberg*, one of the stories I did not sell, dealt with a chapter of naval history that is familiar to everyone. The great difficulty is, of course, that by this time of day most of the world's best stories have already been told, and when an editor merely wants one of them retold he puts a staff man on to it. But I have no real talent for scribbling (though I am not out of my depth in the columns of the popular evening threepennies); and nor, to be perfectly frank, do I wish that I had; for I would much rather find a modest place in the sun as a commercial translator.

And what about other forms of employment? Well, I have already made it clear (I hope) that I am fit only for office work; and here, as I have explained, there are difficulties. There is no prospect, in view of my age and the superannuation barrier, of my entering the service of a large firm, and the only type of small employer who would consider me would be one who was trying to drive a hard bargain. I am not over-concerned with the question of salary, as I have said; but I have not, on the other hand, the smallest intention of allowing myself to be exploited by some vulgar, sickly-eyed, money-grubbing little beast of a grocer. A large, reputable firm could have my services, as a translator, for a fiver a week; the state could have them, in the same capacity, for the identical sum it at present pays me for doing nothing; but the small employer, looking for a cheap general clerk, must pay the full market price.

That is my story. I must confess that I have told it with some diffidence, because, inevitably, it must have all the appearance of a long, sustained whine. But it is not a whine—understand that once and for all. I do not want your sympathy, and nor, despite my previous remarks about the assistance which is lavished upon persons suffering from other disabilities, do I really want your aid, for to say the truth, I prefer to fight my own battles, and win my own victories. I wish merely to be allowed to compete with you on even terms. Only that.

10

The Stricture

by 'N. O. GOE'

THIS TITLE, which so interestingly looks as though it might be that of a poem by Donne or a story by Henry James, simply means what *The Concise Oxford Dictionary* says: 'STRICTURE (Path.) morbid contraction of some canal or duct in the body'. The matter is, in fact, very down to earth, and in every sense of the word, vulgar; and some may well think it trivial. But while I agree that, compared with other disadvantages, such as physical deformity, the lack of one or more of the five wits, or a sexual deviation, the stricture scarcely ranks high, nevertheless it can cause a certain sense of shamed inferiority, as well as bodily discomfort, and may have a considerable influence on a person's life.

I remember very clearly the first time I became aware of it, if only because, never having had any trouble of this kind before, the discovery of anything so unnatural in a small boy's natural world was something of a shock. I was, I suppose, some six or seven years old, and had been ill in bed with some childish complaint, from which I was recovering to the extent of being 'allowed up' while my mother and the maid tidied the room and made the bed. I had washed myself, I remember, while this was being done, and my mother told me to 'make myself comfortable' (as the middle-class euphemism of my childhood had it) before I got back into bed. Accordingly I hauled the jerry-pot out of the washstand cupboard, as I was accustomed to do, and applied myself to it, doubtless in that peculiarly stuck-out-in-front attitude of little boys happily relieving themselves. There was no result whatever. It suddenly seemed to me that not only did I not want to relieve myself now, but that I never had wanted to in the past, and never should want to again. This familiar action, that is to say, was suddenly meaningless. But while I stood there in my astonishment at this, it was borne in upon me that it was the presence in the room of my mother and the maid which was having so curiously nullifying an effect. It simply was not possible for me to make water when other people were there; and from that day it has remained not possible, at least as a general rule, though there are the usual proving exceptions to it.

I suppose my mother realized that something was wrong, or perhaps I said, as I put the jerry-pot away, that I would wait until she and the maid had gone; but after that it was taken for granted by my parents that I always had to be alone for this purpose. That was well enough while I was a child, and at home, where privacy was easy to find (I had no brothers or sisters), and perhaps my parents thought that I was 'a funny little boy' of rather exaggerated modesty, who would 'grow out of it': parents are prone to take refuge in the hope that their children will 'grow out of' their troublesome foibles, whether bed-wetting, nose-picking, or telling lies. Modesty in the ordinary sense seems to have had nothing to do with the matter, however; and meanwhile I contrarily 'grew into it'.

Certain occurrences may have contributed to the onset of this difficulty, though it is not easy at this distance in time to remember the order of events, so that I cannot be certain which of them may have been causes, and which effects. My mother was an extremely fastidious woman, not given to calling a spade anything more exact than a gardening implement, one of whose terrors in connection with me was that I might somehow or other 'disgrace' her in public. It may have been at about this time that I was memorably upbraided for asking to 'leave the room' while she was entertaining some other suburban ladies to tea. In the course of the harangue she delivered after her guests had gone, it was made very clear to me that I had in fact disgraced her in those ladies' eyes; and that in future, however badly I wanted to 'go', I must 'wait'. It may have been at about this time, too, that the garden-boy and I were observed from the house in the act of 'making ourselves comfortable' down by the rubbish-heap. There was another harangue about that, and this time it was made clear to me that my behaviour had been both 'dirty' and 'common', direst words to a nice child's ears. It may also have been at about this time that a little girl at the same school to which I went in the mornings incontinently wetted herself and the floor during 'drill'. This was a severe shock to me, and I did indeed feel that the deepest disgrace was involved for the poor child; I thought her unspeakably naughty, and quite beyond the pale of decency.

It is possible that these things, or one or more of them, happening at much the same time in my childhood as the first appearance of the stricture, did tend to impress it upon me that it was altogether *nefas* to make water when anyone else could see what one was doing; for that is really the point: others must not be aware that this natural function, common to us all, is being exercised; even if one is exercising it in a public place expressly intended for the purpose, so irrational are our psychopathological kinks. I think it very likely that the ordinary training of an ordinary little boy in continence and polite behaviour (according, that is, to the bourgeois standards of the early decades of this century) was in my case carried to such an extreme that I became convinced that really nice little boys must not be supposed to have bladders at all. The probability is that my mother, so determined not to be disgraced, unwittingly laid up for me my future difficulties and discomforts. It is, after all, a way that parents have: the good intentions of the fathers pave the children's road to hell.

The tiresome situation in which I found myself at the age of six or so inevitably grew more tiresome as I grew older. As a child, I was sometimes taken to London for the day, and since emotional excitement of any kind always enhanced my difficulty, while circumstances in any way unfamiliar or disturbing enhanced it yet again, these days in London meant that, from the time of leaving home in the morning to the time of returning there in the evening, my water had willy-nilly to be retained. Towards the end of the day the discomfort was considerable. But it was not the slightest use my parents sending me off to a 'gentlemen' in a theatre, a department store or a railway station. Not only were these surroundings strange enough to put me off in any case; they were also public places frequented by other people.

I was already ashamed of my disability. It quite naturally irritated my father, and my mother soon came to regard it as evidence of my being a 'silly' little boy, rather than a 'funny' one. Shame breeds deceit, however, so I dutifully went off to the 'gentlemen' at the Zoo or a pantomime, and pretended on returning that I had done what I went to do. I do not think I was successful in my deceit, and certainly not when my father accompanied me, but my assurances seemed to be a satisfaction to my elders (if they were not to me), and nobody appears to have feared that I might come to some harm by holding my water too long; nor, indeed, have I ever done so, one's physical organism being remarkably accommodating on the whole.

When I went away to boarding-school at the age of ten there were new difficulties, and new ways of dealing with them had to be found. Generally speaking, it was never a case of making water when one wanted to, but always a case of doing so when one could. I felt it necessary to keep my disability secret from the other boys, since the worst thing that can happen to a boy at his prep. school is to be in any way 'different'; so I went when they did to the school latrines, though nothing happened there but the increase of my envy of my fellows' freedom to behave naturally, and even challenge one another to see how high up the wall they could reach. (I should have liked to join in, but if anyone challenged me, I had always 'just finished'.) I used various stratagems. One was to ask to be excused during class, when the latrines would be deserted. Another was to stay awake at night and use the pot under my bed when the dormitory's other occupants were asleep, or at least when it was dark and I could not be seen.

It is remarkable, however, with what speed and cunning a person will learn to adapt himself to his circumstances, and to re-adapt himself when his circumstances change; a new set of stratagems were required when I moved on to a public school, and adjustments were necessary as I moved up the school. But I certainly do not wish to give the impression that my schooldays were made miserable by my disability, any more than my later days have been. It very quickly became something which one took in one's stride, and only occasionally was one reminded of it or inconvenienced by it; inconvenienced, for the most part (as I now see), in one's vanity, in that curious and conventional vanity which fears the possibility of being thought an anomoly. It was anomolous not to be thoroughly 'manly' about as ordinary a thing as sharing a tree-trunk or a hedge on a walk in the country, or responding to someone's suggestion before a game or an entertainment, 'Let's all go and have a pee before we start.' But I fancy that the fear of ridicule in this context is, like many other fears, largely imaginary, though that I did not understand in my early years, when it was a fear which, imaginary or not, caused me a good deal of distress. In later life one cares less, perhaps because one has learned that one must be prepared to be considered ridiculous in one way, if not in another or in several. But for a child or an adolescent, the very fact that he is not yet a man makes anything in his nature which might be thought unmanly intolerable; and convention seems to say that a male person who cannot piss whenever he wants to is, by some peculiar transference, sexually inferior.

When I was thirteen, and one day taken from my prep. school to a nursing home in the town, an appendicectomy was an event disturbing enough in itself to make my little trouble a great one. The nurses did their kindly best, but nothing availed: hot compresses; leaving me alone with that peculiar 'bottle', the door firmly shut on an assurance that no one would come in for at least five minutes; draughts of water to make me 'want to go' (which indeed they did; but the greater the want, the less the ability); even the sympathetic magic of a tap left running within earshot, calculated to send most boys running too. There was nothing for it but to fetch the doctor; it was now some days since I had passed water, and my distended bladder was no longer considered 'safe', though in the ordinary sense it was of course as safe (from the usual kind of juvenile accident) as any bladder ever was. So the doctor came, and his catheter with him.

Those who have had their water drawn off in this way will know that the operation is not pleasant, despite the consequent relief, if only because it is a very strange and confusing sensation to feel something passing up a part of oneself through which things usually pass down. More distressfully, this passage in a small boy is small in proportion; and although I presume that catheters vary in calibre, and that one of the appropriate size was used, the fact remains that this doctor (whom another doctor, when years later I told him of the incident, described as 'a sadist') used a steel catheter, and not a rubber one. More distressfully still, perhaps, it is embarrassing to a nicely brought up boy to find himself lying prone in bed, with a swathe of bandages round his middle and a sutured wound under it (this was in the 'twenties), while a man does obscure things to his private anatomy, and a woman looks on; for the fact that the man is a doctor and the woman a nurse, and that both are presumably exercising their professions with the proper detachment, scarcely weighs with a boy of thirteen, who simply feels that he is being indecently exposed, to say nothing of indecently assaulted.

Nor does the matter end with the painful withdrawal of the catheter and the removal of the enamel basin. It is pleasant to feel that one's bladder is no longer at bursting-point, but this feeling is in the nature of things a temporary one, so that renewed anxiety quickly succeeds it: since one's organism goes on producing urine willy-nilly, and does so (one feels at such a time) with a kind of ferocious glee, it will not be long before one needs to pass water again. And what then? There is no reason to suppose that one's ill-natured canal will not once more be strictured, or that it will not once more be necessary for that sinister doctor to appear with his little black tube, and his minion with her white enamel bowl. As I lay there, while the inexorable physiological processes went on within me, I felt like a trapped animal.

In this case, as it happened, I was spared a repetition of the doctor's ministrations. Left safely and understandingly alone with the bottle next time it was necessary to make water, something merciful in the scheme of things came to my aid; or perhaps it was something merciful in my own psychology, the alternative to getting rid of my water in the usual way having proved so frightful that it overcame the stricture. But it was a qualified mercy. The pain, as the first hesitant drops of water passed through a delicate channel recently excoriated by a steel catheter, was such that I could scarcely keep myself from crying out (which would have ruined everything by bringing the nurse on to the scene too soon), and certainly could not keep myself from tears. The process of emptying my bladder was extremely slow, partly because the pain made it necessary to release the water a little at a time, with pauses for rest in between, and partly no doubt because my organism was in any case only just willing to fulfil this natural function at all. But it was over at last; and the next time and the next were progressively less painful.

A much later occasion on which the stricture took advantage of serious illness occurred when I was about forty, and had perhaps become philosophical. This time the operation, which took place in a large hospital ward, seemed to be comic side uppermost. For one thing, I was completely harnessed in apparatus of one kind and another, having been admitted to hospital with a suspected duodenal perforation; one arm was strapped to the bed, and tubes fed me intravenously; tubes drained my stomach into something or other under the bed, and these tubes went up my nose and down my throat. Altogether I felt more like some fantastic construction in a laboratory than a human being. But my urinary system was still a human being's, and of my peculiar kind, refusing, as ever in circumstances of stress, one of its normal functions, while applying itself all too normally to the production of what it would not discharge. The doctor gravely felt my lower abdomen, muttered, 'Very distended,' to the staff-nurse who had reported my condition, heard from me that I had this difficulty, especially when ill, and nodded in a way which told me plainly enough what must be done. The screens were put up, and the doctor and the staff-nurse went to work.

Theirs was a beautifully impersonal performance, and that it was so, making me feel that I was indeed something on a laboratory bench, or even not there at all, was undoubtedly an intentional kindness. Meanwhile, however, I realized, as I lay there looking up at them, that these two were at least very good friends; their attitude to each other was by no means impersonal. They were discussing the summer promenade concert syllabus, which had just been issued, and making plans to hear some of the concerts together. Thus two more or less incongruous things were going on at once, a discreet love-scene and a job of work, likewise shared, on a third party's recalcitrant sphincter muscle. At one moment the doctor would have his eye on the nurse (and I entirely sympathized), and at the next its focus was professional; at one moment he would be saying, 'Brahms's Alto Rhapsody—we mustn't miss that,' and at the next, 'Urine extremely concentrated—how many days is it?' A certain confusion arose in my mind between what was happening to the doctor and the nurse in respect of each other, and what was happening to me; but I suppose that both professional detachment and personal attachment are such that this confusion remained in my mind alone.

No doubt it is one of the ironies of life that a person afflicted in my particular way should be a beer-drinker: beer is largely water, and has to be taken in large quantities if it is to have any convivial effect, so that it also has to be expelled in large quantities, and (as an evening progresses) often. Some might say that anyone who cannot be sure of getting rid of his beer when and where he wants to should not drink it, and if we were logical creatures they would probably be right. But, as in the case of people suffering from much graver and more incapacitating afflictions, the reaction to a difficulty of my kind is not to order one's life at its instance, so much as to live one's life in spite of it. Besides, alcohol is the enemy of inhibition, so that I have often found that, after a few drinks, my difficulty either disappears or is considerably diminished, though there seem to be no rules about this, and it is not a thing on which one can afford to gamble.

There has been only one occasion on which the post beer-

drinking dilemma had to be dealt with in a really drastic
way.

Years ago, I spent the summer in a village near the Norfolk
Broads, and there made friends with two of the local youths.
One evening we decided to sneak the keeper's rowing-boat
and take ourselves to Potter Heigham, some distance away,
for a drink (a singular, by the way, which with characteristic
British euphemism almost always stands, as on this occasion,
for a plural). We remained in the pub by Potter Heigham
Bridge until closing-time, and our journey home in the clear
moonlight was as hilarious as it was wayward. By the time we
had reached the open water beyond Potter Heigham sound, we
had also reached the stage of making water in more senses than
one. My companions were for using the side of the boat, a
contrivance as difficult as Uncle Toby's, and quite impossible
for me, since, apart from the company, these were circumstances of a strangeness such as always put me off. In fact it was
a contrivance impossible for my companions, for we giggled
so much, and upset the balance of the boat so much in our
drunken efforts to trim it suitably, that this shift was abandoned
for another, that of making for the bank and a landing among
the reeds. This too was tricky, however. The Broads may, as
some assert, be old peat-diggings, with clean-cut sides to prove
it, but their sides are not clean-cut everywhere, and it is by no
means easy, among all those reeds, to discover where the water
ends and *terra firma* begins. At last, however, my companions
managed to get out of the boat and on to something which
would give them the necessary standing place, I having
cunningly told them that I would take my turn later, and
would meanwhile hold the boat to the 'shore' for them, there
being nowhere to tie it up if we all disembarked at once.

But I already knew that, with them no more than a couple
of yards away, the moon at the full, and no place further
inland to make for that was not still exposed or a bog, my
situation would be hopeless. I returned to the boat, of course,
pretending to be as much relieved as they were, and off we set
again for our own village. Our course (I was rowing part of
the time) was not exactly the shortest distance between two

points, and the journey took a very long time. It was two o'clock before we finally reached the keeper's boathouse, and I suppose it must have been at some time after midnight that I came to the conclusion that my bladder was no longer 'safe', and indeed that the situation was desperate.

I have said that a curious thing about my disability is that there is no difficulty about letting go one's water, so long as anyone else who is present does not know what is happening. If I had, with my companions' knowledge, undone my buttons and attempted to make water into the bottom of the boat, the attempt would have been abortive; but simply to let go, without undoing anything, and while they were noisily rowing and knew nothing about it, was perfectly possible. I was wearing cotton shorts, the kidneys reduce beer to little but water, and the night was a very warm one, so that my shorts were dry, and apparently none the worse, by the time we landed; and we all agreed that, in kindness to the keeper, the boat had better be bailed out when we tied it up in his boathouse.

There are other predicaments involved in the stricture. Emotional tensions of any kind are, as I say, among its opportunities for making itself felt, and, like other young men, I used occasionally to become emotionally tense about young women. While it is annoying to miss trains, buses and appointments, to get left behind by one's friends on leaving parties or pubs, because one's natural needs take longer to satisfy than other people's, or cannot be satisfied at all at the time when one wishes them to be; and while it is also annoying to be thought odd by women with whom one is in intimate relations because the pot under the bed is useless (so that one has to make chilly and upsetting journeys to other parts of the house in the middle of the night or before making love), it is very annoying indeed actually to miss, after a long and arduous pursuit, one's chance of lovemaking altogether, simply because one's idiotic waterworks seize up at the crucial moment. Details are unnecessary; everybody knows that it is better not to swim on a full belly or make love on a full bladder, and most people, having at long last, and with the aid of a few drinks, persuaded a particularly interesting young woman into their bed, take care not to leave her there by herself for long enough to think better of the situation, get dressed, and slip out of their lodgings. So the stricture may certainly lose a man his chances.

One might compare it to a recurrent illness (malaria, say), which one can forget about until one is forcibly reminded of it. Perhaps this is why most of us who suffer from it tend to endure it rather than try, by some form of treatment, to cure it. And apart from the fact that human nature becomes perversely fond of its little oddities, perhaps another reason is that this particular oddity is so irrational in its behaviour, and has, as it were, so mischievous a spirit, that one would find it hard to know how to begin to describe one's symptoms logically to another person. I have often been surprised by the irrationality of my own brand of the stricture; there have been many times when I have been sure that some emotional or physical upset would be its opportunity, and yet have been wrong; and there have been other times when it has plagued me for no apparent reason at all.

The stricture is, of course, entirely subjective; that is no doubt why its behaviour is so naughtily obscure. Could one become quite objective about it and see it steadily and see it whole, it would probably disappear altogether. But that could be said of other tiresome aspects of our personalities, of which we might likewise take leave with a grateful 'For this relief much thanks'.

11

His Father a Drunkard

by JOHN LACEY

I AWOKE with a start. Someone was coming down the narrow corridor. Thuds resounded as a heavy body lurched from side to side against the walls. Each thud was followed by oaths and muttering, which grew louder like an approaching storm. The heavy footfalls stopped outside my door. There was silence except for laboured breathing. Then he fumbled at the door; the handle was rattled violently. The door flew open and in lurched a gigantic shadowy figure. The scream died in my throat, stillborn. I pulled the sheet over my head. The candle-light glowed through it, increasing in brightness as its holder approached. 'Lord hide me in eternal darkness', I prayed desperately to myself. The shadow of an arm fell across the sheet, which was whipped away.

My father peered down to see if I was shamming. I shivered at the smell of whisky. He held the candlestick over me, above his head, at a raffish angle; it trembled in his hand, and he heaved a great sigh.

'Where's your mother, boy?' he demanded rhetorically.

'Where's your mother?' he repeated, shaking me by the shoulder.

He pushed his red face close to mine, and closer as I shrank away. Beads of sweat stood out on his furrowed brow; in the candlelight his eyes glistened as if with tears.

'I don't know, sir,' I snivelled.

'Don't know?' he replied incredulously. 'You're lying as usual, boy. Didn't she tell you she was going away?' I was silent out of loyalty to her.

'Don't lie to me, you rat, damn you,' he roared, shaking me.

Again he poked the slanting candle and his face close to mine so that I blinked in the glare and shrank back.

Triumphantly he hissed out the answer in slurred tones:

'She's lying with that snivelling Captain So-and-So.'

At the age of seven I only knew one kind of lying, so was mystified.

There followed a torrent of abuse against my mother, mingled with dark hints, threats and foreboding prophecies. We were all no good, we'd all come to a bad end, we'd all be ruined. I was forced to say 'Yes, sir' in agreement to various rhetorical questions. But what sank most into my mind, never to be erased, was his triumphant proclamation 'You were born under an unlucky star'. As he repeated this refrain he swung the candlestick like a censer; indeed, in his white night-cap and nightshirt he looked like a heathen priest making a diabolical invocation.

In his other hand was one of his Indian clubs with which he did his Swedish exercises. To relieve his feelings after his harangue, he began limbering up and swinging it. It flew out of his uncertain hand past my head and straight through the window. The noise of crashing glass and the shaking of the window curtain disturbed a bat, which dropped from it like a stone and then flew round and round the candle and my father's head. He began to curse and swipe as if the devil himself had come for him (a thought which the bat's shadow and shape doubtless suggested).

Meanwhile, screaming rose from the adjacent back yard, where the kitchen-maid had been kissing the garden boy. There were running feet and a man's voice below. My father started. A tremor ran through his frame. They had come for him at last. In the corner of my room nearest to him stood my four-ten gun, which I had brought up in order to pot at pigeons on the stable roof in the early morning. It was therefore already loaded (contrary to the regulations of the house). He seized the gun and lurched towards the window, first depositing the candle on the floor. He thrust the muzzle of the gun aggressively through the open window, rested the barrel on the window ledge to steady it, took a deep breath and fired two

shots into the darkness in quick succession. Dead silence.
Cautiously he straightened himself and considered his next step.
By now he had forgotten my existence and was engrossed in
the problem of his enemies' next move.

There was a lull in the attack. So he lurched downstairs with
his candle, leaving my door wide open. Our telephone was on
a table at the foot of the back stairs. I crept to the door and
heard him slump heavily into the chair. Taking up the receiver,
he called 'Police!' He rattled the phone savagely, cursed it,
and muttered 'Damn' and 'Blast' until an inspector answered
at the other end. 'The house is being besieged', he announced,
finding the last word rather difficult. The inspector could not
catch his meaning at first, for my father repeated the word
several times, finally roaring it out in thick tones. The police
were used to this kind of thing and evidently re-assured him
that they would bring up reinforcements. Worn out by the
crisis and his exertions, and with the whisky beginning to tell,
he was soon asleep with his head on the telephone table. I
heard loud snores from below.

Cold and fearful, I crept back to bed. There I remained for
some time as stiff as a ramrod, waiting for the bandits' bullets to
whistle round me and straining to hear their voices in the
yard below.

So many scenes which I remember centre round a gun! Once,
when I was perhaps twelve, I stood in the spring sunshine
pissing in a field. Round a bend along the forest fence comes
my father, gigantic in the shade. I started, so that my four-ten
gun dropped from my crooked arm and went off with a god-
almighty bang as it hit the ground. My panic was shared by the
grey squirrel above me in the solitary oak; it chattered with
terror and disappeared round the other side of the massive
trunk. All around a hundred scuts caught the light, and not
a rabbit was to be seen. Jays squawked their warnings, the
cock-pheasant's call was followed by whirring wings. The
forest fell into a hush as it echoed my father's angry and
upbraiding tones.

'What the devil were you doing, boy', he shouted. 'Haven't

I told you a hundred times not to walk with your gun cocked, damn you?' (*Gun* cocked, mind you—so he *hadn't* seen what I was up to.)

My heart pounded to breaking-point; my breath came in short gasps; terror and guilt overwhelmed me. I mumbled incoherently an unlikely explanation of my aberration. This increased my father's irritable and suspicious mood.

To distract his attention and prevent further questions, I pointed up towards a tall spruce on the forest edge. 'Oh, sir,' I stammered, 'there's the squirrel's nest I told you about last night, into which the wounded squirrel escaped.'

Unlucky diversion! For around two o'clock of an afternoon the repeated whisky begins to tell even on the strongest heads. My father blinked like an owl in the sun. His eyes watered with the effort of concentration. As he looked up, he swayed slightly on his heels like a felled forest giant about to crash. What with the shade, and the sun dancing before his eyes and his spirit-washed brain, he could see no squirrel's nest.

His arm shot out and gripped mine in a vice; he shook me like a rat. 'Damn it, boy,' he shouted, 'you're at your dirty lying tricks again.' Such was my terror and bewilderment that something warm trickled down my trousers.

'What, Sir?' I stammered, not knowing what he meant or what was to follow.

'There's no squirrel's nest,' he insisted indignantly, 'and you never shot a squirrel. With your blasted glasses you can't see a thing, you damn-fool.'

My glasses! My glasses! A daily reproach unto me from my father and mother—and not least from myself. 'Take your glasses off, John, they make you look so stupid,' she would say as the front door bell rang. She snatched them furiously from my face, so that I peered helplessly at the oncoming guest, too confused to know what to say, or even to stretch out my hand in the conventional welcome. At such moments I was little more than a quivering jelly on the floor, a misplaced jellyfish that anyone might have stamped on with stiletto heel.

I looked up again into the spruce. Was the squirrel's nest there or wasn't it? I couldn't be sure now. I couldn't be sure of anything. My father couldn't see it. My eyes filled with tears until even the tree was blotted out. No, I couldn't see it either. He didn't believe me and I didn't believe myself. We walked home in silence, punctuated by my penitential sobs and the call of the cock-pheasant in the brakes.

If he had always been like that, it would not have been so difficult. It was 'the change' that came over him which was hard to understand, so that we did not know where we stood. When he suddenly turned on us we felt there must be something wrong with *us*. For when he was 'himself' he was generous and kind.

I remember a children's party. Fifty of us sat down at the highly polished dining-room table, in which you could see the reflection of your face, of the candles and the family silver. Each child was presented by my father with a carefully chosen present. He wore black velvet knee breeches, white stockings and silver-buckled shoes. As he bent over each child (no smell of whisky now), his dark hair gleamed in the candlelight; at last his face was happy. There was an old-fashioned courtliness, an ease and dignity about him as he moved affably amongst his guests. How dear he was to us!

He was also fun—when my mother was away. In the inner hall stood a large brass gong, ready to be ceremoniously thumped by the butler. There was also a lion-skin (with its family history, of course), upon the snarling head of which many an unwary visitor tripped, entering the gloomy hall; we children would hover expectantly, wondering whether 'poor old' Colonel So-and-So would suppress his instinctive 'God-damn' as he stumbled.

My father once seized the gong, stand and all, and hung it round his neck. He then donned the lion-skin. Its tail, trailing down his back, invited a surreptitious tweak from the nearest child behind him. Its head, with staring glassy eyes and yawning jaws that seemed to saliver, protruded above his own, making him like a gigantic forest creature or one of the fearsome African witch-doctors whose photos we thumbed in his big-game book. He led the procession round the hall, beating the gong furiously. As he flourished the drumsticks above his head like a regimental sergeant-major, they sometimes hit the pendant glass of a chandelier, setting it a-swinging and a-glitter in the gaslight. Each time the procession approached the strategic point we waited hopefully. The gong reverberated up the staircase well. It was all rather eerie, and so we chanted all the louder, 'Whilst the cat's away the mice do play'—referring to my mother's absence.

In this inner hall my father liked to sing Victorian music-hall songs, donning a chocolate bowler for the occasion. In the years of his long decline, guests were hard to come by and had, as it were, to be dragged from the highways and byeways. One evening, the only two outside spectators he could get were a seedy vet with a pink face, watery blue eyes and bristling moustache, and his flouncing common wife, who quite gave herself the airs of the Lady of the House (my mother being absent) and mistakenly thought herself the target of her womanless host.

A servant had arranged odds and ends of chairs in a gaping semicircle, as if there was to be a regular audience. Everyone sat bolt upright and uncomfortable. We had edged away from our hated guests; not all the blandishments and grimaces of the Flouncing Ma'am could persuade us to sidle along the chairs towards her. The gas jets spluttered and dipped, rose and fell; frequently they threatened to go out altogether. They cast a feeble bluish light, which only enhanced the general gloom. The great oak staircase disappeared into the darkness, and the unlit corners of the hall were full of bogies.

At last my father lurched in at the other end of the hall, well primed for the occasion. A servant bore candles after him, and placed them on the piano in the corner. Somebody had been found able to play the few notes necessary for the jaunty Victorian airs. My father's favourite was 'Up I comes with my little lot': it enabled him to crack a great whip at appropriate moments, like a costermonger trotting up to the races at a spanking pace.

He leaned heavily against the piano, the coachman's whip at

the ready in both hands, his bowler at a jaunty angle. We all managed to suppress titters, not being certain whether he was in solemn or jocular mood. As the trembling pianist struck the first note, my father opened his mouth expectantly: out came a great hiccup. In my endeavours to suppress my giggles I emitted curious porcine squeals; my ribs seemed about to crack and there was something seriously wrong in the seat of my pants. He glared at me, his face flushed. I put up my arm to ask for much needed permission to leave the room, in prep. school fashion. 'Stand to attention, boy, and don't fidget,' he said.

As I stood up, white-faced, I felt like a criminal: I imagined that everyone was staring at me. But the others, afraid of being implicated in my criminality or of being thought sympathetic, avoided looking at me, pretending that nothing had happened. If only they had stolen glances at me, I wouldn't have felt so isolated! I began to think of figures in my favourite reading. I pictured Napoleon standing alone on the deck of the *Bellerophon*, his hands clasped behind his bowed back (a coloured card of this painting, which I had bought with my pocket-money, was framed in the nursery).

I was startled out of my reverie by my father's booming but uncertain tenor as he started the first line. His voice went up on the word 'lot', quite out of control; at the same moment he cracked the whip ferociously. This was too much for an un-invited guest on the nursery landing three floors up: my favourite collie uttered prolonged howls. The pianist stopped and burst into tears. My father's mouth was open, but the words of the next line refused to come; even the hiccups were shocked out of him, as though he had received a god-almighty slap on the back. The vet's wife screwed up her little mean features as if in pain, and went into hysterics. Above the pandemonium sounded my father's furious tones, 'shoot that dog'.

He lurched into the gun-room just behind him and got an old service rifle, a souvenir of the First World War. We heard him striking matches in the darkness, cursing to himself and ferreting in the drawer for the ammunition. The drawer jammed and he shook it furiously. Then there was a crash as he pulled it out and it fell on the floor, scattering the contents. 'Bring a candle, damn you,' he shouted to all and sundry.

At last he emerged, the rifle at the ready in his hands. He swung it up in the dog's direction. We all ducked. An age passed whilst he pointed the rifle unsteadily, swaying slightly on his heels and drawing breaths to steady his aim. There was nothing to see in that darkness, really. But in his state of persecution-mania he may have seen the fierce muzzles of blood-hounds baying him to death. Three shots rang out. Each time the bolt clicked as it was shot home and drawn back; the ejected cartridges tinkled on the floor. There was an acrid smell of cordite, and a haze of rifle smoke hung in the air. I cowered beneath my chair, expecting to hear the heavy thud of the dog's corpse as it fell from the banisters above, and afraid that it would land directly on me! But only bits of plaster rattled down.

The shooting relieved my father's feelings. He repeated quite genially, 'That'll teach 'em a lesson, eh, that'll teach 'em a lesson.' (Had the one dog really become many?) As for us, somehow we were thankful to be alive; the storm was over and the air cleared. We pretended that nothing had happened. The guests hastened to escape before my father could start some long-winded harangue which would detain them another hour.

When waves of aggression did not surge over him, he was politeness itself. With old-fashioned courtesy he bowed them out of the front door, though he found it difficult not to fall forward as he bowed, and the straightening-up process took rather long. When he finally achieved an upright position, he swayed slightly on his heels; there was a far-away glazed look in his eyes, and we wondered whether he would crash backwards through the glass of the door. He kept us, as always, in a perpetual state of wonder and guessing; it was always difficult not to expect the worst.

Despite their protests, he insisted on accompanying his guests to their car; being only a vet's, it was parked in the stable-yard across the lawn. He led the way with a lantern, which a servant had hung in the porch. He zigzagged across the lawn in an erratic manner; it was like following a will-o'-the-wisp. Our guests gazed at each other in embarrassment and cast side-long glances at us; nobody could make any conversation.

Gusts of repressed giggles swept over me. Not daring to laugh, cry or scream, despite the unbearable tension, everything inside me came to a full stop. Stomach cramp attacked me; I felt my legs giving way—nothing functioned any more. I was only saved from total collapse and immobility by—as usual in our household—the unexpected.

My father lurched against an old leaning medlar on the lawn. The lantern went out and fell to the ground, leaving us in darkness. As he groped to find it, he fell heavily on his face and started to swear horribly. The vet's wife began screaming again. This was too much for us children. Despite our fear of father we bolted back to the house, half sobbing and half giggling. The front door was locked. Panic seized us as we alternately tugged at the handle and pulled the door bell out to its full extent. We thought we heard its echoing jangle; but no footstep approached the door, no light appeared within, and we waited in vain for the noise of bolts withdrawn. We dared not call out, we dared not pummel in fury and despair on the door for fear of father hearing us. At any moment his gigantic figure would lurch out of the darkness, upbraiding and swearing. Shivers went down my spine as if somebody were approaching me from behind. We felt like trapped animals in the porch, but luckily an obsessive desire to be somewhere else mastered us. We careered like wild ponies along the gravel walk round the house. Every angle of it that we turned put something between him and us.

At length we came to one of the many back doors, the one that led directly into the servants' quarters. There we listened, trembling—listened for sounds of cursing, stumbling and pursuit; listened for sounds of stirring within. But our hearts were beating so loudly and we were so out of breath that it was a little time before we were sufficiently calm to hear anything else! When our ears were attuned to the silence, we heard the gentle rise and fall of snoring from the butler's room on the ground floor. Dare we call out and rouse him, and have *him* swearing at us and reporting us next morning to the Master? Only half aware of what he was doing, my brother tried the door, which was—unlocked! We almost fell across the threshold with surprise. We held our breath and took our shoes off so as not to wake the butler. Then we groped along the corridors and up the back stairs to our rooms, terrified of the darkness and stillness. We crept into bed as we were, without undressing, safe from pursuit at last.

I can see him now, slumped for days on end in his armchair in the Damask Room, alone with his gloomy thoughts, which we dared not disturb. On his right, a coffin-stool with a glass of whisky, constantly replenished by a seedy footman who brought in the fresh decanter and siphon on a silver salver. On his left the books he was *supposed* to like reading (for years now they had hardly been opened)—an old Scots manual on forestry, *The Stockbreeder* and Shakespeare. This was a pocket edition given him by his father for his first boarding school; he could hardly read its small print now, which danced up and down before his eyes and deterred him with a headache. In front of him, carved boastfully on the oak panelling above the mantelpiece, was the long-winded family motto: 'Say, let them say: do well, regard not what they say.' But all his life voices within and without told him he was a failure. The more he heard them, the more he took to whisky; and the more he took to whisky, the louder they became.

He had not been born to inherit the place, but had stayed on to run it whilst his more clever elder brother, David, served abroad with some distinction in the Diplomatic Service, until he died of typhus in South America. My uncle David was a great correspondent; his long letters described the interesting places and people he knew. They were read aloud by my grandfather, and the talk was always of what David had been doing. The first thing a visitor asked was 'How is David?' or 'Where is David now?' He therefore perpetually made his presence felt. Naturally he was fêted when he returned home on leave, so that my father was always thrown into the shade. He seemed to have no standing of his own as long as his father and elder brother were alive.

There was not enough for him to do, the estate being comparatively small. Farming was his hobby, but in those days it did not pay and was not so scientific. He was a good forester, but none of these rural pursuits were then regarded as of national or economic importance. The atmosphere, too, was beginning to change, since we were not far from several socialistic Midland industrial towns. He felt there was no place for him. I seem to have absorbed from the atmosphere this difficulty in finding one's niche, and of knowing how to set about it!

Worst of all, in a family closely connected with the Army and Navy, a physical handicap had prevented him from getting a regular commission. This rankled with him and his martinet father, a retired general with parade-ground manners. My grandfather, himself a younger son and not too happily married, had been embittered by professional disappointments and the deaths of several of his children (who had lived long enough to show promise of various sorts). A lonely widower, he did not long survive his eldest son's death.

By that time my father was middle-aged, with his life behind him: his freedom and position came too late. The servitude of the drunkard to his drink remained.

Now that his father was dead, his main preoccupation was to hide his whisky glass from his wife. As he heard her approaching footsteps he hastily shoved the unfinished glass in a drawer, behind the sliding panels of a sideboard, in an empty chamber-pot in its bedside table. . . . He then forgot where the glass was, and sought it with trembling hands. If my mother found it, she poured it out of the nearest window (I was never sure whether the plants below thrived on the whisky or not); if the footman found it, he poured it down his throat; if the maid found it, she giggled; if I found it, I didn't know what to do or think. I was faintly aware of an air of secretiveness about the house, which has become part of my own nature.

He was as much in bondage to my mother as previously to his own father. How he begged her forgiveness! How he promised to reform! He wrote long abject letters imploring her to return, when all would be so different. 'If only this . . .' 'if only that . . .' He lived in a world of regret and make-believe. When all around him collapsed, he retreated into the imagined glories of the past.

In his dark smoking-room he harangued me about my ancestors, of whom I must be worthy—otherwise he'd 'cut me off without a penny' and strike my name off the entry list of the public school where he and his father had preceded me. 'Do you know, boy,' he'd suddenly say, apropos of nothing, 'the Duke of Wellington sat in that chair in which you are now. Your great-grandfather was asking him to use his influence for a commission in a crack regiment for his son. The Duke replied "Ask me anything but that, sir—it's a favour outside my power to grant".' So sought after was the commission which, of course, my grandfather eventually obtained!

He spun endless family yarns which I drank in. One of his uncles had the best string of polo ponies in India; he ended a promising military career by falling on his head during play. Another lost an eye in the Mutiny when a soda-water bottle (whisky again!) exploded as he hit it with his foot whilst entering his tent. A third was washed overboard from his own quarter-deck in mysterious circumstances (my father hinted that only his early death prevented him becoming an admiral). Rajah-like ancestors had won and lost fortunes in India— 'money which we would have had now, my boy, if we hadn't been cheated by a bunch of beggarly solicitors,' said he, referring to a lawsuit over a contested will.

It was always the past, which he saw in a Claude-like glow, and the might-have-beens. These were like a series of express trains to fame and fortune, which he had always just missed through bad luck. It was almost as if there had been a conspiracy in life against him. So even as a lad I fell into the same way of thinking. '*If only* I was a Baronet,' I would muse; everything would be so different and so easy!

This preoccupation with past glories enhanced the depressing contrast of the present—the empty house, the changing servants, the lack of visitors and friends. Once some kind neighbours called at midday to see what they could do, having heard that things were pretty bad up at 'The House' and my mother away. They hastily left when they found my father sodden in his chair! As they passed through the great gates which opened into the park, they caught sight of my brother and me disappearing round the nearest oak. The carriage stopped. The wife, well-meaning, called out to us to return with her. 'Oh, you poor children . . .' she began. The blood rushed to my face. I was overcome by indignation and a furious rage which made me speechless. Scowling, we turned our backs contemptuously, and made off as fast as we could from the hated visitors. They disturbed our privacy; they spied on us; they knew our shameful secrets!

But we were not united, even in our grief and loneliness. We went in different directions, nursing our miseries alone for the rest of the day at opposite ends of the garden! Every member of the family was uncertain of the other; nobody knew from day to day where he stood. This uncertainty about myself and my relationship with others dominates me even now.

The social isolation in which we lived produced periodic crises. Often during the school holidays we stayed with my mother in hotels and with relatives. But always we wanted to be back in our grand and beautiful home, with *him*. We wanted to be free to roam in the park, ride the pony, boat on the lake, and feed the chickens on the farm. Now and then we were promised that these coming holidays we could be at home—as long as he behaved himself and some relation was there.

Everything was satisfactorily arranged. We arrived back from school, overjoyed. But the relative failed to turn up. Instead she sent some message about illness (as an excuse for her loss of nerve). The solicitors got wind of it. A stern letter arrived threatening that unless father could find a substitute we'd have to leave. An air of gloom and uncertainty filled the house. He sent desperate messages to neighbours, begging them to come up at short notice to tea or lunch. Wires were sent to

relatives with pressing invitations to stay. But all knew what
to expect, and often all declined.

On one occasion an elderly spinster was staying, in fulfilment
of the letter of the law. My father had fallen down the highly
polished oak staircase, cracking several ribs. He did not dare
to summon a doctor and go to bed because the man would
perceive that he had been drinking, scold him and probably
sneak to the solicitors. So my poor father endured, as silently
as he could, appalling agony. Only when he let himself down
slowly into the big chair at the head of the dining-room table
did he savagely exclaim 'Damn my ribs!' Dead silence, except
for the spinster's embarrassed cough. The guests who had come
to lunch glared fixedly at their plates. As usual, we tried to
pretend that nothing had happened. But conversation was
frozen, and we fell on our food to relieve the tension.

These ejaculations at the beginning of each meal were too
much for the spinster; she insisted on going after a few days.
She warned the solicitors and her cousin, who was to succeed
her as guest-guardian: my father was not 'behaving himself'.
An ultimatum arrived from the solicitors. Panic-stricken, my
brother and I suggested various local people who could be
asked up to tea in turn. As each refused, our repeated question
'Why can't so-and-so come, sir?' hurt my father's pride and
nettled him; it brought home to him his undignified and helpless
situation. He began to curse and swear, and we to cry in
bewilderment and foreboding.

Finally an old roundabout spinster with red face, white
wispy hair and twinkling eyes, promised to toddle up for tea
to delay the crisis. An extra-special tea was prepared. We waited
impatiently for the ring at the front door bell. When we could
wait no longer, we trooped forlornly in to tea in glum silence.
The little blue flame was burning under the silver kettle, which
sang and puffed merrily. The buttered crumpets and muffins
were warm under their covers; the table was loaded with all
that the cook could devise to tempt us. We sat at the table in
tears, unable to eat, thinking of our threatened departure on
the morrow. This irritated my father who started damning his
bloody relatives, the bloody solicitors, and his bloody ribs.

Then my mother rang up to ask how we were and who was there. 'Don't you want to go?' she asked. I indignantly replied that we'd rather stay with him, and added defiantly that 'Father was all right.' She rang off abruptly, rather hurt.

Alas, she was unable to enlist our sympathy, despite her courage. My father, as the picturesque and generous figure, appealed to our childish imagination as well as dominating it by terror and uncertainty. Nevertheless, our loyalties were sadly divided. During a Sunday afternoon walk round the estate a quarrel flared up between them on the way home. Their paths began to diverge. Miserably, I trailed further and further behind, trying to steer a middle course! My father turned savagely on me, accusing me of 'hedging'. We were never left in peace, but used by our parents as pawns in the struggle between them. My father favoured me, as his eldest son and heir, and pushed me forward; consequently, my mother favoured my younger brother.

He was bigger than I, didn't wear glasses, was a better shot, remembered the names of trees and flowers, had a natural seat on a horse, didn't bother about reading in a family in which I was the only 'bookworm', was a born conformer in country society, and altogether more suited to inherit the estate. He even looked like one of 'the family', with his aquiline nose and proud face!

The most subtle suggestion that I was a misfit and didn't 'belong' came from my mother. She was never tired of telling people that 'she didn't know who I took after and looked like —not any of the family'; my snub-nose and glasses in particular were remarked on. It wasn't of course suggested that I was illegitimate, but these constant remarks had the same effect! There were numerous portraits of uncles, grandfathers and ancestors, and scrap-albums of photos. It seemed to me that all of them had, like my brother and father, that aquiline nose, eagle eye and jutting chin which I lacked and for which I so much wished! Only after I grew up do I recollect strangers remarking how much I resembled our Romney portrait of an ancestor—incidentally one of the most successful members of the family! And old people who knew my father, seeing me again after many years, exclaim how like him I am.

This only goes to show how easily false legends are imbibed, which a life-time of counter-evidence cannot destroy without the help of an assiduous well-wisher from the outside. He alone may finally succeed in bringing home the absurdity of these enslaving legends—legends about the superiority of our own family or of some neighbour or cousin held up to us as an example by a spiteful parent.

The worst conflict of loyalty occurred when my parents literally fought over me. Although I was only about six, my father proposed to take me to London to see some boxing match. This was part of the toughening process favoured by that generation of empire-builders. The training included (from our earliest years) cold baths, dumb-bells, riding bare-back, boxing and sword-drill with naked cavalry swords.

My mother thought that seeing the boxing-match so young would brutalize me. She barred the way at my bedroom door. They faced each other angrily. Voices were raised, the cursing started. They became locked in struggle; the door split as they swayed and lurched against it. Meanwhile, I remained sitting on the floor doing up my bootlaces, my back to the door! I howled, gripping the long leather laces in each hand. I was divided between my parents, and miserable at being the direct cause of their quarrel. I suppose the servants intervened. At any rate, I never saw that boxing-match—or any other outside my own school!

These youthful scenes were accompanied by all the classic symptoms of psychic disturbance and anxiety—bed-wetting, indigestion, constipation, stealing and outbursts of ferocity, destructiveness and aggression, for which I was heavily punished and disgraced. This was of little importance, since it passed with time. But what never passed is the underlying fear, self-mistrust and anxiety, which still has to find its channels and symptoms!

As a young curate, for example, I was aware of eyes which noted with disapproval all that I did. In the theatre disapproving whispers went round: 'Look at that idle clergy-man', and 'That young clergyman's no good.' I sweated, fingered my dog-collar nervously (it certainly felt like a dog's collar), and wished it off. What a badge of servitude it was! Often I dived into a shop or turned hastily down a side-street to avoid a parishioner, because I anticipated criticism and felt ill-at-ease.

Not only do the patterns of the past remain: its voices are still heard. One Christmastide my sermon was to be about the Wise Men and the Star which announced the tidings of joy. I gave out my text from Matthew's Gospel: 'The star . . . went before them, till it came and stood over where the young child was'. As from a great distance I heard my voice, like the voice of another, explaining 'He was born under an unlucky star'. Something seemed vaguely wrong. So I cleared my throat and began afresh. Like a gramophone record the same phrase came forth willy-nilly, 'He was born under an unlucky star.' The fatal words echoed round the mock-gothic groining of the Victorian church. People in the congregation whispered to one another with heads bent close together and hands to their mouths—'he was born under an unlucky star'. The nave seemed filled with chattering, malicious monkeys, all uttering the same terrible phrase. In fact, I was sweating so much that my glasses were steamed over, so that I could not see what was happening in front of me and below me. I only knew that their chatter echoed through my head with the hollow refrain.

Everything else was driven out, and I could not remember what I had to say next. An overmastering desire to leave the hated place seized me. Luckily the vicar thought that I had been taken ill, and I was allowed to escape unmolested. As I entered the vestry, a voice called after me; pretending not to hear, I hurried to my bicycle propped against the steps outside, and dashed off on it, fully robed.

What did my vicar and parishioners think of me? The worst, of course! But the answer to them came to me in a dream. A solemn Voice announced: 'You can't always judge by the exterior or by the total apparent result. Things can affect you from the outside, or *there are influences from the past dragging you back*'. I awoke with the feeling that I was being sucked back by a quagmire. A solitary, imperious Voice speaking a remembered phrase seldom occurs in my dreams. Always the Voice demands attention and seems to say something of importance. This is the voice which primitive people heed when they examine their dreams for the riddle of life and guidance for the future.

Even in my dreams my father still pursues me. Many years after his death I dreamed that he was approaching me down a long dark corridor. He was dead drunk and being supported by someone. There was nowhere I could hide, and I could turn neither to the right hand nor to the left. I could only retreat endlessly, with him lumbering after. I felt properly trapped.

But he too had been in the same position, retreating from he knew not what—retreating certainly from *his* father and from much else besides. As the Old Testament says: 'visiting the iniquity of the fathers upon the children *unto the third and fourth generation* of them that hate Me.' So a pattern is established in a family and is not easily broken. This sounds like determinism. Christianity claims to be able to liberate from it; but how often does it succeed? Psychologists of several schools, using deep analysis, claim to dissolve these patterns of fear by making them understood and by re-training the individual. At their false claims I laugh. But my laughter rattles in my throat, like a dying man's.

I2

Accused of Theft

by IAN SAINSBURY

I GOT DRUNK on Saturday night, and became involved with a woman of some sort, so I had hardly any money left on Sunday and I had arranged to meet her again. I went over the road to Robertson's digs and borrowed a pound from him. It turned out to be one of the silliest things I ever did.

If it is necessary to produce excuses for being drunk, I had one or two. I was—or had been—an actor, but the necessity for regular meals had driven me, temporarily or permanently, I was not sure which, to being the storekeeper on a building site. The adjustment was proving painful. I was also recuperating from a love-affair of great intensity and more than usual hopelessness, and living in what, from a long and bitter experience of lodging in other people's houses, I have no hesitation in describing as a hell-hole. I can summarize this experience by saying that landladies are like whores; in exchange for a sum of money, usually exorbitant, one gives you a travesty of civilized eating and sleeping, the other a travesty of sexual love. It is widely and erroneously believed of both classes that they have hearts of gold. This particular specimen was deaf, and had the unmusical voice that so often goes with that affliction, together with a tendency to steal any small sums of money I was foolish enough to leave lying about. Her husband was a small ugly man who belched after meals and then said 'Pardon' and put his hand over his mouth. Five nights of the week, the three of us sat in the tiny front room looking at the television, which featured an everlasting snowstorm, until I went, maddened, up to bed to read or out for a walk. On Thursday I went to the pictures and on Saturday I got drunk.

All the same, it was better than selling vacuum cleaners on the knocker, which had been my last job, and better than walking about London wishing I was somewhere else. Spring had started, the pains of love were beginning to subside and I had actually succeeded in putting two pounds into the post office. Boredom had superseded agony, and when they told me about the missing money, I was if anything rather excited; when they asked me, in the usual polite, menacing periphrasis, 'if I knew anything about it? Was I quite sure?' of course I said no, and when they rather pointedly telephoned the police in my hearing, I almost laughed. It was something to alleviate the monotony.

I knew at once that I would be a logical suspect. A pay packet containing about ten pounds was missing from the timekeeper's office, and I was the only person, apart from the timekeeper himself, who had been alone in the room on the day it had gone. I did my storekeeping in a gloomy little hut isolated from the main office block, and rather than spend my meals alone among the pickaxes and tarbrushes, I would eat with the timekeeper. He was a ruddy, irascible little man who had joined up during the 1914 war at a very early age, obtained a commission, and after the Armistice had gone into the Royal Irish Constabulary, for want of other employment. He took a poor view of English methods of subduing Irish rebellion, and resigned after some unpleasantness about a prisoner who had been shot while trying to escape; at least, so it was said, but he refused to corroborate the story. I am an Irishman, so we got on rather well. He had lived a varied life, and though without formal education, was shrewd and independent in his thinking. He also accommodated me with frequent 'subs' or advances on my wages. These, while quite legitimate, are as a rule, granted rather grudgingly. I did not connect them with the missing money.

To be suspected and innocent gave me a sort of furtive, masturbatory pleasure. *I* was the only person—apart from the thief—who knew I had not taken the money; it was like lying warm in bed with the rain rattling on the windows; the proximity of the cold and wet only made the warmth more delicious. I wallowed in this rather febrile emotion until the police arrived.

They wore belted gaberdine raincoats. One was plump and smiling, the other tall and thin with a mouth like a letter-box. The plump one, who was a sergeant, did most of the talking at first, going over the familiar ground while I smoked a cigarette. I agreed that I had been the only person alone in the time office, and that I was the obvious suspect. The packet had been there before lunch, I had been there at lunchtime, after lunch the packet had gone. The plump man said,

'You can't tell us anything more than that?'

'I'm afraid not.'

'And you know nothing about this missing money?'

'Nothing at all.'

'I'd like to ask you just one more question. Mr Sainsbury, did you steal that pay packet?'

'No—I—did—not.'

'You're quite sure?'

Imbecile question, I thought.

'Of course I'm sure,' I said.

'Well, now I'm going to tell you something. We think you did.'

I rocked on my heels a little at this. *I* knew I hadn't. How could anyone think that I had? I said:

'You have no grounds for saying that.'

'No? Who else could have done it then?'

'I don't know. The only possible person—and though I don't believe for a moment that he would—couldn't the timekeeper himself have done it? On circumstantial grounds I mean, which is all you have against me, it's quite feasible.'

'Don't worry, we thought of that. But he was the person who found that the money was missing, and the first thing he did was offer to replace it out of his own pocket.'

Suddenly the thin one with the letter-box lips spoke. His eyes glowed in his lined face like hot coals.

'You been in trouble with the police before?'

'No.'

'Quite sure?'

178

I was getting tired of being asked if I was quite sure so I said icily,

'Yes I am.'

'Funny, that.' Sergeant Plump came back into the act. 'I thought I read your name in a report the other day. Sainsbury. Do you spell it with a T?'

'Without.'

'Ah. That's the way this bloke spelt it.'

'If you think I'm known to the police elsewhere, I expect you have your own ways of finding out.'

'Oh yes,' said Plump, 'we have. But it'd be much simpler if you told us. Save us a lot of trouble. And if you save us trouble, we'll see what we can do for you. It upsets me you know, to see an educated young fellow like you in trouble. My advice to you would be to admit to taking this money, and you'll find the magistrates know how to be merciful. First offence. Probably put you on probation.'

'Thank you. But I don't need anyone's mercy. I didn't take the money.' I spoke calmly, but I was beginning to be frightened. This wasn't Act Two, in which the hero is wrongly accused (only to be vindicated in Act Three), this was sheer nightmare. Plump spoke again.

'You're an educated man, Mr Sainsbury. I can see that. What's a man of your type doing in a job like this, a rough job? You've been in some sort of trouble, haven't you? That's right, isn't it?'

'I'm an actor,' I said wearily, 'If you know anything about the stage, you'll know that actors often spend a long time between jobs. I got fed up with being idle, so I came down here.'

'How much did you earn as an actor?' Letter-Box Lips put in his tuppenceworth.

'Twelve pounds a week in my last job.'

'Not a very successful actor, was you?'

'What the hell has that got to do with it?'

I was stung by this irrelevant insult. Plump came blandly in again; I wondered if he and Letter-Box rehearsed together in the privacy of the police station. He said:

'I think I know why you stole this money.'

'I didn't—' I said. The sergeant raised a flat hand.

'You was out of work, so you came to work here as a storekeeper. Earned enough to keep you, but not enough for much in the way of entertainment. You needed a bit of extra money, met a young lady perhaps, wanted to buy her a present. That's right, isn't it?'

It was partly right, so I said nothing. Plump went on.

'You borrowed a pound from Mr Robertson the other day, didn't you?'

He said it kindly, without menace. He made his accusations always with the air of one man of the world speaking to another. He knew; he understood; tell me all about it, Mr Sainsbury, I sympathize. You could see him drinking a pint in the police club, gurgling over a dirty joke, enjoying a prostitute as the price of not booking her. He would wag a fat finger at her and call her a naughty girl, but he was paid to arrest her and if he was going to risk his job he wanted something to make the risk worth while. . . . He was a model citizen; the man who sinned circumspectly, and exacted tribute from those who sinned carelessly.

I admitted borrowing a pound from Robertson.

'All right then, how much have you got on you now?'

I took out my wallet, and by now thoroughly flustered, counted my money without taking the notes out. Later, I found I had counted wrongly and had a pound less than I thought. It didn't matter. Plump calculated that after paying my landlady and giving Robertson his pound, I should have had a lot less.

'You see what we're up against, don't you? I can't understand why an intelligent man like you should get into a mess like this, I really can't.'

'If you think I'm really intelligent, you should realize if I was going to pinch money I wouldn't do it in such a stupid way.'

'Ah, but intelligent men do stupid things sometimes. I've seen people, moneyed people, up for stealing something that cost only a shilling or two.'

We seemed to have reached stalemate. I lit a cigarette, and Letter-Box's voice cut across the silence.

'Living a bit beyond your means, aren't you?'

'What do you mean?'

'You smoke heavy I see.'

He seemed outraged and contemptuous. Not for him the sergeant's fleshy, saloon-bar tolerance; his eyes glittered with hate, like a minor prophet denouncing the sins of the world.

'And you been drawing your wage in advance ever since you've been here. What did you need the money for?'

'I saw no reason not to have money I had earned. That's not a crime.'

'No sir, it's not a crime, but it shows a very irresponsible attitude towards money in my opinion. Now for instance if you could show me a bank book or a post office book with a substantial balance—a hundred pounds, say—I'd be more disposed to think you were innocent.'

I could not. Till then, I had not realized how important it was to *show* people that you had money, but I had nothing more to show them, nor they me. They thought I was very foolish not to admit the theft, they said, but there was nothing they could do about it. No, they wouldn't want me to admit to something I hadn't done, because then the real culprit would go free. They didn't think there'd be a prosecution, because they had nothing stronger than circumstantial evidence; they couldn't establish my guilt, nor I my innocence. I said I wished they would prosecute, so that the whole thing could be cleared up; they shrugged and said, Well there we were. Then they left, fat and lean, envy and gluttony in a morality play.

I tried to subdue the terrified bird that was fluttering about in the cage of my ribs. Gerry, the van driver who fetched and carried for me, came in. We were not quite friends. He said,

'Who locked the door, then? I bin trying to get in for a half hour.'

'I did.' I said. 'I was being interviewed by two policemen. There's some money missing from the time office, and they seem to think I took it.'

'Eh? That's bad.'

He occupied himself silently in rearranging something on the shelves. The whistle blew for lunch. He seemed glad to go. I ate my sandwiches, wolfing them, seeking comfort from food in my stomach. I began to wonder if I *had* taken the money. Afterwards I went out. Robertson was coming across from the main office with Daneman, the agent. Now why had he told the police about the pound I had borrowed from him? That was something between us two alone, of no concern to the world. He lent me a pound, I gave it back to him, and that should have been the end of it. It had been a private act, but now it was made public. No one except ourselves need ever have known of it, so why did he tell the police? Loyalty to his employers? Or a gratuitous toadying to power and money? I was to find out the answer later. Daneman said, 'I expect you'll understand that after what's happened today you'll have to go.'

'Is it any good,' I said, 'telling you what I've already told the police?'

Daneman shrugged. 'The timekeeper will give you a week's money in lieu of notice,' he said, 'a rail warrant and anything else that's due to you.'

'Look here—'

'The matter is closed I'm afraid.'

'It's not closed as far as I'm concerned. I've been accused—'

I felt my voice rising out of control, like a car engine when the clutch slips. I felt a tightness in my diaphragm. Daneman walked rapidly away, looking sharply at the pile frame to make sure that hadn't been stolen too. I filled my lungs with air, and shouted after him,

'F—— you!'

Nobody could say I was taking it well. Robertson took my arm and led me back into the store. He said quietly,

'I'll be looking after things here until we find someone to take your place. You'd better show me where everything is.'

I looked at him. He was not yet thirty, but his hair was receding and he looked harassed. He was likeable, engaging,

and yet he had told them about the pound. I couldn't understand it. As I showed him round the store, he said,

'Let me give you a piece of advice. When you get another
job, don't sub, even if it means cutting down on entertainment
for a bit.'

Then I went to see the timekeeper. He gave me a week's
wages in lieu of notice, thirty fiftieths of a week's wages in lieu
of holiday pay and a rail warrant to Stockton-on-Tees. Then
he said he felt he was to blame for the whole thing. He should
never have had me in the office, he said, or gone out of it while
I was there. We shook hands. As I climbed the hill that led to
the main road, I met my friend Reg. He was a small, sharp-
tongued Welshman, who, like Sergeant Plump, was half of a
comedy team, his partner being a large blond Yorkshireman
with a broken nose called Ron. He wanted to know where I
was going at this time of the day. I told him where, and why.
He pulled his dirty cap over his eyes and said, looking straight
ahead,

'My word! Ron will be surprised.'

I went back to my digs and told my eructating landlord that
I had received some bad news, and would have to leave
immediately. He surprised me by not asking for a week's rent
in lieu of notice. I caught the next train to London, found
myself a room, and, after a few days, a job. It was in the office
of a factory at Acton; nearly a hundred people sat in a huge
room like an aeroplane hangar, coming and going to the sound
of a dreadful bell. To go anywhere during working hours,
except the lavatory, you had to get a pass and show it to one of
the uniformed commissionaires; they were, surprisingly,
unarmed. It was a revelation to me that people earned their
living by taking pieces of paper out of one drawer and putting
them back in another. I did not find the work absorbing, and
spent long periods lost in my daydreams, which did not endear
me to authority.

I went to see a solicitor to whom my family had recommended me. He wrote to the builders and got a reply from
the company secretary, saying that I had been sacked not on
suspicion of theft, but because I was 'unsuitable,' and ending,

'Our sub-agent, Mr M. L. Robertson, who was present at the time can confirm this.' Poor Robertson! I hope they have given him a directorship by now; he has after all, given them his honour.

The letter was better than nothing; exculpatory but negative, it reminded me of the provincial newspaper editor who, having written 'Half the town council are crooks' and being threatened with litigation if he did not withdraw the remark, wrote in his next issue, 'Half the town council are not crooks.'

To elicit this grudging admission, I had to pay several visits to the solicitor and take time off work to do so. My periodic absences, combined with my tendency to reverie in the firm's time, gave them the idea that they could very well do without me. I left without regret, but when I signed on at the Labour Exchange, I found I could draw no benefit, having been sacked this time for something called 'industrial misconduct'. Like a party to a divorce, I denied misconduct, but it was six months before I got any money. Consequently I had to go on National Assistance, and had rather a thin time for a few weeks. One day I had nothing to eat but a twopenny packet of peppermints (complete with holes in the middle).

I often accuse myself of being naïve and self-centred, but even in those days I was not enough of either to expect life to be fair. 'It's not fair!' is the cry of a child learning that the world is not full of love. I often let myself *feel* that life wasn't fair; when I found that the girl I loved didn't love me, when I was kicked out of the repertory company for being difficult; but then I could see some reason why I had lost my job or my girl. Some deficiency in myself had made me vulnerable. I did, however, believe that life was on the whole *just*, that you didn't lose things you liked unless you had, in some sense, deserved to. Now I could see no reason or justice in my present state.

That I had been the only person alone in the room on the day the money went was mere bad luck, and there is no point in complaining about it. We are creatures of circumstance, and when circumstances are against us, there is nothing to do but take Yeats's advice:

Be secret and take defeat
From any brazen throat . . .
Amid a place of stone
Be secret and exult,
Because of all things known
That is most difficult.

But I do not think that I should be secret about some of the things that happened to me here; some were mere circumstance, but some could have been avoided, and of those that could have been avoided, some are matters of organization, and some go deeper.

On the purely organizational level, I think the behaviour of the two detectives was questionable. They had good grounds for suspicion and were quite entitled to look askance at me, to question me closely so as to confirm or deny those suspicions. What they were not entitled to do was to lay traps for me—however fatuous—nor to wheedle me into a confession by promises of mercy. They were far too interested in finding a scapegoat, and in far too much of a hurry. During the interview I felt as though they were salesmen peddling the Probation Act. I should of course have shut up like a clam and screamed for the nearest solicitor; but I didn't think of that at the time. There has been a good deal of criticism of police methods in the last year or two; if they behave elsewhere as they did here, much of it is justified.

Circumstantial evidence apart, their suspicion was strengthened by my shaky financial position, and by the fact that I had been drawing advances on my salary. This is another organizational matter; some of my misfortune was a result of the practice in the building and engineering trades of keeping employees 'week in hand'. It is a practice that should have stopped long ago.

If you go to work for a building or engineering firm, you will not be paid till the Thursday of your second week. The management recognize, however reluctantly, that in the meantime you must eat, and so allow you to draw an advance not exceeding the amount you have earned on the first Thursday.

Seven days later, you will get your first pay packet from which the advance will have been deducted, so you promptly draw it again, less a pound. This procedure is repeated in the following weeks, your debt being in effect reduced by a pound each time, until the full amount has been repaid. It is a silly system, and the reasons for it are, in the main, sillier still.

A fairly sensible reason is that you are being paid by the hour, and your wages for any week cannot be computed till the beginning of the following week, because it takes two or three days to prepare a payroll of any size. A less creditable reason is that the money provides the employers with a sizeable interest-free loan. Builders and the like are constantly in want of ready money; they put up a structure which costs a million pounds, but they don't get the million until a specified interval has elapsed, and it is reasonably certain that the thing isn't going to fall down. Meanwhile, they must find money to pay men and buy materials for the next structure, so they borrow it from the bank. But if they employ a thousand workers, with an average wage of £10 a week, it is more convenient to borrow from them, especially as the loan only becomes repayable to each man when he leaves. I do not pretend to know which of these theories corresponds more exactly with the truth, but having repaid my original sub, I saw no reason why I should not start another, being convinced that I had earned the money, and that I should be in control of it.

Inefficiency in the police force and inequitable rules are things that can be changed with a little effort. I suffered from them, and I hope they will be. Reorganization is not too difficult; changing human nature is. While I complain against muddle and incompetence, I complain more loudly against the cruelty with which I was treated in this affair, for it was the worst of all cruelties, the kind that, in John Press's fine phrase, 'is slopped out as carelessly as soup'. The most appalling character in the parable of the Good Samaritan is the man who passed by on the other side; he walks in a darkness more terrifying, more impenetrable, than the men who robbed and beat the traveller.

Daneman's attitude to me can be summed up like this: 'This

man is perhaps a thief, perhaps not. We can't be sure, so we'll get rid of him.' Simple, practical and effective; no one need wonder whether justice had been done, for I would be gone, and getting and spending armours the mind against doubt. I had always thought people in authority dense, pompous and obsessed with trivia; I had not realized that they were also as silly as an old woman who automatically sacks a servant when the silver is missing. This is for me the horror of the whole episode: that having incurred suspicion, a human being was swept out of the way as dust under a carpet. Nobody was concerned to see justice done to an individual; nobody said, 'Let's try to prove he did steal, and if we can't, let's give him the benefit of the doubt.' Nobody came to me and said, 'I don't know the ins and outs of this thing, but I don't think you took the money.' All anybody did was to clear their throats and shuffle their feet and look down their noses and advise me to be more careful in future; and ultimately, send me to penury in London.

This is what seems to me universal in my predicament; I had no money, and money is better than virtue. If I had been another sort of person, a man with a house, with something in the bank, of known antecedents, concerned not only to be honest but to appear honest, I might have fared better. But I was not; I was a man from nowhere, 'described as an actor' the papers would have said (is there a more damning phrase?), an educated man doing an uneducated man's job. There must be something wrong with me, or I would not be in that bleak store, and I was, because of all this, more likely to be a thief.

This was not an isolated clash, it was one engagement in a long war of attrition. The opening shots were fired in child-hood, the first skirmishes fought at school. The summons to the headmaster's study after chapel: 'Your refusal to play games seems to me to show a very poor spirit'. My last day at school, the blazing row because I accused him of undermining my position as a prefect: 'How dare you speak to me like that! After all I've done for you!' But this now was a major engage-ment, a full-scale attack; I was out of a job, discredited, demoralized, less, I felt because of what I had done or not done, than because of what I was. Authority is not a series of acts, it is a state of mind, and so is non-acceptance, revolt, the refusal to join the group and wear the correct badges. The penalty of that state of mind is isolation and uncertainty, and now I was uncertain: I knew they were wrong, but that didn't mean that I was right. Now, of course, I can see that I was; my attitude to money, to work is ten times better than Robertson's. What happened that day on the site was not accidental; it was as inevitable as any other battle. If there have been no other battles since, that is because I have not let my flank be turned; it does not mean that there will be no more.

I remember a birthday party at home in Ireland, when I was eight. My host had been given a huge box of chocolates, which was passed round. It was left lying about, and inevitably emptied. The boy's mother turned on me.

'You took them. Greedy little pig!'

'I didn't! I didn't!'

She ran her hands through my pockets, and finding no sweets, said:

'Greedy little beast, you've eaten them all. I hope you're sick.'

I went home in tears, and was comforted by my mother, who said, 'Forget all about it. It doesn't matter now.'

It is four years now since the episode of the pay-packet, and life has been much kinder to me since. If I had ever told this story to anyone, they might well have said, as my mother did, 'Forget about it. It doesn't matter now.'

Up to a point they would be right. It doesn't matter that I was accused of a crime I didn't commit; that was something as fortuitous as the colour of my hair. It doesn't even matter that I suffered a certain amount of undeserved hardship. (It may even have been a blessing in disguise; I might still be in that store). Ultimately it doesn't matter that all this happened to *me*, but it does matter that people behave with stupidity, with a casual, craven indifference worse than deliberate cruelty, with, in Robertson's case, a cowardly disregard of the truth. It matters that they act in utter oblivion of what is due to other people, however shiftless, improvident or eccentric, of whatever sins on whatever grounds suspected.

Be secret and take defeat? No. One of the stock arguments against idealism, against Weltsverbesserungswahn, is that, 'you can't change human nature'. But we must at least try to change it; to do less is to accept the ultimate defeat. The acceptors, the upholders of the *status quo* say that it is foolish to look for much in mankind beyond self-interest and stupidity, that a thousand schemes of improvement have foundered on these rocks. But if the world is in the smallest degree a better place to live in than it used to be, it is because of people who have looked for more than greed and stupidity in themselves and in others, and sometimes, have found it. The privilege of the underdog is to bark; and his barks will be heard.

13

Criminal

by 'JOE'

MY MOTHER is a prostitute. My father I have never known.
I was conceived twenty-five years ago somewhere on Clapham
Common.

My home during childhood was one room in a house in
Somerleyton Road, Brixton. This house is now owned by a
Jamaican brothel keeper who has six of the rooms occupied by
his stable of girls. He once offered employment to my mother.
She answered by giving his face a hard slap. Her verbal reply
was 'I'll never sink that low.'

I went to a local school. It matters not that I fail to name it
here. The often quoted saying that school days are the happiest
days of your life certainly didn't apply in my case. Every
moment was hateful. Most of all I hated the condescending
ways of the teaching staff. They pretended to come down to
my level but all the time gloated over me and my classmates.
We needed their charity but didn't want to accept it.

My mother didn't help much. 'What does it matter if you go
to school in rags?' she said. 'Most of the others are no better.'

As I write this I am what is termed a hardened criminal, but
when I first crossed with the law I was such a soft little creature.
It happened in a Brixton street market and I was twelve years
old. Because of hunger I took an apple from a stall. Only one
apple, I wasn't greedy.

For this felony I was marched to the grim looking Victorian
building which housed the Police Station at the top of Stockwell Road. Two days later at a juvenile Court I was placed
before a heavy oak table and three JPs who were just as heavy
looking. To my small eyes all three of them were full of wind.

I told them the true reason for taking the apple. My frank-
ness was received with hostility. For my 'horrid' behaviour
I was sent away for one year.

When I returned home mother had changed. Before I went
away she never showed any affection for me but now she was
openly hostile. I was a burden to her.

After nine months the Juvenile Court saw me again. This
time I was deemed to be in need of protection as I was exposed to moral danger.

The home I went to was populated by boys of my own age.
During the year I spent there I learnt a great deal. In retrospect
it is plain that it was the wrong stuff to have learnt.

The idol of the home was a boy named Jackie. He was expert
at picking locks, steaming envelopes open and telling lies.
His standard was something to aim for. He was my ideal, my
only ideal. Within six months I was close to Jackie's standard.
When I left to join the Royal Air Force as a boy entrant I had
passed him.

I wasn't particularly interested in joining the service but the
school headmaster thought it was a good thing to do.

My first look at service life was at Locking in Somerset.
I arrived there at four o'clock on Monday afternoon. After
being shown the hut where I was to sleep my guide took me to
the cookhouse for my first service meal. It consisted of sausage,
mashed potatoes and peas. I remember it well.

At 9.30 p.m. out went the lights. That first night was lonely.
During the following six weeks however there was no time to
be lonely. From reveille to lights out our NCO instructors
drove us hard. The whole six weeks were devoted to foot drill
and weapon training. I became skilful at handling a bren gun.

After basic training the thousand boys were separated into
various trade groups. My future trade was that of an armourer
and I was going to Kirkham in Lancashire for eighteen months
trade training.

Sixty of us entrained at Bristol early one morning and ten
hours later alighted at Preston. The local train from there to
Kirkham was swifter than I expected.

We marched from the station to the camp which sits beside

the main Preston to Blackpool road. A long march when one is fifteen years old and wearing full webbing equipment.

We spent a year at Kirkham. Much time was spent on physical training and foot drill. Church parade was compulsory every Sunday.

Our pay was ten shillings a fortnight. By the dictates of our Commanding Officer we were forced to spend most of this on cleaning requisites. A kit inspection was held weekly and webbing equipment was blancoed each day. The wooden huts in which we lived each had two stoves. These stoves were black-leaded daily before we went to our classrooms.

The black lead and many other cleaning materials had to be purchased from our meagre wage. We considered this the accepted practice and were not well enough versed in life to strike up a protest.

Constantly our young minds were bombarded with entreaties to be honest and upright in all our dealings. Yet the same authorities that issued these pleas played many moves against us that were morally if not legally dishonest. I will mention just one.

On a large camp such as Kirkham there were many huts not permanently occupied. Through various causes some of the windows in these huts came to be broken from time to time.

Often the Commanding Officer would order a move around of the boys. We would move into the damaged huts and within a few days they would be repaired by maintenance staff. A few days after this a senior NCO would tour the huts with a nominal roll of the inhabitants. From each boy he would demand a sum of money; usually half a crown to pay the repair bill. It wasn't any good protesting that the windows were broken before we moved in. I tried it once. For a month after I refused to hand over my money I was given cookhouse fatigue duties every weekday evening. At the end of the month the fatigues ceased and I thought I had won. I was bitterly disappointed and angry when at the end of the quarter I examined my pay ledger and found an entry in the debit column 'Barrack damage', 2s. 6d. To have protested would have meant more unpleasant fatigues. I remained silent but I did not forget.

Whilst at Kirkham we had little free time. However, whenever I could I put on my best uniform and went out of camp. My favourite walk was along the ash path leading from the camp down to the village. Then past the Swan public house, up the hill and through the cobbled square to the fields beyond the parish church. I spent many hours walking through the fields. When weather allowed I lay amid thick grass and went to sleep. Sometimes I sat up and watched the trains go by, each one carrying holiday makers to Blackpool's beaches and shell fish stalls.

It was on one of these walks that I met Eileen, the only female for whom I have ever felt any regard. She was seventeen when we first met. I find it impossible to explain why she attracted me. Of one thing I am sure, our friendship soared far above mere physical attraction.

We had little time together because two months after our meeting all the boys were moved to a station near Wolverhampton.

Our friendship could not survive at a distance. Two weeks after saying a temporary farewell Eileen sent a goodbye letter. Perhaps that was the best way. I still remember her as a girl of seventeen and she probably sees me as still a youth.

My stay at the new camp was all too short.

Every Wednesday afternoon all the boys were sent out on a five mile cross country run. On one of these runs I gained new strength from somewhere and reached home with the leaders.

I had a shower bath and went into my hut to change into uniform. I was alone in the hut less than five minutes. Then in came other runners, amazed to see me back so soon.

After tea I was told by one of the boy NCOs, Sergeant Boy Peters to report to the Commanding Officer's office at six thirty that evening. Strange, I thought, the old man doesn't usually work after five. 'What's it about?' I asked. 'You should know,' replied Peters.

Exactly at six thirty I stood before the Commanding Officer. His Adjutant stood behind him. After I had saluted he said,

'Stand at ease, I won't take long over this.' Then he explained why he had sent for me.

I had not been the first to enter my hut after the cross country run. A boy named Horsley had beaten me by about two minutes. He had looked into his wallet before rushing into another hut to see a friend. In his wallet was a letter that had come from his mother earlier in the day. With the letter was a pound note.

When Horsley returned to the hut he found the letter and cash missing, He went immediately to Sergeant Boy Peters. Together they began a search of the hut.

My bed was the first they came to. Peters pulled apart my blanket roll and from it fluttered the envelope with the cash still in it.

When the officer ceased talking I began to protest my innocence. However it was plain that he wasn't paying attention. Then my eyes focused upon the folder on his desk. 'Is that my personal record file, sir?' I asked. 'Yes,' he replied. 'This shows that you have been caught stealing before. I propose to recommend to the Air Ministry that you be discharged. We don't want your type in the service.' 'But, sir,' I protested. 'I didn't take the money.' 'Once a thief always a thief,' he snapped back sharply. 'You may go now but you are confined to camp. You will report to the guardroom every two hours.'

After marching out of the office I was still in a daze. I didn't consider that a conviction for which I had been punished should be held against me.

The Air Ministry replied swiftly to the Commanding Officer's recommendation. Within ten days I was discharged. The official papers stated that my services were no longer required.

Seventeen years old and kicked out of the Air Force. I had a single ticket to London and a few pounds that had stood to my credit in the pay account. I was allowed to travel home in an old uniform for I hadn't any civilian clothing.

It was a Friday evening and Paddington station was thronged with travellers. The tube train to Stockwell was cramped. I walked from Stockwell to my mother's home in Somerleyton Road, Brixton. I hadn't seen her since joining the Air Force. What was the point? She didn't particularly wish to see me.

The second door on the left led to her room. The paint had peeled long ago and the door was ajar. I pushed it wide open. A double bed occupied one corner of the room. The wooden bed frame had been polished at one time. A rickety kitchen cabinet stood by the solitary window. A door of the cabinet was open exposing to view a slice of mouldy bread. Before an ash chocked fireplace stood a paraffin heater. In an easy chair beside the heater reclined a woman. She had once been beautiful. The whole squalid scene was lit by a spluttering candle which was lodged on the mantlepiece.

Mother turned in the easy chair. Her eyes stared for a few seconds. Then she spoke. 'Oh, it's you. What are you doing here? What do you want?'

Seated on the edge of the bed I explained at length what had happened. She let me finish, then in a shrill voice said, 'That was a bleeding stupid thing to do. Why didn't you pick a better hiding place?' 'But mum,' I protested. 'I didn't take the money.' 'Pah, you make me sick,' she snapped. 'Get out of my sight.' As I turned and said goodbye the spluttering candle died and the room was in darkness.

I spent the night at the Union Jack Service Club at Waterloo. Next morning I returned to Brixton and got rid of the service uniform. At a second hand clothes shop it was exchanged for a complete set of civilian clothing. Once more dressed decently I wandered through Brixton Market. A café behind Wool-worths was my first call. As I entered many people stared and appeared to be sizing me up. It was plain that I was completely out of place. Later I learnt that they suspected that I was a new detective who was looking the place over.

After satisfying my hunger I decided to explore Brixton and see what had changed since my boyhood. From the café I crossed Coldharbour Lane and into Electric Avenue. Lying in the gutter was a ten-shilling note all dirty and crumpled. I picked it up and looked about to see if anyone had lost it. As no one appeared concerned I pocketed the note.

Before I was clear of the Avenue a hand grasped my sleeve and its smartly dressed owner said, 'I am a Police officer. Have you just picked up a ten-shilling note?' 'Yes,' I replied. 'What are you going to do with it?' he asked. 'Spend it of course,' I replied. 'Findings keepings,' I said boldly. The conversation continued until I found myself at Brixton Police Station charged with stealing by finding.

Over the weekend I was kept in custody. At ten on Monday morning I was taken to Court in a Police van. I well remember my first appearance at this particular Magistrate's Court.

My case was number twelve on the list. While waiting to be called I had to sit with all the male prisoners in a room connected to the Court by a narrow passage. People continually left the room until I was alone but for three others. These three talked quietly among themselves. They were on a charge of housebreaking. By what little I could hear it was plain that they intended to deny ever having been near the house in question.

My name was called out by the gaoler and I followed him into Court. He ushered me into the dock and I faced the Magistrate. Only twenty feet separated us.

A very fat man sitting between the Magistrate and myself asked 'Do you wish to be tried by this Court or by a Judge and jury at the County of London Sessions? Before you answer I must tell you that if you consent to be tried by this Court and are found guilty of this offence then the learned Magistrate will have power to commit you to the Sessions for sentence if he considers his powers of punishment are not great enough after hearing all about your character.' Then almost in the same breath, 'Do you wish to be tried by this Court or by a Judge and jury?' I replied 'This Court.' 'Do you plead guilty or not guilty?' 'Guilty.'

'Facts please,' said the clerk to the police officer who stood in the witness box.

From his gleaming leather brief case the officer withdrew a sheaf of papers. Reading from these he gave an account of my felony.

The Magistrate leant back in his chair and closed his eyes.

Perhaps he had heard so very many cases and was bored to sleepiness.

When the officer ceased talking the Magistrate woke up. He asked 'Is there anything you want to say about this?' I stammered 'No.' 'Very well then. I will discharge you conditionally for twelve months. If you behave yourself for the next year you will hear no more of this.'

I was back in Brixton within an hour of leaving the Court. Looking back upon that day I see that if I hadn't followed the advice of the police officer and pleaded guilty I might never have started a life of crime. However, that is now merely wishful thinking.

Within the hour I was back in the small café behind Woolworths stores. This time no one stared at me. The proprietor while serving me said, 'You didn't get bird then?' 'No, how did you know about it?' He smiled and said, 'There isn't much happens in Brixton that I don't know about boy.' He left me to carry on eating.

I had almost finished when a dark overcoated figure sat opposite me. 'Hello, Joe,' he said with a smile, 'I saw you at Court today. You were lucky to get discharged. That beak usually gives out plenty of bird. He's given me plenty in the past.'

'I've finished with that,' I said firmly. 'What a hope you've got boy,' he laughed. 'Now you're down you stay down.' 'I shall get a job tomorrow,' I protested. 'Don't waste your time looking,' he said. 'If after exhausting yourself looking for work you're still interested in making a spot of cash come and see me. My name's Max.' He handed me a printed card on which was an address in the SW2 postal district. 'What's the job?' I asked. 'Come and see me next Friday and I will tell you. If you want somewhere to sleep tonight go to 34 Atlantic Street and ask for Mrs Moon. Tell her I sent you.' He then stood up and left the café.

I looked again at the card. On the back was scribbled the address of Mrs Moon. I went to see her.

A knock on the front door of the terraced house didn't bring any answer. The door which was ajar moved easily to my touch. I pushed it wide open. A shout of 'Anybody in' brought a muffled 'I'm coming' from a room at the rear. A few seconds later along the passage walked the thinnest woman I have ever seen. She wore a faded cotton dress which made her appear taller than her five feet. Her greying hair hung down each side of her oval face.

She took me to a small room at the rear of the house. There was a gas stove in one corner so I presumed this to be the kitchen. She poured out a cup of weak tea and whilst drinking it I told her of my troubles.

'You can stay here until you can settle what you want to do. I don't want a penny from you until you start earning.' She escorted me up the stairs to a room on the second floor at the front of the house. It was large and in the shape of an L. There were six beds. The beds looked familiar and when I examined them closely I found them to be ex-Royal Air Force beds.

Pointing to a bed in a corner she said, 'You can use that one. You can come and go as you please. The front door is never locked.' With that she went down the stairs and I sat on my bed.

Half an hour later there sounded footsteps on the stairs. Two small figures entered the room. One wore a black belted raincoat that hugged his figure and the other wore a pair of blue jeans and a vivid yellow sweater.

The coated figure spoke: 'My name's Alfie.' Pointing to his companion he said, 'This is Tony. You must be Joe. Max has told us all about you.' 'This Max seems to know a lot of people,' I said. 'He has to,' replied Alfie. 'If he didn't he would soon be out of business.' 'What is his business?' I asked. 'If Max hasn't told you then I'm not going to,' answered Alfie. 'He will tell you in his own good time.' With that we dropped the subject of Max. We talked about ourselves.

Alfie was twenty years old and prided himself upon being an expert car thief. 'There isn't a car door in London that I couldn't open,' he boasted. Tony was eighteen. His parents had kicked him out of home and two days later he teamed up with Alfie.

In Tony Alfie had a great admirer. 'We've had five cars away this week and the busies haven't even smelt us,' boasted Tony. 'Max will be pleased.' 'Shut up,' snapped Alfie. 'Don't tell him too much until Max gives the all clear.'

The conversation continued about Alfie's skill for a few more moments then it turned to me and my plans for the future. When I said that I proposed looking for work the following morning Alfie said, 'You're not serious. You will never get a job.' 'Why not?' I asked. 'Because you've been convicted, that's why. Once caught you can never get a decent job.' 'Well, I'm going to try,' I said defiantly. 'Go ahead,' said Alfie. 'You'll only wear yourself out trying.'

The pair then went out and Alfie's parting words were, 'I'll be seeing you.'

I lay down and went to sleep. During the night Alfie and Tony came in. They talked quietly but excitingly of a job well done. Max had wanted cigarettes and the pair had obliged him by stealing a whole lorry load for him.

They wouldn't go into detail so I went back to sleep.

When I rose the pair were sleeping soundly. In one corner of the room was a huge carton of 'Players' cigarettes. Part of the night's work, I thought.

After a clean up I walked to the employment exchange. Being a Tuesday morning the waiting hall was deserted. I had no trouble in finding a clerk to answer my enquiry, although when I fully explained my position to him he didn't hold out much hope for me. He did however give me a list of some twenty firms in the Brixton area who required general hands.

My first call was at a light engineering firm in Coldharbour Lane. As soon as I gave my name the foreman asked me to wait and he entered a glass panelled office. He picked up a telephone and I could see his lips moving as he spoke into the mouthpiece.

When he had finished he put down the receiver into the cradle and came back to me. 'Sorry, the boss says no vacancies.' 'But,' I protested, 'according to the employment exchange you have several vacancies.' 'Well we have, but not for you. You see the boss has read the local paper and learnt about the case you were involved in. Sorry but he's the chief.'

And so it was at every place I applied. Either the boss had read the local paper or had spoken to someone who had. Either way it meant no job for me.

I returned to Mrs Moon's house in despair but vowed to continue my search the following day. My supper was a cup of tea. My tiredness overcame hunger and I slept soundly.

The following days proved a repetition of the first. As each day passed I grew more hungry. Thursday evening I lay exhausted upon the bed.

Alfie and Tony came in flush with cash. 'Max just paid us for the cigarettes,' said Tony. 'What's wrong with you?' asked Alfie. He must have seen my pale face. 'I can't get a job,' I answered. 'That's nothing to worry about,' he said. 'I haven't had a job since I was sixteen. So what?'

'Come out and have some food on us.' I agreed and we left the house. As we left we met Mrs Moon coming in. 'Here you are, lady,' said Alfie. 'Have these.' And he thrust into her hands a roll of pound notes. She mumbled 'Thanks Alfie,' and hurried past us into her kitchen.

We walked through the side street into Brixton Road. Alfie suggested, 'Let's go to Victoria. I'm fed up with Brixton.' He hailed a passing cab and we clambered in. 'To Victoria, cabbie,' commanded Alfie.

Once at our destination we entered a good class restaurant and ate in style. I felt no remorse as I ate the delicious food. The money that was going to pay for it had been acquired dishonestly but I wasn't greatly perturbed. When one is hungry the source of the money to buy food does not matter. After a hearty meal we returned to Brixton by cab.

Friday, the next day was spent seeking work. At every application I was given a cold reception. After trying sixteen places I was wild. I checked the address on the card in my pocket and went to see Max.

'Glad to see you boy,' he said. He listened patiently while I told him of my repeated efforts to find a job. He smiled. 'Don't worry. I can keep you staked if you want to do some jobs for me. You'll break the law but what does that matter when you are hungry?'

'I don't like doing it Max but I see no alternative. I can't get honest work so this looks the only way.'

'Right,' said Max. 'Alfie has a job laid on for tonight. Meet him and Tony outside the Town Hall at eleven. Let Alfie guide you. He's a good boy.'

Max slipped five pound notes into my pocket and then showed me out.

At eleven exactly I arrived at the appointed meeting place. Both Alfie and Tony were waiting. We walked to Stockwell and took a bus ride to Battersea.

When we alighted Alfie led the way and I soon lost my sense of direction. After about five minutes of this fast walking we halted in front of a pair of huge wooden gates. Alfie pulled a short jemmy from beneath his raincoat. With this he quickly snapped the padlock from the gates and pushed them open. The gates opened on to a yard belonging to a large warehouse. Another thrust and twist of the jemmy and the warehouse doors slid open upon their runners.

Two lorries stood in the warehouse. Alfie entered the driving cab of one and Tony took the other. They drove the vehicles into the yard and I closed the warehouse doors. The lorries then moved into the street and I gently closed the gates. When they were closed I snapped on them a padlock similar to the one Alfie had broken off. If any patrolling policeman examined the gate he would find it firmly fastened. I worked quickly and was soon in the cab of the first lorry driven by Alfie.

On we sped through darkened streets until we reached Battersea Park Road. Here we turned into Queenstown Road, round the roundabout and over Chelsea Bridge.

Once over the river I was on unfamilar ground. After twenty minutes driving we turned into a narrow street. The lorries were parked nose to tail and we alighted.

'Beat it,' hissed Alfie to Tony. 'See you tomorrow for the shareout.' He grabbed my sleeve and said, 'You're new to this game so stay with me.'

We walked quickly away from the scene and turned into a well-lit road. Ten minutes more walking then into another side street. Alfie began trying the handles of cars parked in the street and eventually found one that was unlocked. 'What are you doing?' I asked. 'You don't want to walk back to Brixton do you? Get in and let's get going.'

We hardly spoke during the return journey. Alfie was intent on his driving and I had my thoughts. It was only as we neared the Town Hall that I spoke. 'What was in the lorries Alfie?' 'Just fags and whisky,' he replied. 'What's the idea of leaving them in the street?' I asked. 'Don't worry Joe. They won't be there more than half an hour. As soon as the scene was clear a couple of boys working for the receiver would drive the lorries away.' 'Who is the receiver Alfie?' 'Only Max knows that and he keeps it to himself.' 'What does Max do then?' I asked. 'He's the brains boy. He finds out where the stuff is and passes the information along to us. We go and lift it, take it to the receiver's boys and Max pays out later.'

The car stopped outside the Town Hall and I alighted. Alfie drove away the car to abandon it away from our living space. Once in the sanctuary of the house I flopped on my bed. My hands and face were wet with perspiration. Fear I guess. This was the first time I had committed a serious crime and I felt utterly dejected.

Alfie seemed a long time returning. Had he been caught with the car? Was he already on his way to the police station?

A sound upon the stair and a 'Good night, Mrs Moon' calmed my fear. Alfie sounded as cheerful as ever. 'Where have you been?' I asked. 'It stalled on Brixton Hill and I nearly had a busy offering to give me some help. I soon gave him the slip.'

The following day at noon we met Max. He gave us each £50 in notes. I didn't want to take my share but was finally persuaded by Alfie's caustic comment.

After the hand-out we parted company for a time. I went into the nearby reading-room of the public library to sit and think over the events of the past few hours.

My coat pockets felt snug with the notes lining them. The room was crowded and it was with difficulty that I found a seat. Most of the occupants wore dejected looks. They scanned the newspapers with obvious disinterest. To most of them the room was just a comfortable place in which to while away their time. The weather dictated the volume of visitors to this reading-room.

Except for an occasional cough and rustling of paper the room was silent. My mind was able to gather thoughts.

I hadn't in my heart wanted to join the raid on that warehouse but now that I was committed to this way of earning money I decided to make the best of it.

Fifty pounds felt snug in my pocket but I remembered Alfie saying that the loads of the lorries were worth £2,000. Three of us only received a paring of the full value. As we had taken most of the risk fifty pounds seemed poor reward. I decided to tackle Max on the subject when next we met.

Max sounded annoyed when I raised the matter next day. However he promised to remedy things on the next job. The next haul I could do on my own and take half. This seemed fair so I agreed. I listened eagerly to his outline of the plan.

A Saturday night and I was on my way to Clapham to do my first job alone. Max told me that he had arranged for a large amount of cash to be left in unlocked drawers of a certain office.

The way to the rear of the building was via a narrow alley along which only one person could pass at a time.

The drain pipe at the rear of the office was secure. I had no difficulty climbing to the first-floor window which Max said would be open. It proved to be closed but unlocked and opened easily. I squeezed through the opening and landed with a slight thud upon the office floor.

A large desk occupied the centre of the room. Only one drawer was unlocked but this one was crammed with bank notes of various denominations. Quickly I filled my pockets.

Through the window again and swiftly down the pipe. As I emerged from the alley on to the roadway a horde of uniformed figures descended upon me. Less than twenty minutes later I was at the police station. I thought Max's planning had slipped badly this time.

While on remand in prison awaiting trial I learnt that Max hadn't slipped at all. In fact, everything had worked out as he had hoped.

Through long talks with other fellows on remand I learned that Max didn't like sharing too much of his spoil with other people. If anyone tried to get more than he wished to give them he squeaked to the police. Then when busily engaged upon their next job the men who had asked for more would be pounced upon by police. That's what had happened to me.

I was told that wise men kept clear of Max. I wondered how Alfie and Tony kept on his right side. Perhaps they were content to work for almost nothing.

I vowed to get even with Max as soon as possible. Because of his double-cross I was sent to Borstal Training. This training gives young men instruction in various trades but from what I have seen there is little point in doing so. It is impossible to make full use of any such training when one returns to the outside world. No one will employ an ex-Borstal Boy.

The most useful part of the training is obtained after the official hours of instruction. After tea each evening the bright boys of the school gathered in the recreation room and gave lessons to anyone who wished to take advantage of their experience.

At Borstal I learned to pick a lock, force a window without splintering the woodwork and in theory learned how to blow a safe with plastic explosive.

Three months after my entry to Borstal news of Max seeped through. He wouldn't be in Brixton when I was released. He had forgotten a fellow he double-crossed two years before. This man who shall be nameless here had been released from prison on a Wednesday and by Saturday had learnt of a plan by Max. A lorry load of stolen whisky was to be left on Max's premises. Half an hour after it had been delivered police raided the place and arrested him. Max tried to bribe the police and that's what helped to make his total sentence five years imprisonment. I decided to forget my vow of revenge. He would have ample time to reflect upon his folly.

On my twentieth birthday I was released from Borstal. When I reached Brixton my first call was on Mrs Moon. She still had her spare beds and she welcomed me.

After a few days of getting used to freedom I had to set to and start earning my bread once again. Alfie was in prison and would remain there for years. He had been foolish one night when stopped in a 'borrowed' car by a constable. He violently attacked the policeman and caused him grave injury. The Judge at the Old Bailey did not show Alfie any mercy.

Tony was completely lost without Alfie. Since my Borstal training I had matured and so took Tony as a partner. We agreed that we would never use violence to anyone. I was committed to a life of crime but did not want violence of any kind. We were after cash not blood.

The first job Tony and I did as partners was a trick known as the till gag. I first heard of it at Borstal.

A Friday was chosen as till day. The victim was to be the owner of a grocer's shop on the Battersea–Clapham border.

First thing we did was to 'borrow' two bicycles and this proved easy. We then parted company.

I rode up to the shop shortly after nine a.m., parked the cycle at the kerb and entered the shop. The proprietor looked up and asked 'What can I get you?' I asked, 'Can you tell me the way to Chelsea?' The woman, aged about forty-five, started to give me detailed instructions but I pretended not to understand. I played my part well for she exclaimed impatiently 'Come outside and I will point the way.'

We left the shop and stood on the pavement near my cycle while she again explained the route to Chelsea. She had left the shop door open. While I held her attention Tony walked into the shop unseen. He quickly emptied the till. He then left the shop and cycled off without the woman being aware of anything unusual.

When I saw that Tony was clear I began to understand the woman's directions. After a few moments I gave her a sincere 'Thank you' and cycled off towards Chelsea.

Later in the day I rejoined Tony and shared the thirty-five pounds from the till. 'The busies will never catch us for this one,' proclaimed Tony. He was right. Our first venture into business together had been a success.

Through information from friends I learned that the manager

of a certain large grocer's shop in Battersea always locked the store himself at six thirty each evening. The building had good locks and heavily barred windows. Breaking in by the conventional method would be too noisy. Therefore a more subtle approach was needed.

On Tuesday evening as the manager was locking the front door of his shop a small motor van was standing in the roadway. His keys jingled and I approached him. I said, 'My mate has locked all his tools in his box and left the keys on a building site in Chelsea. He needs these tools on a site in Croydon tomorrow. Do you think we could try to open the box with your keys?' The manager was co-operative and after completing the locking of his shop he walked over to the van inside which Tony crouched beside a tool box. The box was fitted with a most impressive looking lock. I held the attention of the manager while Tony quickly took wax impressions of the keys under the pretext of trying them in the lock of the toolbox. After three minutes the keys were handed back. Tony said, 'None of these will fit. I'll have to force the lock.' The obliging manager expressed regrets and drove away in his own car.

It took us two days to get a complete set of keys made from the detail given in the impressions.

Three months later on a Saturday morning just before dawn we unlocked the gates to the yard at the shop's rear and drove in our lorry. Every lock in the shop opened to our bidding. We worked quickly and methodically, locking each room as we emptied it.

We had studied the area well and knew there was little chance of being disturbed. The police constable on this beat was a regular chap. He tried the shop doors at eleven pm and five am each day. His routine never varied.

Half an hour after entering we were ready to depart. It seemed our lucky night for the manager had been careless and had left £150 in notes in his desk. Tony drove the lorry away to our receiver and I locked the outer gate to the shop. I then moved quietly away to Brixton.

I only had one regret about the night's work. I would dearly have loved to have seen the manager's face when he found his entire stock missing and not a window in the place broken.

The police were baffled about the whole thing.

Our appetite whetted by success we decided to continue our partnership and look for bigger and better jobs.

We took great care to avoid letting success go to our heads. No ostentation was our rule. Many thieves are caught because of their eagerness to show their full wallets to the world.

Despite the outstanding success of the store raid I was not satisfied with our method of working. Great risks were involved when a third person was introduced into a deal. Having a receiver was risky. Tony and I therefore decided to aim only for ready cash.

By channels known only to a few people we began to look for work. Two days passed before we found our target.

We learned that each Thursday morning at ten a hired car drove the cashier of a South London engineering firm to a bank half a mile away. He would spend twenty minutes in the bank and emerge with a small suitcase grasped tightly in one hand. The car would then carry him back to the factory.

The car was always hired from the same firm and always it was driven by the same chauffeur. The cashier and chauffeur were good friends and upon their return to the factory would chat for several minutes. The car would then be driven off leaving the cashier standing on the pavement waving goodbye. Once the car was out of sight he would walk quickly up the eight steps into the factory.

We observed this routine for six weeks and had timed every yard of the journey. We decided to strike on the seventh week. As the factory stood in a quiet by-road it was planned to take the cash from right outside the door. Tony was to drive the escape car and I was to grab the suitcase containing the money.

On the morning of the operation I was outside the factory in time to see the hired car take on board the cashier. As the car threaded a way through the traffic it was closely followed by Tony driving a 'borrowed' taxi cab.

With the cash on board the car returned to the factory.

Outside the offices the cashier and chauffeur had their usual chat. Their conversation over, the cashier stepped on to the pavement with the suitcase. The hired car drove off. Once it was out of view the cashier turned towards his office. As he did so I pushed him over and grabbed the case. He staggered and seemed to be in a daze.

Meanwhile Tony had been kerb crawling in his cab. As I ran towards him he revved the engine. I opened the cab door, clambered in and lay on the floor with the case. Once out of view of our victim I left the floor and took my seat as a normal passenger.

At Waterloo Station I paid off the cabbie and went to the left luggage office. I deposited the locked case and placed the receipt in an envelope addressed to Tony. I sealed the envelope and posted it in the nearest box.

After dropping me at Waterloo Tony drove the cab back to the place in South Lambeth from where he had borrowed it. The owner only worked at night so he would still be in bed. His cab was regularly parked on a piece of disused land a short distance from his home. Tony left the vehicle in the same position from which he had removed it and then travelled to Brixton by bus.

Fortune smiled upon us. The cashier was too bewildered to have noticed the cab at all. The owner of the cab was so careless about his records that he never noticed the extra miles recorded on his speedometer.

The police worked hard on the case. Every big time thief in South London was questioned. No one questioned Tony and myself. Perhaps we were considered incapable of such daring.

A fortnight later Tony went to Waterloo and retrieved the case and contents. He brought it back to Brixton in a cab. One legally hired.

We had no difficulty in forcing the locks. Inside in neat rows lay £7,000 in bank notes. At the bottom lay a blue cloth bag containing £50 in large silver. Mrs Moon was well rewarded that evening.

For nine months we remained inactive. Our pockets were full and life was enjoyable. Then one day in Brixton I met

Peter. He was a pal from my schooldays. At school I was very shy and made few friends. Peter was one of the few.

He certainly had troubles. After listening to his story I silently vowed to help him. My method of helping would be outside the law so I could not tell him about my plan. But first let me relate what he told me.

Up to two weeks before our meeting Peter had been living with his wife and baby daughter at his father's home in Camberwell. Then one day without warning his father told them to leave the house. He would not listen to any pleas.

For two days the family wandered about Camberwell and Brixton seeking accommodation. Eventually they found a room at a high rental in Acre Lane.

Peter's father was a tyrant and a rich one at that. He didn't trust banks and kept his money at home. Peter let slip the location of one of the cash boxes. I decided there and then to right a wrong. I didn't like to see people trodden upon.

I managed to sneak Peter's front door key which, in his hurry to throw them out, his father had forgotten to ask for.

Knowing that the house would be unoccupied the next afternoon I went there and opened the door at precisely two pm. The cash box was in a cupboard in the sitting room. I pulled out the box and looked about for something with which to force the lock. The poker proved too thick and the blade of my knife much too weak. Oh, well, only one thing to do; take the complete box and force it later.

Five minutes after entering the house I left. The cash box was the only thing I took. I was out to right a wrong, not line my own pocket.

I slid the front door key down a drain and hurried along the street. A passing cab caught my eye and I was tempted to hail it. However, by the time I had made up my mind the cab had gone from view. I continued walking and kept to side roads.

I was only two streets from safety when it happened. Two furtive figures in workmen's overalls caught my eye. I quickened my pace. They quickened theirs too. I ran but they caught me. The taller of the pair said, 'We are police officers. What have you got in that box?'

My bluff was to no avail. I had to go to the police station quietly.

Despite a lengthy bout of questioning I did not mention Peter. No sense in implicating him.

When the box was opened my eyes had a feast. It was crammed with bank notes. There was a total of £550. Why, oh why, didn't I hail that cab?

Two months later I stood trial at the County of London Sessions. I pleaded guilty for the sake of time saving. My sentence might have been far heavier had I wasted Court time by pleading not guilty.

When the Judge asked if I had anything to say I replied, 'No'. He then delivered his little speech. 'Joseph——, you are guilty of a most impudent case of housebreaking and the theft of a large sum of money. Fortunately that money has been recovered otherwise your punishment would have been greater. As it is you must go to prison for twelve months.'

No description beyond 'Deadly dull' is needed for my time in prison.

When I was released I soon teamed up again with Tony. He had not been idle during my absence. When we met he had news of a pay roll that, to use his own words, 'Begged to be lifted.' The scene was again South London and the money was going to an engineering firm.

Each Thursday morning the pay roll was carried from the bank to the works by an old and well trusted employee. His route took him past an underground station and it was here Tony and I planned to strike. The station was on the corner of a busy road junction. At eleven in the morning the place would be thronged with pedestrians.

Two minutes before eleven on the day, I arrived upon the scene. Tony was in position. My eyes took in the scene. All seemed normal except, 'curse it,' the automatic traffic signals had a fault and a policeman stood in the centre of the junction directing vehicles.

Should the plan be called off? No, I thought, with luck that policeman will be too busy with the traffic to notice us.

Exactly at eleven the firm's employee walked past the opening to the station. I approached from behind him and threw a clean sack over the grey haired figure. With all his cries muffled I snatched the case from his hand and walked quickly into the station. After booking a ticket to Morden I boarded the escalator. Tony followed a few paces behind and booked to Charing Cross.

On a crowded platform it was a simple matter for me to pass the case to Tony. While he sped towards town I travelled to Morden. After spending an hour there I returned to Brixton. Tony didn't return that evening. Three days later I found out why.

When he reached Charing Cross he had alighted from the tube train intending to cross to the main line station and deposit the case in the left luggage office. However, as he walked up Villiers Street a careless cab driver ran him down. Tony was flung unconscious to the ground. When the ambulance arrived he was lying on the road still clutching the case.

Later when he awoke a stranger was sitting beside the hospital bed. This detective wanted to know how Tony came to be carrying a stolen case containing £2,000 in banknotes.

At his trial Tony pleaded not guilty but the jury didn't believe him. The Judge must have had an intense dislike for wage snatchers for he gave Tony three years.

The police thought Tony had done the operation single-handed and fortunately for me he didn't dispel their mistake.

Now that my partner is going to be away for a while I am going to suspend operations. I intend to settle for a while. This doesn't mean that I intend to marry. In my business there is no place for a woman. A woman would mean living a more or less settled existence and for me that cannot be. Now that I am committed to a life of crime I cannot ask any girl to share that life with me. There is no chance of putting back the clock.

There is only one way now that I can know a different life and that is through the medium of books. With Maugham I can go to China. With Churchill I can see the North-West Frontier and the Sudan. Stanley takes me along the Congo. Howard Spring can show me the gore of Peterloo.

As I have done bigger and better jobs I have had more free time to improve my academic education. Even in prison I was able to do this. I never caused trouble and was always a trusty with access to the prison library.

Upon discharge I always returned to my native Brixton and there made use of the public library. I thank the ratepayers for this service. I was going to write thank God there, but remembered in time that I don't believe in God.

Some days it is difficult to obtain a seat in the reference section of the library. The place is usually crammed with coloured students avidly reading or writing. A white student is a rarity. Is this the reason why the coloured peoples are steadily gaining ground? They are prepared to go to great trouble to gain just a little learning. The average white person of my acquaintance is not the least bit interested in improving mind or body.

Millions of pounds may be spent upon education in this country but the spending will be to no avail if the principles of self-help and the exercise of initiative are not thumped into the pupil at an early age. Initiative is at a premium even in my line of business.

My mode of life is simple and my savings from my work provide ample for my needs. These days I have more time to stand and stare.

Whenever I walk in Brixton I am amazed at the large number of pregnant women that are to be seen. They are a varied lot. Varied in shape, size, colour, deportment, breeding, speech and dress. I suppose to a doctor they are all the same; just bearers of the next generation who will in their turn bring forth another generation and so on. This will continue until either war or disease destroys mankind.

Looking back on some of the jobs I have done I have reason to feel satisfied. Self-satisfied that is. I have initiative and would have been willing to be a worker and follow a normal occupation had I been allowed to do so. However, society has rejected me and I am forced to use my talents in pursuit of criminal activity.

When I first took to crime I was ashamed. Now I have no illusions. I still feel shame but no longer for myself. The only shame I have now is for Society.

14

Brought up in an Orphanage

by 'JACKIE'

IN ATTEMPTING to convey what it was like to be an inmate of an orphanage in the twenties I have resisted an impulse to present what might be termed a 'balanced view', preferring to let my untrammelled feelings and memories, as they rise like long-imprisoned bubbles, dictate the pattern of my account. The resulting picture may strike a reader as morbidly subjective; nevertheless, I believe it to be a truthful one. I begin with a memory of P—— C——

I see him, as I so frequently saw him: stripped to the waist, with his shirt and vest tucked into the top of his trousers, waiting for Sister G——, the terrifying scourge of us all, to scour his cropped, eczema-covered head in the steaming washbasin against which he stands. She seems to enjoy her task, if the vigour with which she attacks it is any guide to her feelings. But I, stealing a wary glance now and then as I scour the plughole rims of the nearby basins with brickdust—my morning task—I wince with P—— as Sister kneads the smarting, scab-encrusted skin of his scalp and pours on the too-hot rinsing water from the gaping beakspouted kettle. It puffs out its steam so menacingly that I can imagine a horrible tongue appearing as the 'coal-tar' lather is washed away and P——'s scored and shining scalp is nakedly revealed. I see him also, in his nightshirt, carrying an armful of wet sheets—for P—— is a bed-wetter—making his way towards the bathroom in the early morning.

The sheets he dumps in an empty bath and then, half-wearily, half-apprehensively, strips off his nightshirt and goes to the shower-bath cubicle where Sister G—— has already turned on the cold water and now waits for him with her golosher. She is impatient and begins to hit him before he gets under the streaming rose, although she has ample time and there is plenty of room for her to swing her arm in the spacious cubicle. Scorning the water she hits him haphazardly: on his head, buttocks, back, arms, anywhere, and wherever the golosher lands on his streaming body the skin splits, for P——'s eczema is not confined to his head: it covers his whole body. For us who watched and heard, it was as terrifying as murder.

I see P—— again, wearing a jester's cap and bells in place of the home-made black skull-cap which he usually wears, and a red and green-quartered jester's outfit hired for this occasion. In one hand he has a stick with an inflated pig's bladder at the end and in the other a collecting box which he rattles and brandishes at the grinning people lining the route of the Home's annual procession through the streets of X——. It is hot in the sun and as he hops about now like a shambling ape, now like a stilt-gaited penguin, now zooming with outstretched arms like an aeroplane, I think of him sweating and itching beneath his motley. He incites laughter from the crowd, as he often does from us, his companions, when we are safely out of sight of Sister G—— with his grotesque, calamine-whitened face, his red-rimmed eyes without eyebrows or lashes and his lipless mouth from which comes an insane, gabbling chatter. I remember also how he sometimes enlivened the one-mile homeward run from the day school which we attended at X—— with this same meaningless gabble—French he called it—so that the anxiety which customarily quickened as we approached the Home and Sister G—— was mingled with breathless laughter. As I think of these daily runs I am reminded of how they often ended in shame and misery for D——, N—— and P——.

As soon as we arrived home from school these three had to remove their underpants for Sister G——'s inspection. I see them standing in their stockinged feet on the highly-polished floor of the 'dayroom' with downcast eyes, while she minutely examines their inside-out underpants. The slightest mark was enough to get them two strokes from the 'spade', and one stroke from this seaside toy was enough to set your hand alight. One or other of them was sure to get it. I remember how degraded, hot and breathless with apprehension I felt while the search went on and how, strangely, relieved when I heard the sharp slap of the spade and the weeping that followed it. I suppose that the other boys felt the same desperate sorrow as I did, although fear of being 'reported' to Sister prevented us from showing any sympathy to the sufferers or talking about it amongst ourselves as 'free' boys would. Reporting was endemic among us and I was one of the few who managed to resist its sweet temptation. I suppose that they did it to ingratiate themselves with Sister. Since we lived in continual fear of what she might do to us it was natural to try to divert her attention towards someone else. (Remembering this aspect of Home life I was not shocked, as many were, when I read about similar behaviour in the German concentration camps.) However, even tale-bearing was fraught with danger.

I remember that one bath day, P—— C——, with whom I shared the bath, reported me for scrubbing my feet before my hands but got the golosher himself because that was the proper order of things and by reporting me he had betrayed his own ignorance. Even so it was impossible not to feel sorry for him, or indeed, for anyone who got the golosher, once you had tasted its hot pain yourself, especially on buttocks made tender by hot water. My own great fear on bathdays was that she might again make me get into a bath too hot for my fair skin. It was no use wincing and no one ever dared voice a complaint: the only time I was ever more afraid of the heat of the water than I was of her, she forced me to sit in it but after a few minutes I leapt out and was sick and she gave me two with the golosher. To return to the order of washing: the last parts to be washed were the 'privates' and these were dealt with by Sister G—— herself; we were not allowed to touch them ourselves. Sister always brought the golosher with her to the bathroom and someone always got it on their wet skin, so that my memory of bathdays is a phantasmagoria of rising steam, wet bodies and the anguished cries of weeping children. Our greatest danger of getting the golosher, however, was in the early morning, just after we got up.

At the end of the long narrow dormitory where we slept there were two enamel pails which stood on squares of linoleum close to Sister G——'s room, and each of us in turn had to use one of these pails after we got up in the morning. To use the pail you knelt on one knee while hugging the pail with the other and then passed water with infinite care, directing it obliquely down the side of the pail so as not to make the slightest spot on linoleum or polished floor, for you knew that if the 'pail monitor' or the boy who followed you found one you would be reported and you would get the golosher on your bare behind. No one used the pail without first anxiously scanning the linoleum square and the floor around it, and by the time twelve boys had used each pail it was a pretty hazardous undertaking. When every boy had used the pail P—— B—— and another boy, whose name I have forgotten, emptied the contents into a low sink and then carefully washed and dried the linoleum squares and the surrounding area of floor. I sometimes wondered why we were not allowed to use this wide basin directly, or indeed the w.c. which stood in the far corner of the dormitory, not realizing then that Sister G—— was obsessively interested in urine, excreta, scabs and the infliction of pain, besides reading the lives of the great Christian divines.

Like P—— C—— we all had some household task to do before breakfast and at various times during the day. Mine was to clean the washbasin plugholes with brickdust after the porcelain had been washed by another boy, so it was difficult not to mark the basins themselves, but whenever I did I always got the 'spade' so most of my days began in misery. However, I was more fortunate than J—— H—— whose evening task it was to peel a bucketful of potatoes for next day's dinner. I can see him anxiously watching Sister G—— as she dredged up handfuls of peelings to examine them for thickness, for if they were 'too thick' he knew that, besides getting the 'spade' he would also have to eat a plateful for his next day's dinner and J—— often had to do this, having only an ordinary table-knife to work with. It was a sad spectacle, made worse by the fact that one could never commiserate with him for fear of being reported to Sister. It is unusual to find children so much on their guard as we were, but circumstances made us learn. One such remains in my mind.

R—— (I have forgotten his surname), was something of a pet of Sister G——'s. He attended the grammar school at X—— to which he travelled daily, including Saturdays. This particular day was a Saturday but for some reason R—— had not gone to school as usual. Instead he had played in the field with the rest of us. When we were called in for dinner at twelve o'clock we had to pass Sister G—— greeting her as we did so. R——, first in and still rosy from the excitement of the game, wished her 'Good afternoon Sta' (*sic:* Sta was the permitted abbreviated form of Sister), forgetting that he had missed morning school at X—— and that it was still morning. If he had spat in her face she could not have reacted more viciously than she then did. She slapped him hard across the face again and again with her hard, ringed hand—she had once been married—and I felt almost sick with the injustice of it. We never dared duck or try to shield ourselves which shows how much we feared her.

Another incident which exemplifies the extent of her domination over us occurred one summer afternoon when we went into the 'grounds' for tea. The tea urn was carried out, the mugs, and the regulation two rounds of bread and margarine for each boy. Although, as indoors, we ate in silence, we enjoyed the novelty of an al fresco meal and we enjoyed this one until a cloud of midges descended on us just as we were about to be dismissed. Sister G—— from the midge-free eminence where she was sitting, immediately ordered us to sit absolutely still on pain of having the spade when we got indoors. She dismissed us one by one at what seemed unbearably long intervals, keeping those who appeared to be suffering most, to the last. I cannot forget S—— P——'s face with the thick tears coursing down as the tiny midges settled on his ears, in his hair, and on his sweating forehead. There were many other incidents which seemed to show that she enjoyed inflicting pain on us in other ways than by hitting us with the 'spade' and the golosher: one, I remember, concerned myself.

A large boil had developed on my back and Sister G——decided to 'squeeze' it immediately after I got into bed. She made no attempt to bathe it but tried to burst it by applying pressure with her thumbs. It must have been obvious that she was inflicting needless—and fruitless—pain but she continued until my screams brought another Sister running in from the dormitory of an adjoining house. This, I realize now, must have been a serious breach of etiquette, but it saved me from any further pain: which, incidentally, must have been pretty fearful for I remember that I screamed for my mother who had been dead for three years. Another time I remember her squeezing a whitlow on a boy's finger until he fainted from the pain. I remember the white, dead-looking end of his finger and his white lips. He like P—— C—— had come from another branch of the orphanage although at a later age than P—— had done, which probably accounted for his once attempting to defy her: the only boy I ever knew to do so. He had dared to sell a pair of football boots to a boy in another house because they would no longer fit him. She found the money in his clothes and this gave him away for we were never allowed to have any. He told her the boots were his to do as he liked with and she beat him unmercifully about the face until he broke down under her blows and wept. He had a handsome face and he was fifteen years old. D—— S——was a more frequent sufferer. . . . Sometimes his eyes discharged during the night and his eyelids would be stuck fast by morning. I remember his stumbling down the long dormitory once to ask permission of Sister G—— to swill them, for he could see nothing as they were, and she slapped his face and the tears burst through his gummed-up lids.

I hope that I have said enough to show what may happen when orphaned children are entrusted to the care of such people as Sister G——: untrained, themselves seriously maladjusted, their only qualification being membership of the appropriate church. Sister G——, one imagines, now lies mouldering in her grave. For the sake of present and future generations of orphans, one hopes that her spirit does not go marching on.

15

Brutal Husband

by 'ANNE KAYE'

I MUST GO back to August 1941, when I first met the man who was to become my husband.

I was a tracer, working at an Ordinance Factory in Lancashire and Percy was a clerk in the Pay Corps. We travelled to our respective jobs by the same train and were mutually attracted from our first meeting.

We became engaged on January 13th, 1942, but did not plan to marry in a hurry. The following August, Percy was sent to Northumberland and I missed him terribly. There were letters of course; I wrote daily and he replied to alternate letters approximately.

In December 1942 I joined the WAAF and became a plotter at Fighter Command, Stanmore. I was in the Intelligence Branch of the Service and found the life full, exciting and interesting. I met many people far above my normal social circle and lost my shyness, when I realized how ordinary and likeable they were, when one dug beneath the veneer.

During the early part of the year Percy was posted to Aldershot for an officer's course. We met most week-ends in London and had a wonderful time. There was always so much to do and we danced, skated, swam and saw all the interesting places in Town. The bombs became commonplace and we were young enough to take them in our stride. The war seemed to be an excuse for cramming our waking hours with every possible enjoyment. We saw all the best shows, learned to enjoy serious music and appreciate museums and beautiful architecture.

We made wonderful plans for the future and spent every

penny of our pay. There seemed to be so much time to save later and we were determined to enjoy London to the full.

Perhaps it was the hectic life which made Percy fail his OCTU. He was returned to his unit and had to apply for a further course.

Eventually, after a struggle, he was sent to the famous Sandhurst for another officer's training course.

From the beginning, Sandhurst seemed to alter Percy. He told me that when he was commissioned, he would expect me to salute him, as my rank was merely LACW! He became very mean and I found myself drawing out money from my savings to pay for meals and shows. He explained that most of the chaps at Sandhurst had private incomes and it took all his pay to provide drinks etc., when they called in at the local.

I was still very much in love and heeded not the advice of my colleagues who thought he was making a mug of me.

His attitude became ever more domineering and I usually went to bed weeping after an evening out with him.

I had made friends with a family at Bushy in Hertfordshire where I spent most of my off-duty time, when I was not with Percy.

The son of the family had been training in the USA and came home as a fully-fledged pilot. He was a huge, blonde, kindly fellow and we became good friends. He spent a lot of time with me and did all he could to cheer me up when I had been depressed by Percy's condescending manner.

Eventually, he asked me to marry him and told me he thought I would forget Percy if I became his (Ron's) wife.

I knew I was not in love with Ron. He was so sweet and kind though, that I realized life would be much more peaceful with him, so I wrote to Percy and sent back his ring.

Two nights later, Percy arrived at my billet at about one a.m. I shared a room with another WAAF who was a very timid girl. I went to the door and told Percy to go away as we should be in serious trouble if we allowed him inside. He refused to move until I promised to put on my great-coat, so that I could continue our conversation out-of-doors.

I told him I was not moving from the porch because I had no right to be absent from my billet. However, he put one hand across my mouth and half carried me across the path until we entered the orchard.

He held me down and told me I had better be quiet if I knew what was good for me. I was terrified and promised to be quiet if he would only let me go back to my room. He told me he had a lot to say first and I must listen.

He then told me he would never let me marry anyone else and swore to dishonour me if I refused to take back his ring. I was so afraid that I promised I would, providing he let me return to my room at once. He did so eventually, after making it clear he would force me to marry him if I tried to break my promise.

We married by special licence on Christmas Eve 1943, then returned to our respective units.

We met as usual each week-end and I was reasonably happy although fear of my husband made me very tense and nervy.

My mother-in-law, who had twice been divorced, had always claimed part of my husband's pay, so he told me I should send her fourteen shillings each week from my marriage allowance. This I did, banking the rest and living on my WAAF pay.

In October 1944 I discovered I was expecting a baby and was discharged from the WAAF.

This was a blow, as we had no home and very little money.

I went to my parents' home in Salford. It was a grim four-roomed house, with no modern amenities and in the Dock area. Such a contrast to beautiful Stanmore. However, there was nowhere else to go and I was very short of money.

When I asked my husband for money for clothing (we had a joint account incidentally) he told me I was fit and ought to work for some months to earn money for clothing for myself and the coming child.

I managed to find a job as an assistant to an auditor and I was able to work until early 1945.

During this time my husband was commissioned and came home resplendent in kilt and sporran. He was a 2nd Lieutenant in the Cameron Highlanders. He certainly looked very smart in his uniform but his pride and arrogance were painfully obvious and he was rude and churlish to my parents.

This hurt me of course and we had a quarrel almost the first day he was home. He told me he hated Salford and he ended up by spending the remainder of his leave at his mother's home in Wallasey—whilst I remained in Salford.

He wrote about once each week after he returned to his base at Inverness. Just before the baby arrived he did not write for three weeks as he was 'too busy'.

My baby was born in May and when my grandfather asked my husband if they were having a drink to celebrate the birth of a son, he was told, 'It has cost me enough to celebrate this,'—'this' being the 2nd pip of Lieutenant.

My husband came on leave when our son was three months old but spent only two days with us because he objected to the district. I begged to go up to Scotland and live near his camp but he refused to hear of it.

When the baby was five months old, I managed to rent a lovely flat in Old Trafford, near to the cricket ground. I was thrilled to have my own home and was sure Percy would spend his leaves with us as it was such a pleasant district.

Friends helped me to furnish it and my husband bought a dining-room suite, a bed, wardrobe and chest of drawers. It was a humble start but I loved painting and decorating so it soon looked cosy.

However, my husband did not come home for leaves and I had an unsigned letter from Scotland, telling me he was living with a Scots ATS girl. I burned the letter and tried to forget about it but I was desperately lonely and unhappy. I told nobody about the letter as my family and friends were already so bitterly angry about my husband's behaviour.

When he was eventually demobbed, he lived with his mother at Wallasey and visited me at week-ends occasionally. He gave me very little to keep the baby and pay the rent of the flat and it was a hard struggle.

I told him I could not carry on as we were and he told me he thought he would be able to settle down if we had another child. I agreed to this and he started to come home each week-end. He had returned to his pre-war job at Ellesmere Port and could not travel daily so he continued to live with his mother during the week.

His behaviour had improved and when I knew I was expecting another baby he seemed happy and was quite helpful in the flat, although terribly jealous of our little son. He was very strict with him and said he must be 'treated like a recruit.' He gave commands continually and never made any requests.

The second baby was also a son and we called him Christopher Douglas. I didn't like 'Douglas' but my husband was most insistent and I later discovered it to be the name of the girl he had been living with in Inverness.

Whilst I was in hospital, my husband told me he did not intend paying the bill. He said, 'You've had the child so they can't do a thing about it.' This was typical of his attitude. He thought the country owed him a great debt although he had never been out of England and had suffered no hardship at all.

We moved to a pre-fab in May 1948 at Ellesmere Port, near to the factory where Percy worked.

The baby was six months old and the elder boy was three years. They were quite a handful but Percy refused to help to clean the pre-fab when we moved in. It had been left with paint on floors and windows which had to be cleaned off and there was cement to be sandpapered off kitchen tiles. He was out each night and I had to slave for eighteen hours a day until the place was straight.

He then decided the furniture was not to his liking and he bought more, including a console radio. We hadn't a decent carpet in the home but he bought luxuries and did not give a heed to essential furnishings.

Whenever I protested about him leaving me alone each evening, he merely said, 'A woman's place is at home.'

However, the district was pleasant and the children were bonny and thriving so I was not too unhappy.

Once, when I asked why he had married me, he replied, 'I wanted somebody plain, whom I knew I could leave at home and be sure no other man would be attracted to.' In those days

I was not quite plain but it hurt a lot and I found myself cringing whenever he came near to me, after this remark.

He drank quite a lot and he was bestial when he came to bed after these drinking bouts. The more I tried to protect myself, the more violent he became and I often dared not go into the garden in case neighbours noticed my bruises.

He started stealing on quite a large scale. I could have understood it if he had taken articles which he needed, but he became like a magpie.

One night he stole a spirit level, a surveyor's tape, a set square and a huge wheelbarrow from a building-site. I begged him to return them and said the wheelbarrow was so easily identifiable. He merely took a hacksaw and shortened the handles and then painted it black.

On another occasion, he went to some new houses, unscrewed the hinges on a coal-place door and brought the complete door home. I was horrified and lived in terror of him being sent to prison.

We later moved to a new brick house a little nearer to the shops. This was a council house but brand new and very nice. I had the same job of completely cleaning it, but by this time, the elder boy was at school and the younger child was running about. Also, I had made many friends and often I had one or two girl friends in to cheer my lonely evenings.

If by any chance, my husband happened to be in when my girl friends called, he would simply exude charm and they were nearly all very impressed by his good looks and fine physique. Sex was his hobby and he certainly knew how to attract women.

His evenings out became even more numerous and sometimes he would be away from home from Friday evening until Monday evening. If I asked questions, he either ignored me or delivered a blow. If I retaliated as I occasionally did, he would hold my head under his arm and punch the back of my head with his fist. He said he had been taught this way of combat in the Army and I would eventually have cerebral haemorrhage and he could deny any knowledge and nobody would be able to prove a thing.

My nerves were becoming very ragged and I dreaded his

footsteps. The life he was leading was showing in his face and he looked very haggard after his weekends away.

On one occasion he brought home some soiled pyjamas and ordered me to wash them. I picked them up with the coal tongs and dropped them into the boiler fire. He flew into a rage and beat me about the head until I became unconscious.

When I recovered, I was in bed and he was trying to force brandy down my throat. I felt terribly ill and had a violent pain in my chest. I begged him to bring the doctor but he refused.

The next morning I managed to go downstairs, with a tremendous effort, and I rang up the doctor and asked him to call. My husband threatened to kill me if I told the doctor what had happened and he stayed at home so that I was unable to talk to the doctor. The latter told my husband I must stay in bed and ordered the children to be sent to relatives for a few weeks.

Soon after this, I told my husband I could carry on no longer and we agreed to separate. We went to a solicitor who thought he was being a friend to us by asking us not to do such a thing. He said the boys would suffer. We reconsidered it and I decided to stay for their sakes.

However, my husband's behaviour became even more violent and he stopped the housekeeping money completely. I sewed for money for essentials, and my brother sent money for clothing and shoe repairs etc.

My husband took to parading the streets at night in a kilt and tam-o-'shanter he had worn during the war. His table manners were atrocious and he began eating meat and even stews with his fingers.

Eventually, he started threatening me with fencing-foils and thin canes. He tried to force me to partake in disgusting sexual rites which he said he had enjoyed with his former ATS girl-friend. He became utterly loathsome to me and I could not even bear to look at him or handle his clothing. He refused to bath and went frantic each time I had a bath. He would turn off the light which was outside the bathroom and would run to the kitchen and try to run off all the hot water.

In December 1953 he was unable to continue his work. The

people opposite to our house had complained that he had been standing at the bedroom window unclothed and people on the bus which passed our house had also complained.

He saw a psychiatrist who recommended that he should go to a rehabilitation centre at Belmont, Surrey. He flatly refused.

On Boxing night of 1953, he threatened me with a Service revolver and kept loading and unloading it. I was terrified in case it went off and either harmed the children or killed me and left them at his mercy.

At about six a.m. the following morning, I dressed the boys, put a few of their clothes and a couple of towels in a bag and the three of us left the house.

We called at the Police Station in case he reported us missing and told them we were going to Chester and gave them the address of a friend who we knew would put us up for the night.

As we waited at the bus stop for the Chester bus a police-woman came running up to us and told us to hide in a side street and she would let us know when the bus came. She said my husband was at the Police Station and was raving like a madman.

We stayed at Chester overnight and I then took the boys to my parents' home in Salford.

I returned alone to Ellesmere Port, hoping to get a job there and hoping I might obtain possession of the council house in Ellesmere Port.

It proved impossible to find work there and the Council refused to let me have the tenancy of the house, even though my husband was living at Wallasey with his mother and the house was unoccupied.

He had changed the lock and I could not get in for clothing or any of my personal effects.

I went back to Salford and the clergyman at the church where I had attended all my life, gave me a room at the rectory for myself and the boys. He and his wife were wonderfully kind to me and would accept nothing by way of payment, even though we were there for four months.

I immediately found work in Trafford Park as a tracer, which was my old job.

I fixed up the boys in a local school and we began to collect a few articles towards a new home. My husband had taken all the furniture from the house at Ellesmere Port and left us with only two single beds, an old kitchen table, a rocking chair and a collection of cracked and broken pots. He took three kettles and even the bed-clothes from the children's beds.

I applied for a Separation Order but the day before it was due to be heard in Court, my husband served divorce papers on me, alleging desertion.

All this time there had been no maintenance at all from him. I complained of this to the solicitor at Ellesmere Port and he said he could be forced to pay back-pay from December when the maintenance was agreed upon. This was not so however, and I did not receive anything for all the weeks he escaped paying, but he apparently claimed income-tax relief for all three of us.

I understood that a husband was responsible for all debts contracted by his wife whilst they were living together. I ordered some books for the children before I left him. When the bill came, I sent it to him but he refused to pay and the solicitor said I must foot the bill.

When I eventually got a flat of my own, it was a very old and dreary place but at least it was a start.

In 1955, the divorce case was heard at Chester in the High Court. I had to pay £22 Legal Aid fees to bring the cross prayer alleging adultery and cruelty. I was assured that I would receive most if not all of the £22 back if and when I won the case.

I was awarded the case and my husband's charge was dismissed. I was also given custody of the boys and costs of the case.

I repeatedly asked my solicitor about the costs and each time he put me off by saying my ex-husband had not paid up and I would have to wait until he had finished paying costs.

In 1956 both boys won scholarships and went to different schools. The elder boy was accepted as a boarder and the list of necessary clothing and equipment worked out at £57. I wrote to his father asking if he would help. He ignored the letter and for three months he did not send a penny maintenance.

My solicitor prepared a case to be heard against him, but the day before it was due to be heard, he paid up.

We had by this time a Court Order making him responsible for thirty shillings per week for the boys and fifteen shillings per week for me.

My ex-husband had access to the boys and saw them approximately every six weeks or so. He spent his time questioning them about my salary and made them tell him exactly the amount of furniture we had in every room. They returned from their visits like small ghosts and were upset for days afterwards.

Whenever I suggested to the solicitor that we apply for the the visits to be stopped he said it would merely be my word against their father's and did not seem to worry about the effect on the boys' health.

In the meantime, my ex-husband married and his wife had a very well paid job. They were living in apartments at Wallasey and they told the boys that they were going to buy a big house so that they could reduce the maintenance.

My elder boy seemed to be quite well at his school but my younger son did not appear to be very well at all. He had all sorts of trivial pains and never seemed to be really fit.

After a great deal of thought I decided to look for a small house in the country.

Whilst I was doing this, my husband arranged for a Court Hearing because he had bought a large house at Wallasey and was paying £5 per week mortgage. In his affidavit, it stated he had only £50 worth of furniture and he was paying a pound per week HP terms for furniture. He took over £200 worth of furniture from our house in Ellesmere Port. The whole of the affidavit was false and he claimed to have only two shillings per week for food. No mention was made of the fact that his wife was earning a large salary.

I filled in my own affidavit and sent it to my solicitor, (I had changed to one in Manchester). I heard nothing more for some weeks and then I managed to secure a small cottage at Marple in Cheshire. It was very humble (not even a bath) and cost £500. I borrowed £300 from my father as a deposit and arranged to pay off the rest at a pound a week.

Unfortunately, I had to give up my job in Manchester and take one at Cheadle which meant a drop of nearly thirty shillings per week.

However, I wrote to my solicitor in Manchester and told him I would need to fill in a new affidavit of means as my circumstances were considerably altered. He calmly wrote back and said the case had been heard the previous week and my maintenance had been reduced by fifteen shillings per week. I had not been notified of the date or given the chance to go to hear the case. I was told my ex-husband had *offered* to pay all costs and I need not worry about paying anything.

What right had this solicitor to make private arrangements without even consulting me?

I did not receive a farthing back from the costs of my divorce case and when I asked about claiming some of the furniture, I was told it would cost about £50 to take my case to Court. Don't solicitors like Legal Aid cases? It appears to me that the laws are made for men, regardless of the fact that the children suffer mostly.

I have now changed to a solicitor in Cheadle who seems to be a genuine help and puts rights before his bank balance, but I know of other women who have been cheated of their costs and have been unable to demand what is rightfully theirs.

My younger son has just joined his brother at boarding school and the £22 costs owing me would help tremendously towards winter raincoats and shoes for them both but what hope is there of even getting it now? None, if one happens to be a woman!

16

'Uncharm'

by 'ANN LORNE'

I BELIEVE in 'uncharm'. I believe in it because I have it; I know how it works, intimately, from the inside and (perhaps because I have it) I have carefully observed its working in other people. I am sure it is quite separate from either virtue and vice, mental health or ill-health—though its effects are liable to cause the latter; and I am sure that, among the many causes of underdogmanship, uncharm must cover a lot of territory.

Further, underdogmanship is no problem, except where it produces feelings of injustice and grievance; uncharm typically has this effect and so should merit serious consideration.

What can cause failure—or underdogmanship? First there are deficiencies: limited intelligence; limited education; limited money; weakness of character; physical defects such as illness, being crippled, excessive ugliness or disfigurement. Allied to any of the physical deficiencies (and sometimes caused by them) are mental ill-health, from the serious to the mild, undiagnosed, neurosis. And last but far from least, the positive repellent: *uncharm*.

'Charm' and 'personality' are often wrongly used as synonymous; I should like to be explicit about how I distinguish between them. Charm is a talent to attract and please—irrespective of any other factor. I regard what we call 'personality' as a sort of supercharge—quantity not quality; we all have *a* personality; to 'have personality' means to have it with a bit PLUS.

A person with 'personality' we see through a magnifying-glass; a charming person through rose-tinted spectacles; an uncharming person through distorting lenses that produce grotesques—clumsy parodies of men and women such as one sees in those cleverly designed mirrors at fair-grounds.

Charm functions best and most naturally at the intimate, personal level. 'Personality' is essentially for an audience (the individual is affected, but mainly because individuals are what audiences are made of); accordingly it is the essential quality for such people as entertainers and leaders.

There is another not insignificant basic difference: charm may often go with a somewhat gentle, reliant character; charm appeals to our protective instinct, it belongs naturally to the unspoilt young (and young animals); but 'personality' goes with a forceful character. These dazzlers tend to be the ambitious ones and generally they *arrive*. But it is easier for a person to succeed without a dazzling personality (which in some walks of life would automatically be suspect) than it is for a person who is essentially uncharming—because the aura of uncharm throws up a distorting mist through which it is almost impossible to observe and evaluate fairly.

Contrariwise, I would say that people may be underdogs *in some way* at least, although they do have charm. But I think that having a good measure of uncharm makes it almost impossible to realize one's potential; though a good combination, and quantity, of the other assets may compensate considerably.

I know that in spite of the distinctions I have drawn there is an enormous amount of overlapping, but that does not invalidate the distinction; the sea and the sand are quite different although large quantities of sand may be saturated with sea water.

Before going any further I think I should indicate why I insist on the *existence* of uncharm, as the opposite of charm. Can you think of anything in our world, as we understand it—intellectually, spiritually, artistically, legally, politically or in any other sense—which exists without its opposite?

It seems to be a basic truth of our universe that light can only be identified by means of darkness; good by evil; beauty by ugliness. You may say: 'But people can be *more* or *less* charming, and we should call those who are more charming "charming", as we do; but this does not mean that some people need be the opposite of charming, in fact, repellent.' Why not? Do we deny deep black? In the broad range of human behaviour do we not accept the superhuman excellence of the saints at one end of the scale, and the inhumanity of Belsen at the other? Do we not accept as a necessary evil that some children are born imbecile and that a person can be so ugly or so disfigured that it is an effort to look at them calmly? We cannot deny the existence of things because they are distressing.

Most of my belief that charm or uncharm are inborn qualities is the ultimate conclusion based on my personal experience. I have battled persistently and sincerely to make myself more acceptable and inevitably, it seems, I fail; just as I should fail to wish away my piggy eyes or my short thick neck. (In case these words may be misleading I must admit my face has not been my misfortune and I received my fair share of female-appeal).

This argument based on a single case is, I know, utterly unscientific and proves nothing except that it is what I believe. But how could one examine a satisfactory number of cases? Even the Americans, dearly as they love a survey, would balk at sending people round asking: 'And to what, Mrs Clambake, do you particularly attribute your total lack of charm?' (Might the Australians try it? They are said to be dedicated to plain speaking).

When I was young I used to think that one could *earn* love, therefore I had an excellent incentive in trying to develop the virtues. I was also very enthusiastic about psychology (on a personal, amateur, level, I mean) because I believed that it would help one to overcome all sorts of difficulties. There is a little truth in both these ideas: but rather, I think, on a better-than-nothing basis from the uncharming person's point of view.

I think a similar type of ameliorating treatment can be given to disguise or camouflage the uncharming. But it does not create charm nor cure uncharm. Acceptable behaviour in as many ways as the person can manage is bound to help. And an understanding of the dangers of not facing facts squarely, and cultivating a sense of proportion, will work against those feelings of grievance that make uncharming people go from bad to worse. Apart from religious belief and spiritual progress, such objectiveness, and the cultivation of a sense of humour, are the best possible compensations for the uncharming. (Middle-age seems to help too: I am expecting people soon to go round informing each other that I have '*mellowed*'! Whatever this means, it feels most comfortable).

I also believe this quality is inborn because I seem to see the same uncharm as my own in other members of my family; and I seem to see patterns of charm, or its opposite, in other families I know.

But if you round on me and say: 'But your uncharming ways may well have been taught to you by your uncharming relations (who caught it from their uncharming relations) at an early age, when you were most susceptible, and which you would be unaware of.'

Then I reply: 'Well, how do you explain away the fact that my adopted brother had more charm than all the rest of us put together? He was brought up in just the same way as we were.'

Searching for a simile for my idea of an uncharming person —this person whose behaviour is not exactly wrong, but is nevertheless objected to—I am rather attracted to the idea that the uncharming person is not necessarily singing the wrong tune; it is the right tune, but in a different key from the rest and so it jars. But I am too ignorant to pursue a musical analogy in the opposite direction, towards charm. Perhaps it will not hold? Nevertheless, the idea of an ordinary person *transposed* into a different key does fit exactly my idea of uncharm being independent of the other aspects of personality.

To examine more closely my contention that charm and uncharm exist separately from the other qualities of a personality, would you please look at it this way for a moment: think of all the really charming people you know, or have known, in your life; do they resemble each other in any way apart from their charm? 'Nice people,' you would say; yes, but are not some of the most appealing of these charmers rather weak? Some are lazy, some drink too much, most have a marked and sometimes not too innocent, preoccupation with the opposite sex; some are dishonest, if only in a mild way; some spongers, some sycophants—are not most of them at least as selfish as other people?

I think I would venture to accuse the majority of being more selfish than the rest of us—and who am I to blame them? If I were naturally charming, and therefore popular, without bothering to produce my best behaviour, would I try very hard? I doubt it.

Or is it the other way round? Naturally, I have asked myself secretly in the night, to tell me honestly if there are not some specific personal characteristics I have that could show, without my realizing it, and be irritating or repellent to others; and if this could be the secret of what I call my uncharm. And I say to me: 'Yes! You criticize people in your mind an awful lot, even if you say nothing—and you know you have an expressive face; perhaps it shows more than you think; perhaps it shows a magnified version of what you are really thinking! After all, you can't see it from outside.'

What a horrifying thought—because there is some truth in it. 'But, wait a minute,' I protest, 'would it not be more true to say that I have an analytical mind? (Very common among the Scots and perhaps a main factor in keeping us comparatively undistinguished in the creative arts?) 'Is it not fair to say that I am equally incisive in my criticisms of my own behaviour; that my observations are largely an interest in and a desire to understand this world we live in? After all,' I add, 'you generally realize when you are merely thinking cattily!'

'Is it not also fair,' I continue more complacently, 'to say that you are always pleased to pick out good qualities, often in the most unexpected places; and that you really want to find more and more good qualities in people, so that the world may seem a happier place; don't you always prefer (if only on a Do-as-you-would-be-done-by basis) to extend the 'benefit of the doubt' rather than risk being unfair—though it is in this way you have often been hardest hit? (But it still remains a good principle.)'

'You say to yourself, you take no credit for your standards of right and wrong—the "Scottish Calvinism" of which you have sometimes been teasingly accused—because you realize that they are inborn and inbred and you have no power to act any other way, when it seems important. Yet in your mind do you not criticize other people's standards? Might not that basic "Calvinism" (of which intellectually and emotionally you yourself heartily disapprove) be the simple cause of your dislikeability; what need is there to postulate uncharm?'

But if we pursue the implications of this argument we are left with the assumption that it is mainly the people who are willing to take liberties with right and wrong who can be charming—which is just as absurd as the assumption that virtue automatically goes with charm.

'And, of course,' I conclude to myself, 'think of all the "delightfully catty" people you have met! That should dispose of the too-critical-and-it-shows theory.'

Finally, I have sometimes asked me whether, since no one could seriously think I am a prig or a prude, for all my basic 'Calvinism': 'Is it because they somehow realize intuitively, that I have standards above my moral station?' And that could be: nobody likes a phoney—except, of course, for the phoneys they do like.

Another quite small fact which seems to show that uncharm can be quite independent of character, virtue, mental health and so on is that the same person can be charming in the flesh but not in his writing, or the other way about; I am given to understand that I, myself, am 'much better on paper!'

I am not entirely satisfied that my whole argument of uncharm may not be a symptom of ill-health. We all know enough psychiatry nowadays to know that what is the root of the trouble is most strenuously resisted by the subject—often with very ingenious arguments. But, by analogy with the body, I think it is at least arguable that there may just as well be structural defects of many kinds in the psyche as there are varieties of defective performance.

Turning with a sigh of relief from all that introspection, I suggest the idea that charm and uncharm are totally unrelated to reason or virtue is well illustrated in the way both provoke the word 'but'.

'Of course she's a frightful liar (drunk, snob, cat, moron) *but* you can't help liking her.' Or: 'Yes, I do understand why he takes that attitude, *but* I can't bring myself to like him.' One of the dons in *The Masters* says something like this, and it shocked me because I felt that such highly-civilized people *ought* to be able to make such a mental adjustment successfully. (This book is an interesting example of the interplay of characters charming and uncharming—though I could not for the life of me see that Jago was fit to be in charge even of a good kennels. It is unusual because the uncharming people won. Normally, in books at least, the charming people are the winning team and losers are uncharming.)

Honesty compels me to acknowledge the possibility that charm can be related to a well-fed ego, because the two tend to coincide—though there could be a confusion of cause and effect. Hungry people have bad table manners and the unloved become unlovely. Conversely, happiness tends to overflow and attracts in the same way as Nothing-succeeds-like-success: such truths are platitudinous.

But, thinking of charming people, I find a proportion of them do not seem to have the history for a well-fed ego. One can circumvent this difficulty by arguing that a rather stupid person may need less food for his ego because he is insensitive, so there is less wear and tear; rather as if his ego had a slow metabolism and so needed less stoking. But I do not really find this theory satisfactorily covers the remaining cases.

There is no doubt that emotion can modify the *appearance* of charm, at least temporarily. Ugly thoughts may distort a charming face, while the uncharming person, bursting with a great and sudden joy can, for a moment, be radiant. (I have seen this phenomenon reflected in other people's faces and in their kind looks).

But generally there is a downward spiral with uncharm. I believe it is not to be cured, one just has to learn to live with it, and to disguise it in as many ways as possible, hoping that people will not notice it too often.

In addition to the hard luck of being born with such a handicap, uncharm is made harder to cope with because it is really not recognized: firstly, to exist—as charm is and, secondly, to be inborn and no more blameworthy in civilized society than a club foot.

If, instead of an ugliness of the personality called uncharm, one were markedly lacking in good looks; if one had not a single feature that was the right size or shape or in the right place; and if one's skin, hair and colouring looked as if they had been disinterred from the municipal rubbish dump, two things would follow without fail: one, horrified though they might be, people would be very sorry for one and would do their several bests to be kind; two, sooner or later one would be aware of the truth oneself beyond any shadow of a doubt.

Not admitting our uncharming position may be well-meant, but I, for one, wish our best friends would tell us. And I freely admit that I want them to because this would take the sting out of my ridiculously consistent succession of failures, large and small. I want a good excuse; and I claim I have a legitimate one.

Imagine what it is like to be uncharming. Accept, if only for a moment, that such a quality exists, and that its function is the opposite of charm, antagonizing, and inviting hindrance at every turn. What happens is that, first, you realize that you are not exactly popular; being a sensible person you do not weep too long about this unhappy fact, you set about making excuses; when you really accept that excuses will not do (time goes on and they can't be 'all out-of-step but wee Jock') then you realize you must re-read your Dale Carnegie and anything else you can lay your hands on—use your wits, and not be proud. Because not being liked, even if you mean well, *especially* when you mean *best*, is one of the worst things that can happen to people and must be tackled with perseverance.

But time passes and it doesn't seem to matter what you do, it just will not work. Every time you make a great fine splendid effort to drag yourself into the boat someone cracks you over the knuckles with an oar. And what is so incomprehensible about it all *is that they are all nice people*—often including your best friends. (The friends of an uncharming person are very, very kind).

So you start turning over in your mind what you know about one or two mental conditions which could be relevant —but that does not work either. Not so much because people treat you as fully responsible and, one assumes, some of them would not if you weren't; but because, getting pretty tired of the battle, you have got around to wishing it were over, and to wondering if mentally ill people suffer worse than people who have to behave normally when they are in considerable distress; and the probabilities are, you feel, that this wish that one could escape from the reality is the one thing that proves one is sane; if it were not so, surely one would be off, away downhill in a dizzying spiral to insanity? But it does not happen.

I know there is a lunatic in the cellar of my mind. I accept him because this seems to me psychologically healthy. But I rarely think about him, he is not let out, it doesn't do. He is very dangerous and tears me into ribbons over what is long dead and done with. I know it is a lunatic because he wants me to climb, screaming up the walls: *literally*. Which is absurd. So he stays in the cellar, not entirely forgotten but under control.

Still one cannot be *sure* one is mentally healthy if nobody will admit that one is uncharming—because it is the only thing that explains to me the inexplicable in my personal life. If they would, one would be helped to withdraw fairly gracefully from the battle and not go on battering oneself against the brick wall of an incurable personality defect—risking, in the meta-phorical sense, mental injury, just as in the literal sense one would be inviting concussion.

Perhaps, in some cases, it would be just as well not to admit the truth; such a revelation is strong meat and (particularly if the uncharming person has no close relations or others who will be sure allies) the tumbling along in a fool's paradise may sometimes be the best thing. But the implications of refusing to tell are basically uncomplimentary, if not insulting. Consider someone like me: reasonably intelligent, educated, a sense of humour defensively well-developed, brought up to be independent from an early age and of good, tough peasant stock. (It is a Viking call that rallies me in times of stress).

With someone like me, I think there is every chance of the 'bitter' truth being not only understood and digested but even —this you may find strange—coming as an enormous relief, and a great comfort. And why not? It is not so remarkably heroic, we take it for granted that a cripple must learn to live with his disability, hard though it may be. Blind people tell us that they wish the public would accept them as being merely blind—not also deaf and rather half-witted. Uncharm, I think should be accepted likewise, honestly and without fuss. (One could think up some lovely beat-nikky jokes about it).

After all, once uncharm is recognized for what it is, surely it becomes all the easier, without shame or guilt, to do the little that can be done about it? And a little can be done about it—just as ugliness can be camouflaged and made the best of.

If one accepts that one is often disliked because one has uncharm—and people are not yet enlightened enough to realize one cannot help it—then it is easier to forgive them and not mind so much. The ego is even boosted a little by being able to look down on the barbarians! Which helps towards shrugging the whole thing off with something like a chuckle. It follows from this, it seems to me, that one is less likely to develop neurotic symptoms due to the unhappiness and frustrations of this condition. It seems to me good mental hygiene to know the truth and face it, and *digest* it.

Above all, the neurotic symptoms which may, and often do develop, should not be confused with the uncharm itself. This is bitterly unfair to a person who, by the very nature of the lonely, uncharming condition, is battling year after disappointing year, to keep mentally healthy in spite of it all. When one is trying to laugh at one's absurd condition as often as possible and come to terms with it, it is outrageous for people to say 'It is neurotic to think people don't like you.' Or: 'You're just imagining it—of *course* not!' Or: 'What's the matter with you? Inferiority complex—or have you got some sort of persecution mania?' (Peals of merry laughter.)

I would go further and say that this type of suggestion, that one is not quite 'in touch', is both dangerous and rather reminiscent of our ancestors poking sticks through the cages at the lunatics. If we cannot help being uncharming, give us the benefit of the doubt, at least, for doing our best; and don't insult our intelligence and undermine our security any further.

Changing my tune, after all this rather humble stuff, to end on a more challenging theme: I suggest that it is not only chivalry (or squeamishness?) that makes people unwilling to recognize uncharm. I think another motivation is shaped something like this: our conscious mind accepts that a lot of things are unfair in life and this unfairness (at least nowadays) is deeply to be resented—all the more reason not to want to add another item to the list. On the other hand, so ruthless is our subconscious mind that any incident or situation which makes us feel slightly superior is pleasant to our egos; thus we resist (unconsciously) any signal from our intelligence that tends to deflate the ego, such as: 'This poor character can no more help being as attractive as a sackful of litter than that unfortunate young thing can help having a face like the back of a diesel engine.' So People have plenty of 'reason' not to recognize uncharm, for all the arguments one may put forward.

But there is one consolation: if you are wild and tough as I am, you can end your days as an eccentric old lady. This I mean to do.

Eccentrics can do and say what they like—a good vocabulary is an asset, and some wit. Charm is blessedly redundant. Only old age is needed, and that will come.

17

Mother of Four

by RUTH COLYER

I WRITE OF the time when I was the mother of four children under seven, born between 1939 and 1945. Some of the conditions described, therefore, no longer apply to the same extent. Nor do they apply universally: many young mothers can still turn to spinster aunts or grandparents for some relief; but with nearly all women earning their living, the supply of the former is dwindling, and with increased mobility of labour, family units of more than one generation are becoming rarer. Moreover, not all young mothers would feel the intellectual frustration so keenly as I did, as I had been lucky enough to have a University education. However, the recent spate of babies being given away seems to indicate that all is not yet well.

When war broke out we already had a baby girl, and as young mothers were not called up, the most worth while thing for me to do seemed to be to continue with our intended family of four, Hitler or no Hitler. We naturally expected that many of our rosy dreams of a wonderful family life would not materialize in wartime, but I was not prepared for the many frustrations not due to the war: for the attitude to the mother of several, of a society of which the unit was clearly not the family but the individual. As a proud Materfamilias it was a humiliating shock when people looked askance at me and my trail of children, clearly considering us a nuisance. The scant courtesy we frequently received when trying to make our way through crowded streets, for example, made me feel as if I had done something slightly immoral in producing the four of them.

Granted that the nutritional needs of young children were

and still are admirably catered for, it seemed surprising that other vital needs were completely ignored. It was splendid to get cheap milk, orange juice and codliver oil, but I was horrified to find for example, that in public conveniences the needs of mothers with two or more small children too young to be left outside, or sent into the convenience alone, did not seem to be considered at all. There was never a cubicle large enough to contain Mother, baby and one or two toddlers at the same time or a second and third seat, graduated in size such as I had seen in Sweden. What a nightmare it was, when circumstances forced me to use these places, wondering whether the toddler left outside would have wandered off or been abducted before I could get out, or whether the child sent in alone would fall right in. What is more, there was never a low wash-hand basin, and seldom one at all, nor a capacious shelf for the inevitable shopping basket so that it did not have to be put down on the often filthy floor. (I found my teeth a help in solving this problem, but only when the basket was light!) These seemed to me reasonable expectations in an age of scientific marvels.

The same thing applied to trains. Travelling with a carricot and three under-sevens in an overcrowded train was a nightmare: faced with the inevitable request by the three-year-old, I had to extricate myself and her from the compartment, abandon the others with a prayer, struggle and push our way through the corridor and then, the seat being far too big, perform a difficult balancing act with one foot braced against each side of the swaying toilet and the child suspended over the aperture. At buffets a request for milk or orange juice earned me as scornful a look as one for opium might have done. How I longed, too, for at least one carriage for families only, with facilities for changing a nappy, laying a toddler down to sleep (the small ones are not much taller than a bulky man or woman is broad!), and giving a feed in reasonable comfort and without disturbing other travellers. My ingenuity was taxed to the utmost to keep the children fairly quiet and still, and my heart ached many times for those told constantly and acrimoniously, and usually quite uselessly, to keep quiet, not to touch, to sit still, to stop it, etc., the instructions being often accompanied by slaps. We used to arrive smeared with dirt and chalk and with plasticine in our hair, and once I relaxed too soon and all but lost a child under a car.

Shopping, unaccompanied by small children was a fairly pleasant occupation, but I found it most exhausting with the family. First it meant walking with the pram instead of bicycling, which trebled the time taken. Secondly it meant spending a quarter of an hour at each end in winter dressing and undressing them, and thirdly it meant making purchases with one eye on the pram outside and another on the toddler inside, a most tiring busines. I never risked leaving any of them behind for fear of an accident. I did not want to find the house on fire on my return from just 'slipping round to the shop for a moment'. It was a great temptation to go alone but the few minutes away might have spelt death to one of them. I once just saved one daughter from severe electrical burns, but if I had not been there. . . .

The almost non-stop preparation, serving and clearing-away of meals was a formidable task. To this day I eat twice as fast as any other member of the family, a habit bred of the need to snatch a few mouthfuls as quickly as possible in the intervals of feeding the others. With a baby being fed every four hours and the others in the intervals between, I used to feel like a donkey working a treadmill; and when I tried the obvious expedient (ruled out for many on the grounds of expense) of having a meal out it was almost impossible to find anywhere to go where the special needs of children were catered for at all in the shape of high chairs or children's portions. The inevitable black looks from superior unencumbered individuals when a child gave a yell or tried out the sugar sifter on the tablecloth soon made me prefer to cook all meals every day at home where we could have fun. Unfortunately too, large families are not often invited out to a meal except by relations. This seemed very hard, and I now make a point of inviting large familes *en bloc* to a good meal.

Going to church on Sundays had always been the order of the day for me and many young mothers until the children arrived. But though many churches stressed that children were welcome, I shall not easily forget the embarrassment endured when trying to make several lively tinies keep reasonably quiet during long prayers and lessons, or when a dropped penny provoked most unchristian expressions. It could be managed with one or sometimes two, but there was no chance of a moment's concentration on my own prayers, except at the risk of an escape up the aisle or other catastrophe. If my husband was available, one or other of us could stay at home, but this was a poor substitute for attendance by husband and wife together and most couples usually ended by not attending at all. Moreover, attendance at services planned for young children deprived me and my like of the normal adult ministrations offered to non-underdogs. Spiritually I grew in patience but in little else, I felt cut off from one source of help in standing the strain of constant adjustment to the needs of the very young. I used to wish that the girl members of every church youth fellowship would each 'adopt' a family in the parish and look after the very young children during one service every Sunday, and possibly also during one evening in the week, so that the parents could go to church and to some recreational activity together.

I remember the contempt I felt for a moral welfare worker's lack of understanding when she expressed critical and sad surprise that young couples were not always content to stay at home every evening. Had it never occurred to her, I wondered, that the young wife, accustomed perhaps to the sociability of an office or factory, had not spoken to a soul but the milkman all day? Society, it seemed to me, apparently expected parents either never to go out, or to go out separately, or to break the law and as likely as not ruin the mental health of their young children by leaving them alone in the house while both went out. The first course was on the face of it acceptable to me and many others because all energy was exhausted by the time the children were in bed; it was also the only possibility for widows and grass-widows, but lead inevitably in the long run to feelings of depression and victimization. The second course made a mockery of the idea that one married someone in order to be his constant companion. The third lead, I knew,

to all kinds of disasters: headline-hitting ones reported inter-
mittently in the Press, and secret ones revealed in the troubled
minds of maladjusted children. So I almost never went out for
years. Admittedly all married couples were not in such straits:
some could import a relative for the evening, and others
could exchange evenings with a neighbour or afford to pay a
reliable baby-sitter, if one could be found. However, I still
remember the Cinderella-like misery of not being able to go
to the only dance of the year when no Fairy Godmother turned
up to whisk me away from the nappy pail and mopping-up
operations.

Houses were another cause of frustration, though I person-
ally was luckier than most. Human habitations were presumably meant to be the human version of a rabbit's burrow or
a wren's nest, or any other dwelling admirably constructed by
brute beasts with the rearing of their young in view. But
houses seemed to be designed for 'Adults Only' and without
any reference to the needs of a young family. The term 'Family
House' merely meant that there were one or two more bed-
rooms, instead of a totally different layout. (Here I welcome
Dr Greene's recent call for 'houses suitable for Shakespeare's
seven ages of man' at the Royal Society of Health congress,
at Torquay). With nappies festooning the sitting-room and
the pram jamming the hall, I longed to be able to decree that
every architect's training should include a month in winter as
Mother's Help in an ordinary small house with four or five
children under ten. I regularly cursed door handles out of
children's reach (try opening the door for them with hands
covered in dough!), electric sockets in their reach, dangerously
steep stairs and the absence of such things as a dado for
chalking on, and an observation hatch from the kitchen to the
next room so that one could keep an eye on the children and
cook at the same time, and a lavatory low enough to be used
without my help. In a tiny kitchen I went in fear of scalding
a toddler always liable to trip me up, and my nerves suffered
accordingly. Home, in fact, seemed to be a very dangerous
place.

Another bitter experience, which reinforced in me the growing feeling that nobody cared and that one was expected to carry not only the inevitable burdens of rearing a family, which one did gladly, but also those of which one could have been relieved, which caused resentment, was when I visited the government day nursery. I enquired hopefully as to whether they would take my two older underfives for a few hours in the morning so as to give them more scope and me a better chance to cope with the baby, cooking and chores. But the answer was No, the nursery was only for Working Mothers. In vain did I timidly suggest that what I did all day for seven days a week might properly be called work. Apparently one could only qualify by working for money and not for love.

Later on I found the state schools equally uncompromising, with their all or nothing policy. At 5 years, I was told, my child might attend from 9 to 3.30, but not for the morning only. Was I odd, I wondered, in thinking that such an abrupt transition from all day at home to all day at school (and with bed-time at six it really meant all day) was liable to upset quite a number of the more sensitive children? Apparently I was not, to judge from many excellent private kindergarten schools which expected the youngest children to attend for a limited time only to begin with. Many conscientious parents therefore stinted themselves in order to gain the privilege of a graduated start to their child's education. It was all the more maddening since I knew that the shortage of teachers and overlarge classes would have made the voluntary afternoon attendance of the 5–6-year-olds a desirable thing from the schools' point of view, as well as mine.

To turn from school to facilities for leisure activities, or rather the lack of them for the mother of many: here too society catered for the individual and disregarded the family. The knowledge that there was nowhere to go when it was unsuitable weather for the park produced in me an acute loneliness. I used to wish I lived in Peckham, near the 'Peckham Pioneer Health Centre', which catered so wonderfully for family health and leisure needs and which had to close, I believe, for lack of financial support. Perhaps being unique, it could not be classified and so failed to qualify for a grant. I

do not know. Had I lived there I could have turned up with all
four children and each of us could have done something
interesting within the building. With baby safely in the pram
park with an attendant to call me if necessary, the other children could have gone to various playrooms and joined in
activities such as roller-skating, and I could have had a swim
or a quiet read. We could all then have foregathered for tea
and returned home *together*. True, there were various clubs,
where we lived, which catered for this age group and that age
group, but they all functioned at different times and places
which made it impossible for one adult to get children to and
from them, and in any case ignored the needs of mothers with
very young children altogether. I can still feel the despair I felt
at having nowhere to go. I was not surprised that tiny children
were taken into cinemas to see quite unsuitable films and kept
quiet with bags of caries-producing sweets. Gradually I came
to feel I was some kind of second class citizen. This state of
mind no doubt bore a very faint but just recognizable affinity
to that of the wearers of the Yellow Star of Bethlehem under
Hitler.

I had always loved sport and felt acute disappointment
when I could no longer take part in any after the children
came, and just when I needed to do so to regain my figure.
Not even walking was possible except on a pavement where
a pram could be pushed. I seriously considered tying the
youngest on my back like a papoose in order to be able to go
across country, but never had the energy to do so. One could
not go to a swimming bath or a tennis club with three under-
fives, and later the CCPR rejected my request for only one
course in August when sport-loving parents could take school-
age children with them and both take part in separate courses.
Recreational sport seemed to be just another thing one was
forced to give up.

A visit to a theatre had always been one of my favourite
relaxations, but now that I wanted to take my children with
me I found it impossible to find a suitable play. The cinema
catches a child young so that he forms a life-long habit of
attendance, but the theatre, apart from the often quite

unsuitable annual pantomime, seems to ignore children's needs. A notable exception was the Young Vic Company, and great was the thrill when they actually came at my request and performed in our town.

It was most trying, adore my children as I did, never to be able to be just myself for a few hours, but always someone's mother. Having been educated to use my brain, the longing to do some academic as well as domestic work was almost overpowering. It was some help to install the wireless in the kitchen instead of the drawing-room, so that the chores could be done while listening to the excellent schools' broadcasts. Fortunately I was able to mark exam scripts and check articles written in English by a Pole and this gave me intense pleasure although it meant battling against sleepiness and turning a blind eye to even more things neglected in the house. When I managed to acquire some afternoon help with my children I disappeared joyfully into the Library, or the Record Office or the Citizens' Advice Bureau, and after a few hours of being just myself I was a better mother.

To feel ill is always unpleasant, but to be ill and be unable to knock off with a nice medical certificate is pure misery. Never did I feel such an underdog as when there was nothing for it but to carry on when suffering from migraine. There is a Home Help service now and I believe that at least in many big towns a phone call will bring help in an emergency. No such help was available twenty years ago and I have crawled upstairs on more than one occasion. Waiting in dentists' waiting rooms, doctors' surgeries and hospitals' Outpatients' Departments was a nightmare. I do not know which was worse: to be the patient myself and have to bring lively healthy children with me because they could not be left, or to wait with a fretful child. There was never anything for them to do or look at except women's magazines and posters urging one to brush one's teeth, etc. I wondered how many mothers never got their minor ailments attended to at all because of these and transport difficulties. When I was living in a village I lost several teeth in this way.

I once pushed the pram several miles to a clinic when

dentistry was made free for expectant mothers and under-fives. When I arrived, exhausted, and the child was in the chair, the lady dentist suddenly asked if she attended school. On my saying that she was at a private nursery school, we were brusquely told that the service was only for children at State schools. Too shattered to argue, though I believed and still believe that the dentist was in the wrong, and too tired to press my own claims as an expectant mother, we set off, untreated, on the long road home. Next day I made an appointment with my own dentist, preferring cash and kindness to being treated like an outcast.

The worst thing was when I was advised to go into hospital for some non-urgent but necessary treatment, and was unable to do so as there was no one to replace me at home.

Holidays were another problem. In the majority of cases the sign 'Children Welcome' was a mask for accommodation which none but the mothers of many, excluded from better accommodation, marked 'No Children or Dogs', would put up with. With some exceptions of course, particularly on farms, the 'holiday' proved to be a long humiliating sequence of asking nicely for hot water to warm bottles, space to wash and dry nappies, and every other basic baby need, combined with abject apologies for the boisterous toddler's every yell, sticky fingermark or breakage. Most mothers gave it up and never went away for all the years their children were small. So-called holiday towns showed a lamentable lack of imagination concerning what their child visitors were to do when it rained, a contingency they had apparently never thought of. There were no vast indoor play halls, or children's films to be shown on wet mornings, and yet many landladies insisted on visitors being out of the house for a large part of the day. So we went camping, for me an intensification of the difficulty of most domestic tasks, though in good weather there were compensations. It was certainly no rest.

Domestic help was clearly a Must, but I soon found that those who simply had to have it were those who simply could not get it. What domestic helpers there were went to those who could offer enormous wages and advertise 'Two in family, staff three'. Those who, like me, had to confess to having several young children were scorned by these superior and elusive people. In fact, domestic help was available in inverse ratio to need. Desperate solutions like hiding one or more children in a shed crossed my mind but were dismissed as impossible, and such staunch child-lovers as did come from time to time earned my undying gratitude.

Paradoxically enough one was still expected to carry out the traditional voluntary work one's own mother had had the time to do. I myself was asked to run a girls' club but had to refuse, and schoolmasters' and Dons' wives I knew, whose mothers used to perform such a valuable function in entertaining pupils and students, could no longer carry on to anything like the same extent the tradition of keeping open house, a sad loss to education in the widest sense of the word.

The strains imposed on young mothers like me inevitably caused family life to deteriorate. Even today the 1960 No. 5 Monograph of the Christian Economic and Social Research Foundation reveals that 59 per cent of wives with one child are unable to go out of the house regularly, 67 per cent of those with more than one child and up to 80 per cent of those with several children. It also says that 'Apart from financial strains . . . the loneliness arising from this state of affairs accounts for most of the psychological stress imposed upon the young mothers.' Many of them, it says, begin to smoke excessively.

I did not expect or want the coming of children to leave me the same liberty as I had enjoyed before, yet the frustration was for me, and clearly still is for many, all the greater because of the much fuller life independent women may now lead. The contrast between my life as a mother and as a single girl was much starker than in the days when a single girl was confined to her parents' home and was largely occupied with the care of younger siblings. Then a home of her own spelt more and not less freedom, as she was at least its mistress. I knew that contrary to the promises of romantic films and novels, the wedding bells would not automatically inaugurate a life of bliss. I expected a family to involve sacrifice, expected to have less freedom, less money, less leisure, and more work, more worry and more need for patience. But I was not prepared to feel such an underdog in a society which had apparently failed to realize that the family was its natural unit and to organize itself accordingly, thus denying to a whole section the chance of living a full life. As a young mother I had no Trade Union and no spokesman, and as a conscientious one I carried on as best I could and hated myself when the strain every now and then caused me to take it out of the children. I came to understand how many cases of sudden cruelty to children could simply be due to impossible conditions of family life causing a parent to reach breaking-point. My mental and physical health suffered. I was tempted to give in and by becoming feckless, to unleash all the helpful people society paradoxically reserves for families which get into trouble. I had been quite unprepared for my job as a mother. Unlike animals, I did not know instinctively what to do with a tiny baby, a screaming toddler or a stealing seven-year-old. Infant Welfare Centres were a great help to me here, but gave no guidance about the psychological side of rearing children. How it would have helped to have known approximately what to expect at different stages of children's emotional as well as physical development, and how many later troubles could thereby have been avoided 'if I had only known'. In desperation I sought out in libraries the books which might well have been conspicuously available at clinics for all mothers, just as friendly advice from an expert about Tommy's tantrums should have been available as easily as a diet sheet. A County Librarian, when approached about the possible loan of books to the Clinic, was quite agreeable to lend them, but I was quite unable to persuade any Clinic to display and issue them.

I wished too that the Registrar of Births had enclosed with each birth certificate a pamphlet setting out the details of such services as were available to parents in the rearing of their families, as a disproportionate amount of help seemed to be lavished on the unmarried mother, and the ordinary one left to sink or swim alone.

The feeling that Society set little store by the job a mother did in rearing children was reinforced when I recently took a teaching appointment. In assessing increments for war service, the years I had devoted to rearing my family, surely of considerable practical value to a teacher, counted for nothing whereas had I farmed out my children and spent the years as a clerk in the Forces I should be earning a reasonable salary now instead of that of a young girl only recently out of College.

Having felt an outcast for many years I welcome any signs of an improvement in the status of the family. I would like to see occasional activities open to 'Parents and Children Only', just to make them feel appreciated. I would like to see a playwright write a play spotlighting the efforts and struggles of young mothers as 'No Medals' did those of the Housewife. I would like to see the 'Family' rather than the 'Child' become the concern of innumerable social organizations. In fact I would like to see a woman prepared to give birth to and rear four or five children given a square deal and honoured, instead of being allowed to emerge exhausted after fifteen years or so of what many men would consider the equivalent of 'C.B. with Hard Labour'. But perhaps the most hopeful sign remains the fact that despite society's indifference, most women, including myself, still feel that the most worthwhile occupation is to be a mother of many children.

18

Illegitimate and Rebel

by 'ROBERT POWELL'

I AM SUSPICIOUS of the great hulking piece of machinery called civilization. When its Bishops and Merchants and Psychologists get to work I expect trouble. And when I hear of 'genuine psychological and social contributions' I reach for a gun.

This is because civilization has created the Underdog and is creating more of his sort every day, and when it describes him it is looking in the mirror. You need only think for a moment of the men who are furthest away from him in everything that matters to realize that society is never likely to go the whole hog in working for mental, spiritual and physical balance. The Romany gipsy and the saint come nearest to being in possession of their own souls. Civilization outlaws one and still martyrs the other.

I have spent several years dealing with feelings of humiliation and the sort of mis-treatment that comes to those who protest from a position of weakness. The only thing I ever needed was inspiration, something to raise me up. You have to look very closely at the hard face of civilization to find that—the Higher Medicine Men seem to reckon that uplift is a matter of corsage design. Minds are left to sag.

So I shall take a few brisk swipes at the undergrowth around me in the hope of driving something interesting out into the open and perhaps raising the spirits of my companions.

One grey morning a few years ago, when I was gardening at a small country hotel, the police arrived and, putting a ladder to a first-floor window, smashed the glass and entered. The would-be suicide was a psychiatrist.

I don't of course know the truth of the matter. But it is easy to see that the healer may come to grips with the mental distress of others by way of his own suffering—healer and patient balanced together on the edge of understanding or tragedy. It is not so easy to see that the Underdog—the man digging in a garden or weeping in a doss house—may steer away from tragedy and, through his understanding of suffering, become healer. The Underdog is a man under pressure, but that does not mean that he must move downwards.

Society seems too ready to think of its relationship with the Underdog as one-way traffic, in which he alone receives the blessings. But suffering calls for resistance and, in his case, a firm allegiance to life whilst the sense and justice of it are still obscure. He may be the evidence of oppression, but he may equally well be an agent of change.

I thought it would be as well to add these few points to re-inforce accepted definitions before getting down to business. . . .

My mother was a domestic help, and my father was at his best a sort of itinerant handyman. I saw him once only, at an age when I was just old enough to notice such things as the smell of the gasworks around which we walked and his prickly, farewell embrace. He was no Valentino, but may have had a poetic streak somewhere deep down, since the only letter I saw from him—written to my mother when I was twenty-five years old—spoke nostalgically of lilac time and remembrance. There was nothing the matter with his memory, but he forgot to marry my mother.

My first few years were nomadic, followed by twenty years with grandparents in the home from which they had previously ousted mother.

One late evening in my twelfth year I was awakened by loud voices. I crept to the head of the stairs and stood there in fear as my favourite uncle shouted at his father that it did not matter a damn who I was, I should not be sent to work so young. My gratitude remains. (Grandfather was strong and tigerish to the end. Walking across the floor of *The Grapes* a few days before he died, a fit of coughing took him and he dropped his beer. A rag man, thirty years his junior, laughed; and then stopped laughing as Grandfather lunged forward into his last earthly battle).

Anyway, Uncle lost that night and I became Butcher's Boy at 3/6 the week, soon bettering myself by moving to Draper's Boy at 4/6 and finally Wool Boy at 6/–. Inflamed, no doubt, by these successes and having passed the test I made for the secondary school, only to be sternly checked by Grandfather. 'Who the Hell do you think you *are*?' he asked, and that was that.

These I recall as mainly happy times. At school, as in the Army later on, I may have been respected for my ability to kick or fling a ball or punch somebody's nose; sport, man or boy, enables you to get away with near-murder. I left the elementary school at fourteen and, although never having heard of The Buddha, proceeded to work out my salvation with diligence. Thirty years have gone by, but salvation has never been within firing distance. In the roles of washer-up, clerk, soldier, divorcee, tar ganger, farm labourer, tramp and gardener I have sometimes heard the Devil's hoof-beats—and nearby at that—but nothing more.

My boyhood friends and I lived in small terrace houses on the edge of the town, spending much of our time camping on nearby downs and tramping through the woods and lanes of the chalk country. This was the background of much happiness for us all and I returned there when, with our laughter hardly off the hills, the Top Dogs started to bite.

Having seen a good report, my first prospective employer closed the interview by saying he would contact my Headmaster. Meanwhile I was to bring my birth certificate. It wasn't available, and I returned to say so. On being asked my father's name I said I didn't know it, and was then told that the firm did not employ people in my position. Whereupon the interview ended. (Certainly there was an illegitimate boy in the room; there was also someone who in the sight of God and most men must have ranked as a pure bastard. This thought gives me satisfaction of a sort now, but at the time I was unaware of differences between the letter and the spirit of the law).

I was hurt and the memory of what followed is very clear. I went out into the evening drizzle to sit in a cart-shed at the foot of the downs. There were raindrops on the tin roof and teardrops on the earth floor. And then I was away over the hills, slipping on short turf, blundering into resting sodden sheep, searching for a dew-pond landmark—lost, without and within. Towards morning came a track to a gate, a field to a lane, and so onwards over a countryside I knew very well towards things I no longer understood.

Very soon I was back in the groove from which my Head-master had tried to prise me, a café hand, living in a sort of dungeon bed-sitter well below street level, and taking most of my money home where I was not myself wanted. But he sent for me, heard my tale and followed it up with a note directing me to the District Council offices. The interview raised emotion of a different kind, for all the Clerk told me was he would like me to come and work in the Rating Department and that someone would find a £200 surety for me later on.

I would rather have rotted in Hell than let either of those men down. They were both dead when the Top Dogs started to bite again, but by this time I had grown a few teeth of my own. I was always out and about in the countryside, pockets stuffed with drawing pad, catapult (not by any means a toy), hand lens—and, I suppose, dreams. I might walk thirty miles in a day or spend a morning against a bank in the sun. I had never known anyone raise the question of who owned these lanes, fields and hedgerows. Not even Grandfather, who could find trouble anywhere, had hinted of fighting over this country (could he have heard of his grandson's sharp encounter he would have raised a shout of approval—and he may yet reach across the smoke and flames to shake my by the hand.)

It would have been an autumn evening, as I was moving into an unfenced lane from rough pasture, when we met. He was a newly installed tenant farmer, bustling and red-faced, and he ordered me off the land. I said I was going, which may have pleased him; but that I should be returning the same way with-in an hour, which did not. If he saw me, he said, he would fling me off. Arriving back I called to him in a nearby field so that he could start his flinging without delay. In the ensuing encounter I was obliged to loosen several of his front teeth, and in the fullness of time was charged and convicted of assault and battery, with trespass.

The matter did not rest there. Within hours a land-owning baronet had called on my employers (I had then moved to a commercial office) demanding that 'the Gipsy' should be dismissed or that the estate business would be withdrawn at once. From another quarter came a note with a returned club subscription. The hunt was on.

I went to earth, getting into the countryside more often and for longer spells. Peace is where you find it, and I found it there. But peace is a transient thing for the young man, a sort of brief inter-campaign period in which he steadies up and probes for the truth of his situation. And one segment of the truth of the Underdog's situation is that he is sharply aware of the cruelty, stupidity and chaos of our industrial civilization. He must get out of it for a while; he cannot stay there listening to a lot of clap-trap about Realism and Responsibility. Can you bring sanity to a madhouse if you never leave it? And if you lose your self-respect while you are there where can you hope to find it?

In 1939, as married man and Territorial, I joined the Army and in the sudden demand for fitness everywhere except in the head, was carried into the ranks of PT and Battle Instructors. These were a mixed bunch ranging from the highly trained ape to the untrainable genius. Our CO was a useful athlete and fashioned subalterns who preached physical fitness with all the enthusiasm of men who had just heard of it. One of these failed to break himself of a cold-weather habit of shaving with scarf and greatcoat on, but he did not last.

At home my wife was working in an Army Depot and predicting that I should soon run the mile quickly enough to become an officer. I was in fact put forward as 'officer material' but interviewed—such is the luck of the draw—by a colonel whose interest in PT was limited to the use of a walking-stick. He spoke briefly of the importance of background; how one had to have great loyalty; that he had my papers but would want to see my birth certificate. Meanwhile, a few questions. 'Have you,' he asked, extending a bony palm, 'have you got your men like *that*?' and he fiercely closed and shook his fist. I said I had not. 'Do they obey your command instantly?' I could not claim that, either. 'Then what bloody good are you, eh?' He could not see that as a volunteer in charge of volunteers, in a small isolated unit, the relationship he had described could not exist. If he could have proved my father drank schnapps—and that he was my father—I should have been shot for security reasons.

Once back with my unit I handed in my stripes. Thereupon my wife lost much face and believed that I was indifferent to her well-being. This was not true; but she sought and found consolation elsewhere. The advent of peace found me free to enjoy the fruits of victory. I had somehow managed to lose wife, home and job in exchange for £90, cash.

It might be said of this interview that I was running away from responsibility, and afraid of having to produce a birth certificate. Let me deal with the affair without talking about Defence Mechanisms and a Philosophy of Retreat.

In the first place I had not sought promotion. Someone—so help him—had thought I might further the war effort. So far from asking favours I was offering my services. Secondly, that colonel was a menace to the cause he represented, incompetent, having no grasp of the type of command necessarily exercised by the men he was interviewing. Lastly, I was—and am—tired of being asked for my certificate as though it were public property that any fool might demand and base a judgment on. I may be asked; I may refuse—and I take the consequences. This is the heart of the matter. This is where the Underdog may be driven down, unable to take the consequences of backing his right to be judged on what he is. And God help anyone who blames him for that.

('Ah,' you say, 'but this is sheer romanticism, heroics. You are fooling yourself. You hint of defending values, like a Crusader, when you are only afraid of what you are').

Are there values, or are we living in a cesspit? Does society regard its childless wives as prostitutes; or Christianity as the biggest and most contemptible piece of blackmail ever to go on record or those Crusaders—with their chastity belts at home and their slaughtering matches abroad—as distrustful and dirty minded pirates?

If society wishes to keep its own values it must approach those of the Underdog by the hard way of truth and understanding. If it seeks to dissolve values—even the Underdog's —then *it* will lead the slide into chaos.

Illegitimacy, the result and cause of social instability among other things, is said to be on the increase, so that the habit of demanding certificates will be a greater aggravation than ever. But what of legislation? Won't that deal with the problem? It does not seem so. The new shortened version looks like creating a situation where all the legitimates carry the long, and all the illegitimates the short certificate. Understandably, I suppose, no one will risk his status to save three shillings.

In 1946, as we have seen, the world was mine. Going into the chalk country again I marched towards London (how easy it is to understand the Englishman's attachment to that great city—where else can you hope to find Foyle's Bookshop?) but I did not take the place by storm, being held up in Surrey by the loss of my savings book. This led to the discovery that, so far from having global wealth, I could not even get a bed in Woking. The savings book was duly returned. but two nights in the open country drained my confidence and I retreated to the Salisbury–Winchester area.

I am recording a few things that seem significant; the theme is that of a man searching, not in possession. And the man who searches soon finds that definitions are not very much use— put them through the grinding stones of experience and very little is left. What is a tramp? Is he Underdog or Overseeer? It depends on the state of his soul, shall we say; whether he is lost and searching or firmly poised, in possession. I was tramp lost.

And so when I reached Winchester again I felt the same old impact of delight and then wholehearted thankfulness for what it was. The soft flow of chalk waters, the dignity and strength of cathedral, the quiet elegance of withdrawn houses, the tenderness and compassion of true remembrance carved in stone and touched by the spirit—these things lifted me up and held me steady for a while, they 'ministered unto my condition'.

Going there again, without centre, distracted, sure that the nature of things was against me and that nothing was on my side, I saw old Winchester and felt new hope. Everything there would have been torn down or mutilated if something in the hearts of men had not stayed their hands. You can see now in the shadow of the Cathedral, the shifty deal, the low wage, the look of contempt. Take-Over Men would move in on the High Altar itself and sell the Roll of Remembrance at so much the line if they could get away with it. But they are held back. And what is holding them back is on the side of the Underdog.

From Winchester I was away to the water meadows of Salisbury for the ever-startling sight of that great spire stabbing up into the sky. Then on to Old Sarum and Stonehenge. Words do not get us very far here. Out of my experience with that last place I could write the perfect guide book, in a few sentences. 'If you have heard anything about this place forget it, and if you have any books then burn them. Choose a mild and friendly-looking winter's afternoon and get there as light fails. Stay there, remembering that no one will hear you if you scream and nobody will find you if you move. In the morning you will know as much about Stonehenge as the people who put it there.'

Once or twice during this period I slipped down into Dorset, crossing Bere Heath to Lawrence's old home at Clouds Hill, squatting on the small lawn, cut off from the world by banked rhododendrons. In those days he was perhaps too much of a hero, a target for worshippers and gutless literary saprophytes alike. Although he remains, for me, a source of inspiration I could not bear to finish reading *The Mint*, being unable to follow a man of his stature into a defeat which seemed more complete than anything I could anticipate for myself. There is something wrong with that book. It does not feel right, but I shall leave it alone until experience leads me back to it.

The physical wear and tear of seven months' tramping halted me. I had touched and re-touched points of interest and inspiration. Now the meaning of what I was seeing began to escape me, and I drifted back to the pre-war scene, the country-side of my early days. Once the pleasure of reunions had died down it was necessary to face the truth of the matter: I had no link with them stronger than that of memory. It was a painful moment, carrying as it did the shock of loneliness *there*, at the last ditch. It seemed to me that they had gone on living in the right way, that they were what they should be; that I was all to Hell.

Meanwhile cash was running short. I applied for a Civil Service vacancy involving skills I hardly knew existed and spent a week in day and night practice. I even gave up smoking to steady my hands, but the work remained shaky. It then occurred to me that I might be confusing a physical with a mental problem and that if I could reduce tension—particularly that of the interview and test—all might be well. In a short experiment I found that ten or so aspirin tablets brought me to the edge of sleep, blunting my sensibilities and steadying my hands. It worked, and the job was mine. (But balance should be gained in this way only when being interviewed by senior Civil Servants, service chiefs and the like, over whom one is almost certain to enjoy considerable intellectual super-iority; one becomes rather too stupid to deal with the normal employer.)

All was well here until I persuaded myself that ten feet square of semi-darkened room was no place for a fit man. A year earlier I had felt the same about several hundred square miles of superb downland landscape, but how can you search systematically when you don't know what you're looking for? Two counties westwards I joined a small family farm in an idyllic setting, a landscape that must have remained un-changed for centuries. If a fresh start were possible it would have been there, where the only link with past was in the memory of the one who had lived it. An eighty-hour week gave little time for reverie, reading, or correspondence.

Amongst my duties here was the self-imposed one of

visiting an outlying flock of sheep—ewes, heavy with lamb— that were always going over and being pecked about the head. The eyes would be a mass of pulped flesh. It distressed me. The farmer seemed untroubled; more likely he had made a mistake, or had his hand forced in putting the fodder field so far from the house; it lay on the very edge of his land some three quarters of a mile away. Four times a day, in my own time, I trotted down the hill, through a marsh and coppice and up the far rise to set one or more of these sorry creatures upright. I cursed the birds, I cursed the farmer, and came close to praying for the sheep. On Sunday evenings he and brother lay preachers would gather in the drawing-room and a fat ginger-headed aunt would take her place at the harmonium. 'Oh, yes', they would bawl, 'we'll gather at the River' or 'down by the river', or something similar. Wherever it was, I used to think it was a bloody shame they couldn't change their rendezvous and see what they could do for those sheep. Nine months with the farming community was enough. I packed my haversack and set off southwards to the sea and westwards with the sun.

The repetitive 'I' is beginning to annoy even me, and permission is now sought to record some experiences in another form. Here is

A FABLE

Once upon a time there was a large and fierce pack of hounds called The Bigs and they hunted the country killing many foxes and always having a full larder. Then one day a Big Big said they were making a mistake and would do better if they changed their rules. Whereupon there was a great row in which some Bigs followed him and other Bigs followed their own noses, so that many packs roamed the land. So great was the confusion that the hounds started killing each other and the foxes laughed. Then a weak and ailing hound called on one of the First Bigs and said that he had had a bellyfull of the chaos and thought there was after all only one way of killing foxes. 'Very well' he was told, 'but you must obey all the rules. To

hunt in any other way is to be flung out.' And even before the
new hound had learnt the rules and been sworn in he stopped
thinking and started to be happy again.

Then one day he felt that he would like to mate and he
approached a Small Mating Master, who refused him saying
'You have mated before, in another pack, under other Rules.'
Straightway he protested, claiming that he had not always
known the rules, that he had mated and de-mated according
to the rules of Outsiders, and that he would put his case before
a Bigger Mating Master. 'But it does not matter,' cried Small,
'even if you go to the Biggest Big. You will get nowhere. The
thing is settled.' On hearing this the new hound considered
things, saying to himself 'They are wrong in this matter, therefore
I can no longer trust the law of the First Bigs.' And he made
his way back to chaos shouting 'To Hell with the First Bigs, the
Second Bigs, and all the other Biggers. I will find me a mate.'
And he did.

Any one who sets out to live off the land and at the same time
hold to the Cornish coast should plan his affairs with a little
care. I had a light one-man tent, a few shillings, and no interest
in the technical problems, which seemed fewer than those I
had met elsewhere. And yet within the first fortnight I was
often very hungry, once half-dead with thirst, once half-
poisoned by sewage effluent and once carried semi-conscious
from a cliff path. This last incident formed the basis of experience for such 'Philosophy of Existence' as I have, and must
be put down in detail.

I had finished my flask somewhere beyond Polperro and,
walking in the heat of the sun along a cliff path, felt the need to
get down to the sea. There was no path to the shore which may
have been 100 feet or so below and so I went down by way of
boulders, loose shale and soft mud gulleys. On stripping to
swim I was thirsty and trembling with weakness, but the sea
refreshed me and I came out in buoyant mood and made
off along the shore. Somewhile later my way was blocked by
deep water. The trembling and thirst returned and thinking
that I could not reach my original point of descent I made for

a shale scree that seemed to end in a negotiable rock outcrop near the cliff path. Going was bad here. I clambered a few feet, rested, clambered again and then lost ground in a clawing, stamping slide. When I reached the outcrop it proved to be an overhang, unclimbable, The path was a dozen feet away. From this point onwards I can recall only falling and rolling to the shore again and vomiting and sweating in another attempt to reach the path. Anyway, I was found there on the path and driven into Fowey to enjoy a day and night of fine hospitality. (I recall a drenching gale on the Redruth By-pass and a Scots engineer offering me a lift. Water was running out of my boots and I said I should ruin the upholstery. 'Don't you worry, Professor,' he said kindly enough, 'I am a sensible man and it's my duty to look after fools.' No doubt the cliff rescuers thought the same way; they were certainly entitled to).

Now although this incident may sound merely silly it disturbed me. It is one thing to realize you are unhappy, but quite another to find that after years of near-hoboing you cannot carry through an extended seaside stroll without making an absolute fool of yourself. I at once pitched tent near Lansallos and established a firm rhythm of eating, working and resting. I needed £10 to carry me round the coast to St. Ives; the money could be earned where I was, pea-picking for 2/– the hour; the farmer would feed me well; I could swim in the evenings and sleep well on a bracken mattress.

With my capital assured I spent a few evenings in a nearby pub and on the last visit a tough-looking character in an old blue suit, sweat rag and leather belts, started to ask questions. Where had he seen me before? I gave my home town. No, it wasn't there; he looked again, hard, through half-closed eyes. My name? He shook his head, finished his cider and left. The bar hand had heard the talk. 'Something funny there,' he said. 'Gipsies don't ask questions for nothing.' I asked where this one had come from. No one knew. He talked about —— sometimes, that was all. I went back to the farm. Almost the only thing I knew about my father was that he'd lived most of his life within a few miles of the place they had just mentioned.

Having finished the journey without further trouble I turned eastwards. The cliff affair had convinced me of the unlikely-looking truth that it is possible to get so far away from reality as to invite self-destruction. On that occasion I had made no provision for food or water; had given way to a stupid desire to swim under any circumstances; had aggravated thirst and fatigue and misjudged appearances as a consequence, and so on. It is a practical matter to talk about being 'out of touch with reality,' because I had taken no account of things that were essential if I was to exist at all.

At that time I was preoccupied with various problems—the Odd Man Out theme, finding roots, etc. These things were of course significant enough, but they were secondary problems. The primary problem is to exist—or, at any rate, not to die by accident. Civilization tends to obscure priorities. It leads a man to step under a bus whilst checking a football coupon that is thought to hold the key to everlasting joy. It persuades nations to risk annihilation for the privilege of flying aeroplanes at specified heights. The Underdog is double cursed: he may step under a bus whilst pondering the fact that he cannot afford to do the coupon at all.

Since the days of my Cornish walk I have tried to keep one eye on the reality of my situation; with the other I have searched for inspiration, the flash of truth somewhere, understanding, a reason for the sudden effort. I suppose you could say that this contribution is a sudden effort to maintain something about the truth of the Underdog's situation, which would otherwise be swamped by too much protest, too much complaint. And too much conscience-stricken atonement by the oppressors.

I carry around with me the memory of humiliation and injustice. I am liable to erupt into fits of blasphemous violence when certain things are mentioned. But these fits are luxuries. Let me remind the reader—always supposing the level of this discussion has allowed him to forget it—that I am living on an Agricultural Rate wage packet, a manual worker. Expendable. I cannot afford to go around feeling humiliated or oppressed, it would aggravate my condition. It would weaken my efforts to exist and to secure existence for my wife and family. It would be bad for morale.

There, in my opinion, you have it. Life is war, so far as I am concerned, and so far as any respectable underdog is concerned. We cannot afford to lower our morale; other people can be relied upon to do that. Our first job lies in precisely the opposite direction. We must search the mess around us for some link or achievement or vision—anything at all—that will restore our pride and give us inspiration and guts to tackle our condition.

It is not easy to find inspiration in this Industrial Madhouse. But that is our need and we must search for it. No doubt we shall have to lift and turn and shake and turn again the debris of our times, but it is there, somewhere, under the heap.